Empire *of* Horses

ALSO BY JOHN MAN

Searching for the Amazons

Empire of
Horses

*The First Nomadic Civilization
and the Making of China*

JOHN MAN

PEGASUS BOOKS
NEW YORK LONDON

EMPIRE OF HORSES

Pegasus Books, Ltd.
West 37th Street, 13th Floor
New York, NY 10018

Copyright © 2020 by John Man

First Pegasus Books hardcover edition February 2020

ISBN: 978-1-64313-327-0

10 9 8 7 6 5 4 3 2 1

Printed in the United States of America
Distributed by W. W. Norton & Company

For Ge Jian, with thanks

献给葛健先生

Хүндэт Гэ Жиан танд зориулав

CONTENTS

LIST OF CHANYUS

MONGOLIAN TRANSLITERATION	ALTERNATIVE SPELLING	REIGN DATES
		BC
Tumen	Touman	c.230–209
Modun	Modu	209–174
Jizhu	Laoshang	174–161 (or 160)
Gunchen	Junchen	161 (or 160)–126
Ichise	Yizhixie	126–114
Uvei	Wuwei	114–105
Ushylu	Wushılu	105–102
Guilihu	Xulihu	102–101
Chedihou	Quedihou	101–97
Hulugu		97–85
Huandi	Huyandi	85–68
Hyului-Juankui	Xuluquanqu	68–60
Yuan-Guidi	Woyanqudi	60–58
Dispute between Yuan-Guidi, 4 pretenders and . . .		
Huhanye		58–31
Zhizhi	Zishi	56–36
Fujulei-Jodi	Fuzhulei-Ruodi	31–20
Seuxie-Jodi	Souxie-Ruodi	20–12
Guia-Jodi	Cheya-Ruodi	12–8
Ujiuli-Jodi	Wuzhuliu-Ruodi	8–AD 13
		AD
Ulei-Jodi	Wulei-Ruodi	13–18
Hudurshi	Huduershi	18–46
Wudadi-Hou	Wudalihou	46

NORTHERN CHANYUS

Punu		46–48
Youliu		c.48–??
Youchujian		91–93
Feng-Hou		94–118

SOUTHERN CHANYUS

Bi (born Khailoshi)		48–56
20 others		56–216

XIA (XIONGNU STATE IN CHINA)

Helian Bobo		407–425
Helian Chang		425–428
Helian Ding		428–431

TIMELINE

CHINA (DYNASTIES)	DATES	STEPPES	ELSEWHERE (approximately)
	BC		
XIA (legendary)	2205–1600		**Middle East:** Early cultures in Egypt and Indus Valley. **Sub-Saharan Africa:** Spread of farming and pastoralism.
SHANG	1600–1122 c.1500	Pastoral nomadism develops.	
ZHOU: WESTERN ZHOU	1122–770 c.800 (–AD 200)	Ordos bronzes.	**South America:** Cultivation of maize.
EASTERN ZHOU: SPRING & AUTUMN PERIOD	770–480 c.750–650	Arzhan 1 and 2. Mounted archers appear.	**Greece:** Democracy (of a sort). **Italy:** Foundation of Roman republic.
WARRING STATES	480–221 c.350	Pazyryk culture. Ordos golden coronet. Xiongnu in Ordos.	**Inner Asia:** Alexander the Great builds empire.
First written mention of Xiongnu.	244		
	c.230	Tumen becomes chanyu of Xiongnu.	
QIN Zheng reigns 246–, from 221 as First Emperor of unified China.	221–206		**Italy:** Hannibal's march over the Alps starts Second Punic War with Rome.
	214–210	Meng Tian drives Xiongnu out of Ordos, and builds Great Wall and Straight Road.	**Peru:** Nazca culture flourishes.
Death of First Emperor.	210		
	209	Modun becomes chanyu.	
QIN collapses. Civil War.	206 206–202		**Mexico:** Teotihuacán founded.
WESTERN HAN He-qin policy starts.	202–AD 9 198	He-qin policy starts.	
	176	Xiongnu take Loulan.	**India:** Fall of Mauryan dynasty.
	174	Death of Modun.	
	162	Xiongnu expel Yuezhi from Gansu. Yuezhi migrate to Ili Valley.	**Persia:** Persians conquer Seleucids. **North Africa:** Rome destroys Carthage.
Emperor Wu (141–87 BC)	140s	Many Xiongnu attacks.	
Zhang Qian starts expedition to west.	138		

CHINA (DYNASTIES)	DATES	STEPPES	ELSEWHERE (approximately)
	133–2	Pushed by the Wusun, the Yuezhi start migration to Bactria.	
Wu starts Han–Xiongnu wars.	127	Wu starts Han–Xiongnu wars.	
Zhang Qian returns.	126		
Great Wall heads west.	119	Great Wall heads west.	**Peru:** Foundation of Moche state.
Li Ling defeated.	99	Li Ling defeated.	
Sima Qian's *Shi Ji* (*Records of the Grand Historian*) finished(?).	94		**Northern Europe:** Julius Caesar takes Gaul and invades Britain.
	54	Xiongnu split between Huhanye and Zhizhi; Huhanye turns to Han China.	
Huhanye visits Chang'an	51	Huhanye visits Chang'an.	
	44	Zhizhi flees west.	
	36	Zhizhi killed at Talas.	**Italy:** Augustus becomes first Roman emperor.
	AD		
XIN	9–23	Possible start of élite graves (terrace tombs) by Xiongnu aristocracy.	**Southern Africa:** Arrival of nomadic pastoralists.
EASTERN HAN	25–220		**American North-West:** Hunter-gatherers form complex societies.
	48	Xiongnu split into northern and southern sections. Southerners move into China.	**Middle East:** Rise of Christianity.
	87	Xianbei invade northern Xiongnu.	
	89	Northern Xiongnu defeated by Han at Battle of Mount Yanran.	**Mediterranean:** Roman Empire reaches greatest size.
	155	Northern Xiongnu fall to Xianbei, and many migrate westwards.	**South-East Asia:** Foundation of Champa empire.
THREE KINGDOMS	220–280		
Disunion (six dynasties, including ZHAO dynasty set up by southern Xiongnu in north China (304–329).	265–581		**Rome:** Constantine adopts Christianity. **Peru:** Rise of Tiahuanaco.
	376	Huns appear in west. Battle of Adrianople.	**Italy:** Visigoths seize Rome.
Southern Xiongnu chanyu Helian Bobo builds Tong Wan Cheng, capital of Da Xia (407–431).	413–419		

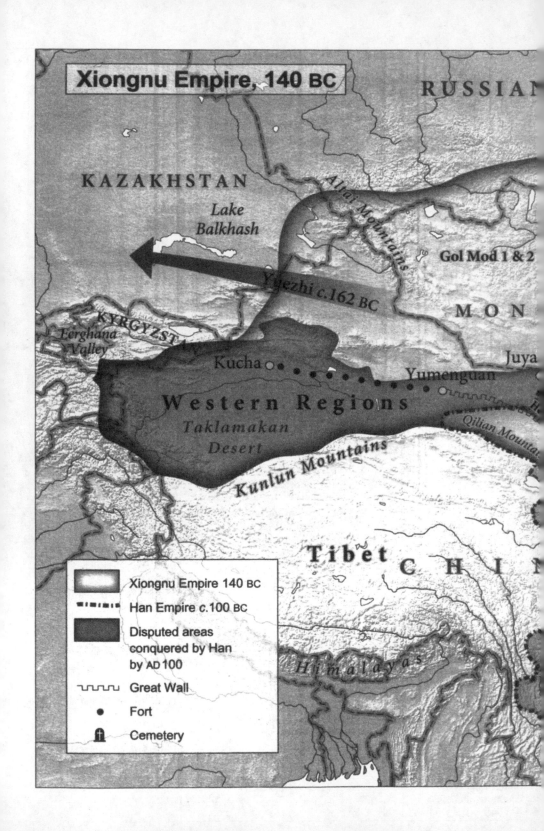

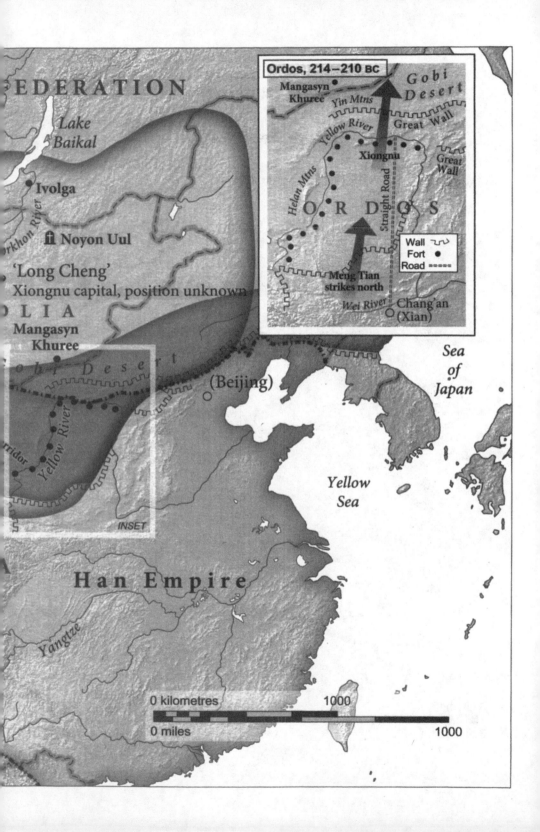

EDERATION

Lake Baikal

Orkhon River

Ivolga

🏛 Noyon Uul

'Long Cheng'
Xiongnu capital, position unknown

OLIA

Mangasyn Khuree

Gobi Desert

(Beijing)

Corridor

Yellow River

INSET

Sea of Japan

Yellow Sea

Han Empire

Yangtze

Ordos, 214–210 BC

Gobi Desert

Mangasyn Khuree

Yin Mtns

Yellow River

Great Wall

Xiongnu

Great Wall

Helan Mtns

ORDOS

Straight Road

Meng Tian strikes north

Wall ∿∿
Fort ●
Road ▪▪▪▪▪

Wei River

Chang'an (Xian)

| 0 kilometres | | 1000 |
| 0 miles | | 1000 |

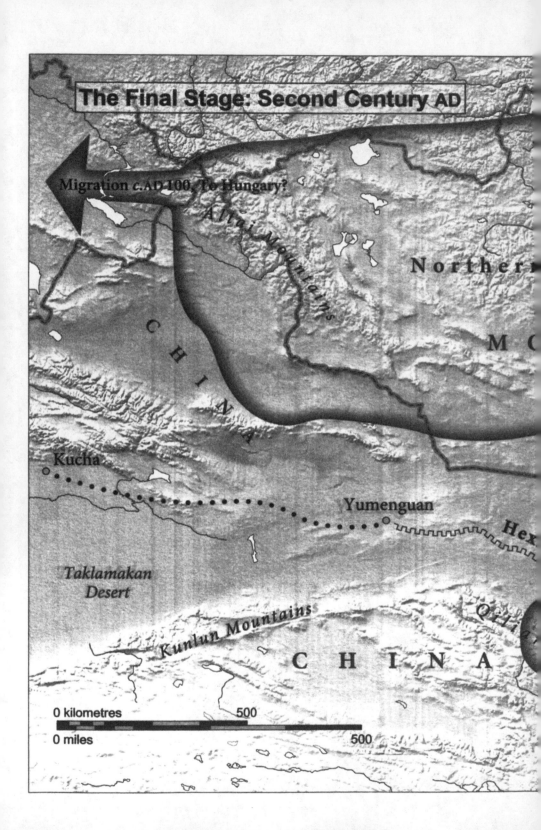

The Final Stage: Second Century AD

Migration c.AD 100, To Hungary?

Altai Mountains

N o r t h e r

M

C H I N A

Kucha

Yumenguan

Hex

*Taklamakan
Desert*

Kunlun Mountains

C H I N A

Qil

0 kilometres   500
0 miles   500

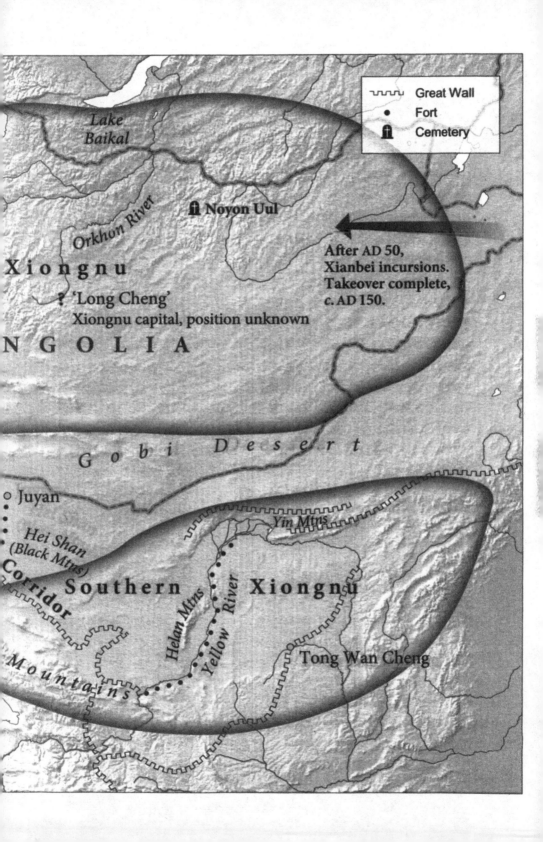

Introduction

A NEW BROOM SWEEPS
THE CHINESE SKIES

IN THE SPRING OF 240 BC, ASTRONOMERS EMPLOYED BY THE nineteen-year-old King Zheng of Qin, deep in the heartland of modern China, reported the appearance of a comet. It was in fact the comet now named after Edmond Halley, the British astronomer who in the early eighteenth century discovered that it returned every seventy-six years. To Zheng's astronomers this comet, like all comets, was a heaven-sent omen of change – possibly good, possibly disastrous. Comets were commonly called 'broom stars', because, wrote a sixth-century Chinese historian, 'the tail resembles a broom ... Brooms govern the sweeping away of old things and the assimilation of new ones.'[1]

As in the heavens above, so in the earth below: King Zheng,

---

[1] Fang Xuan-Ling, *Jin Shu* (History of the Jin Dynasty AD 265–419), quoted in Joseph Needham et al., ' "Spiked" Comets in Ancient China', *The Observatory*, Vol. 77 (1957).

ruling with the Mandate of Heaven, was already something of a comet himself, the newest of brooms. In the course of five centuries of incessant warfare, states, mini-states and city-states had whittled themselves down to seven. Among them, Qin (pronounced 'Chin') was the hardest of the hard, with an army honed for conquest. Being the first among equals was not enough for Zheng. He wanted to be the one-and-only ruler. It took nine years of war. In 221 BC, Qin emerged as the core of today's China, with Zheng as its First Emperor, ruling in this world and (he assumed) the next, as tourists by the million can see when they admire his spirit warriors, the Terracotta Army.

But the Great Comet of nineteen years earlier foreshadowed more than just change. Disaster also loomed, from beyond the borders of Zheng's new empire. To the north, in the vast grasslands and semi-deserts of Inner Asia, were tribes with a very different lifestyle: no cities, no farms, an endless supply of horses, and fearsome skills with bows and arrows. For centuries, they had been little more than gangs, making pinprick raids on the Chinese heartland. But now they suddenly became a real danger.

Though famous in China and Mongolia, few westerners know about this people. To Mongolians, they are Hunnu or simply Huns. The Chinese for Hun is Xiongnu, pronounced 'Shiung-noo'. Because Chinese written sources dominate the history of this relationship, that's how they are generally known today, though mainly to specialists.

They deserve better. They lacked many elements that are in theory essential to statehood, yet they forged the first nomadic empire – the third greatest land empire in history before the rise of modern super-states (the first and second being the Mongol empire and the medieval Muslim empire). They are the reason China reaches so far westward. They inspired one of the world's best-known monuments, the Great Wall. They were remarkably successful, lasting some three hundred years, making them the most enduring of the many successive nomadic empires. And they are possibly the ancestors of the tribe that under Attila helped destroy the Roman empire in the fifth century AD.

Finally, their emergence is evidence that opposition – in this case from China – inspires divided peoples to unify. Until recently, the explanation for the rise of the Xiongnu was based on Chinese xenophobia – that the nomads were dreadful people, the antithesis of everything civilized; that the violence was all on their side; and that China, the fount of civilization in Asia, was the innocent victim of their predatory habits. Today, many academics claim the opposite. They argue that the rise of the Xiongnu backs a great historical 'truth', an equivalent of Newton's Third Law: For every action there is an equal and opposite reaction. Let world historians argue about how generally true this may or may not be, but it seems to explain what happened around 200 BC, when Chinese force begot a counter-force on the grasslands of Inner Asia. Or, in human terms, a powerful charismatic leader on one side inspired a leader of similar qualities on the other. In this view, it was the First Emperor, China's unifier, who started the confrontation. His empire-building acted like a hammer on heated iron fragments, forging the nomads together for the first time. For over three centuries, the two remained in a precarious and violent balance, despite the vast 40:1 difference in population, until China proved there was no law after all, by using overwhelming force to shatter and scatter the Xiongnu.

But their way of life remained. Over the next 2,000 years, it underpinned another seventeen nomadic and semi-nomadic 'polities' – chiefdoms, super-chiefdoms, kingdoms, empires – with an average duration of 157 years.[2] The greatest was the Mongol empire (1206–1368), which at its height ruled all China and most of Inner Asia. Its founder, Genghis Khan, saw himself as the heir to a tradition of imperial nomadism reaching back over a thousand years to the Xiongnu. Mongolians today claim them as ancestors, with both cultural and genetic links.

This is the story of the Xiongnu: how they arose, how they affected history, how they vanished, how we know about them, and how archaeology is adding another dimension of understanding to the written sources.

---

[2] Claudio Cioffi-Revilla et al., 'Computing the Steppes', in Ursula Brosseder and Bryan K. Miller (eds), *Xiongnu Archaeology* (see Bibliography).

I
RISE

1

MASTERING THE STEPPES

IN THE SPRING OF 1913, A RUSSIAN GEOLOGIST NAMED Andrei Ballod, working for a newly established gold-mining company, was surveying among the pine-covered hills of northern Mongolia. He came across mounds that had been dug up some time in the past. Thinking these were old gold-workings, he organized a team to excavate one of them. Almost four metres down, his diggers hit a covering of wood and reeds. Underneath, they found an open space and a puzzling collection of objects – a jug, an axle-cap from a wagon wheel, bits of horse-harnesses, and some strangely shaped pieces of gold and bronze. Ballod realized this was a burial mound. The finds were obviously important, so he sent some of them to the Imperial Russian Geographical Society's East Siberian branch in Irkutsk, with a covering letter headed 'The Ancient Tombs of Unknown People'. The Russian scientists were as puzzled as Ballod, but there was nothing to be done, given the imminent chaos of the First World War and revolutions in both Russia and Mongolia.

Ballod died. His finds remained in limbo for eleven years.

Then, early in 1924, the famous Russian explorer Petr Kozlov arrived in what is today Ulaanbaatar on his way to Tibet. A member of Ballod's team mentioned the finds to Kozlov, who despatched a colleague, Sergei Kondratiev, to check out the site. It was March and the ground frozen, but Kondratiev's workers hacked further into Ballod's mound and found a timber-lined shaft. Realizing this was a major discovery, Kozlov changed his plans – lucky for him, because he had been recalled to face charges of 'anti-Bolshevik leanings', which might have meant a death sentence. It turned out that Noyon Uul (Royal Hills) as it is now named was one huge burial site, covering almost 20 square kilometres, with 212 tumuli. A few test shafts revealed that the graves had been robbed, and had then become waterlogged and deep-frozen – which was fortunate, because everything the robbers had not taken had been deep-frozen as well.

Kozlov's team excavated eight mounds. Under coverings of rock and earth, they found sloping approaches to 2-metre-high rooms made of pine logs, carpeted with embroidered wool or felt. Inside each was a tomb of pine logs, and inside that a silk-lined coffin of larch. The construction of the rooms was superb, with silk-covered wooden beams neatly inlaid into side walls and supports set in well-made footings.

Every grave was a mess, with treasure troves of objects, some 2,000 in all (most of them now in St Petersburg), all strewn about among human and animal bones. Not a single skeleton had been left intact. Almost all the gold had been taken, but enough had been left to show that these had been wealthy people. They loved handicrafts and foreign goods: some objects suggested links with China, even Rome and Greece. Amongst other things, the graves contained patterned felt, lacquered wooden bottles, bronze pots, spoons of horn, knee-length underpants of wool and silk, bronze buckles, fur hats, jade decorations, axle-caps, golden jewellery, silver plates with yaks and deer in bas-relief, felt carpets and tapestries embroidered with male heads and animals. The men braided their hair, often using bone hairpins. In Noyon Uul, 120 braids were found, cut off and thrown on to the floors in the rituals of mourning. In the words of one Xiongnu expert, Ts. Odbaatar, 'Perhaps the braids were a symbolic way for the attendants and servants to join their master in spirit, while not having to sacrifice themselves.'[1]

Who were these people? When were they buried? We know now that this was the first evidence of the Xiongnu. At the time, no one had a clue. The answers came slowly, and then – after the collapse of the Soviet Union and China's post-Mao liberalization – with a rush, detailed in later chapters. But the Xiongnu did not exist in a vacuum. They were the products of a long historical process that had opened up the Asian heartland – a new way of life adopted by several major groups and many smaller ones, all sharing similar traits and all commonly treated as a single culture: the Scythians.

For 99.9 per cent of our 2.5 million years on earth, we humans were hunter-gatherers, making the best of seasonal variations, the habits of animals and nature's bounty. About 12,000 years ago, as the glaciers of the last Ice Age withdrew,

---

[1] Gelegdorj Eregzen (ed.), *Treasures of the Xiongnu* (see Bibliography).

warmer climates gave rise to two new ways of living. The first, from about 7500 BC onwards, was farming, which allowed for permanent settlements and larger, more complex societies. Populations rose. Villages became cities, and life became both political (from *polis*, Greek for a city-state) and civilized (from *civis*, Latin for 'citizen'). As every schoolchild used to know, early civilizations arose around the continental edges and along the great rivers of Europe, the Middle East and Asia.

But there was another world in the heartland of Eurasia that was no use to anyone – an ocean of grass stretching from the Far East to Hungary, from the northern forests of Siberia down to the deserts of western China. Gazelles and horses and wolves thrived, but not hunter-gatherers, because grassland creatures were hard to kill. Here, most large rivers, which elsewhere were the life-blood of civilizations, flow north, into Arctic wastes. Winters are cruel. Grasslands were best avoided.

But once farming had provided herds of domestic animals, farmers spread into the oases that dot the deserts and grasslands of Inner Asia. From these islands of agriculture, farmers could develop another lifestyle entirely, known as pastoral nomadism, the formal term for wandering herders. It was not an easy step, nor was there a clear division between new and old, for the evolving culture still relied on hunting, agriculture and animals.

Before those on the margins of the civilized, citified, farming world lay that universe of grass which, when they learned to use it, would provide for food, mounts, increased populations, armies, and eventually empires. No such ends were in sight, of course, when people first dipped their toes into the sea of green. Progress out on to the grasslands must have involved countless trials, errors, dead-ends and retreats, as animals that were once prey were captured, bred, tamed, and at last ridden. Several species proved amenable: reindeer on the borderlands of Siberia and Mongolia, yaks in Tibet, camels in the semi-deserts. One in particular became the key that unlocked the wealth of the grasslands: the horse.

Horses were first domesticated around 4000 BC on the steppes north of the Black Sea. The evidence is a bit with tooth-marks and horse teeth with bit-marks. People were breeding the wildness out of these flighty creatures, reconfiguring them for tractability, strength and endurance. A knife dating from around 2000 BC, found on the upper Ob River, shows a man holding a tethered horse. A thousand more years of enforced evolution produced a creature that was still stocky, thick-necked and shaggy, still as tough as ever, but with the inbred guts to gallop to the point of collapse, even death, as happens occasionally in Mongolia's long-distance National Day races.

Horses were used to pull lightweight chariots, used in warfare, and heavy wagons, which allowed for long-distance migration. They were also ridden. That's what really opened up the grasslands. With nothing but a bit and reins, riders could herd horses, sheep, cattle, goats, camels, reindeer and yaks. Saddles helped, but were not a necessity. Iron stirrups even less so, because a rope looped round the toe does the job (the first iron stirrups probably date from the second century AD). To stay with your herds, you needed a tent – which evolved into today's warm, cool, wind-shouldering domes of felt – and a wagon or a few camels or horses to put it on. With herds and horses and the expertise to use them properly, grass became food, fuel, clothing and more – the stuff of new life.

It was still a harsh world, a second best. People on the brink of nomadism were probably pushed into it. In the borderlands of China in the second millennium BC, when Chinese civilization was well under way, farmers from the fertile but densely populated regions moved north in search of new lands. They put pressure on marginalized local groups, who were forced to explore other ways to make a living in the even more marginal grasslands. They were also pushed by a change of climate around 1500 BC, when colder and drier conditions forced people to abandon agriculture and take up herding instead. Evidence for these changes emerged from the soil in the 1960s. The pottery was of worse quality – coarse red or brown clay fired at lower temperatures – and horse bones appeared alongside other animal remains. It seems the farmers were halfway to becoming nomads.[2]

Which turned out not to be quite such a marginal way of life after all. This new grassland culture received a boost when a decline in solar activity brought a further climate change around 850 BC. As the milder, damper climate spread, pastures became richer, life easier, and herds and populations grew. These new nomads had more than their horses and herds. They knew how to forge bronze and then iron for swords and arrowheads.

Why bronze? Ancient peoples had long known how to mine and extract copper, lead, gold and silver. Copper was the most widely used metal, but it is relatively soft. If it is mixed with tin (among other constituents), it becomes harder, as some genius discovered in south-eastern Europe about

[2] Xiajiadian Lower and Upper Periods, Liu Guanmin and Xu Guangji, cited in Adam T. Kessler, *Empires Beyond the Great Wall* (see Bibliography).

4500 BC. The discovery spread across Eurasia, which is why bronze is used as the name for an age in human social development between stone and iron. By about 1600 BC, kingdoms of today's China were using it to make pots and other big ritual items, and steppe people, who had no use for heavy bronzeware, began to use it to make lightweight belt-buckles and horse decorations (on which more in Chapter 2).

Pastoral nomads were natural warriors, their skills honed by hunting, both as individuals and in groups. One tool used for hunting made a formidable weapon. This was the recurved bow, which ranks with the Roman sword and the machine-gun as a weapon that changed the nature of warfare. Who first invented it and when is much debated, but there are rock drawings of bows in Spain and Norway that are over 5,000 years old. Homer made it an object of power when he wrote about the Trojan War, which may have taken place around 1250 BC. By then it was the weapon of choice across all Europe and Asia.

This bow looked like a three-foot semicircle of nothing much. The curve is like part of a spring, turning away from the archer. (Later designs had a flat belly and 'ears' that seem to curve in the wrong direction. We will get to these.) The elements – horn, wood, sinew, glue – were all readily available to steppe-dwellers. The trick was to combine them correctly. This must have occurred as the result of chance discoveries. A hunter breaks his basic wooden bow and discovers that a strip of deer-horn is whippy enough to make a rudimentary bow. He finds that boiled animal tendons produce a powerful glue. Perhaps he learns that glue can also be made from special bits of fish: fish-glue was a prized item of trade across Asia. A tendon pulverized with a stone reduces it to threads, which prove useful as binding. He notices that the bow, now mended with glue and sinew, actually works better. Wood has wonderful qualities, as the English longbow shows. That's fine for infantry. But smaller bows for use on horseback need more than just wood. Horn and sinew are both whippy in their own way. Horn resists compression, and forms the bow's inside face. Sinews resist extension, and are laid along the outside. Bowstrings are of gut, arrows of wood. Feathers, which both direct and spin the arrow like a rifle bullet, come from any large bird's wing or tail (they have to be from the same side of the bird, because the feathers from opposite sides are not parallel and counteract each other, slowing the arrow in flight).

Arrowheads had their own sub-technology. Bone served well enough for hunting, but warfare demanded points of metal – bronze (early) or iron (later) – with two or three fins, which would slot on to the arrow. The method for mass-producing socketed bronze arrowheads from reusable stone moulds was probably invented in (or spread to) the steppes between 1000 and 500 BC, making it possible for a rider to carry dozens of standard-sized arrows with a range of heads. To produce arrowheads, pastoral nomadic groups had smiths who knew how to work bronze and iron. Blacksmiths were crucial members of their societies, and remained so – Genghis Khan's birth-name was Temujin, given him by his father after he captured an enemy of that name, or possibly profession: it means 'blacksmith'.

Expertise with horses and pastures combined with archery and metallurgy came together in the mounted archer, who could load and shoot his bow at the gallop, delivering arrows in three directions, forward, to the side, and over the shoulder.

Some no doubt were ambidextrous, which gave them a 360-degree field. A demanding way of life had produced the most formidable warrior known before the age of gunpowder.

The many groups scattered over this vast region intermingled and kept apart, remained in one place and moved about, and migrated and fought and traded in a shifting kaleidoscope of cultures to which archaeologists give many names, depending on the nations they work in. They offer indirect insight into our subject, in that almost every group would be aware of precedents, and copy, adapt or reject, choosing different ways to display wealth, or worship, or bury their dead. On the last, which left the most obvious and the most enduring remnants, there were traditions by the dozen and tombs by the ten thousand – burials under great piles of rock, or in vertical graves, or circular graves, or 'slab graves' made of flat rocks stuck in the ground, or huge pits, and all varying according to the grave-goods, coffin fashions and the status of the deceased. No culture on the ocean of grass was an island.

In the early first millennium BC, pastoral nomads established themselves from the borderlands of China to the Black Sea, where they became the distant neighbours of the Greeks. They were known then and now as 'Scythians', a vague term grouping untold numbers of clans and tribes that spanned all Inner Asia. Persians and Assyrians knew them as Saka, the term still used in Kazakhstan. Scythians get their name from a mythical Greek hero called Scythes, who was one of the sons of the famously strong Hercules and the only one able to bend and string his father's bow, and therefore in Greek eyes a fitting ancestor for the Scythians.

Some Scythian groups had settlements of their own, where

they produced fine works of art, especially gold ornaments. They had no writing, so, as Greek civilization rose in the seventh and sixth centuries BC, the Greeks knew about them only from peripheral contacts. The Greek historian Herodotus is the major source. In 460 BC he travelled to the Black Sea port of Olbia, then a thriving Greek frontier city on today's Ukrainian coast, now a fine archaeological site. From here, trading caravans run by Scythians set out for Central Asia and vanished into who-knew-where. Herodotus spoke only of big rivers and much pastureland, which remained a mystery to him. As he wrote, 'I have never met anyone who claims to have actually seen it.'

The Scythians and their many sub-groups proved so successful that they built substantial kingdoms, recalled not by cities but by the tombs of their leaders. How many tombs? No one knows. Certainly tens of thousands, perhaps hundreds of thousands. They run from north of the Black Sea, across present-day southern Russia and Kazakhstan into Mongolia and southern Siberia. To my eyes they are like Braille, dots on the pages of history that reveal truths to those with the skill to read them. Many were treasure chests of possessions, presumably to sustain the rich and powerful in the afterlife, so for centuries they were literally gold mines for grave-robbers.

The contents of the tombs give a sense of the culture that was common to all on the steppes, including in due course the subjects of this book. Here is a selection of a few outstanding finds.

A new age of archaeology opened in the early eighteenth century, under Peter the Great, when Russia began her great expansion eastwards into Siberia and southwards into what is now Ukraine and the various 'stans' of Central Asia. Russian colonists and explorers could not miss the grave-mounds, which became known by the Russian term *kurgans*. Grave-robbers had not taken everything. In 1716, sixty items were given to Peter the Great, starting the ever-growing collection of Scythian gold that now fills the Gold Room in St Petersburg's Hermitage Museum.

During the second half of the nineteenth century, archaeologists opened dozens more of the Black Sea kurgans, unearthing skeletons, golden plaques, cauldrons and other grave-goods by the ton. Since then, they have opened hundreds more, in ever more remote areas. The truth about Scythia and related places and peoples is far richer, far more complex and altogether far less barbaric than Herodotus could possibly have dreamed.

'Scythia' was not like a nation-state, with a capital and a centralized government, or a land empire like Genghis Khan's, controlled from the centre. No Pony Express linked east and west. Scythia was a collection of cultures, spanning all Central and Inner Asia, unified by a few main traits: funeral mounds, horses, weaponry and a love of the so-called 'Animal Style' of art, made up of convoluted creatures, part real, part mythological. Every Scythian tribe and culture would have known, traded with, intermarried with and fought with its neighbours, slowly spreading ideas and customs. A few sources in literate cultures suggest that there were many Scythian languages. Herodotus was told that Black Sea Scythians who traded across all Inner Asia needed seven lots of interpreters along the way. Trans-continental links were strong: Black Sea gold came from the Altai Mountains of western Mongolia; amber in western Mongolia came from the Baltic.

Scythian sub-groups organized prodigious grave-sites, often

burying vast amounts of wealth. In southern Siberia, for instance, the Minusinsk Hollow is prime pastureland some 200 kilometres across. It and its surrounding territory have some 30,000 kurgans acquired over 1,000 years (c.750 BC– AD 500). The biggest, the Great Salbyk Kurgan (fourth century BC), is surrounded by twenty-three gigantic stones, weighing up to 40 tonnes, each cut and hauled from a quarry 60 kilometres away.

Tuva, 200 kilometres to the south-east, is the heartland from which the Scythians originally came, and has the earliest evidence for Scythian ways. The objects were in two immense kurgans, known as Arzhan 1 and 2, after the nearby village in the valley of the Uyuk River. This is a fine, gentle pasture, with not much snow in winter – a rarity in these austere regions, and a focus for Scythian nomads for many centuries as they migrated between summer pastures in the mountains and winter pastures along the Uyuk. The valley – an arrowhead of grass, 50 kilometres long and 30 wide at its base – has some 300 burial mounds, so many in such a small area that locals call it the Valley of the Kings.

The Scythians of the so-called Uyuk Culture were not just simple nomads, surviving off their herds. They ate freshwater fish, grew millet, built log cabins and made stone tombs with domed roofs. They mined for copper and iron, which demanded specialist miners, tools and good knowledge of the geology. Stone pillars carved with spirals, rosettes and circles suggest they worshipped the sun. They believed in an afterlife, and made sure their leaders were well prepared for it, preserving their bodies wherever they died and bringing them back to ancestral cemeteries for burial. They worked metals into animal shapes, like curled-up snow leopards and birds of prey, which were admired (perhaps) for their strength, agility and vigilance.

The Valley of the Kings: Arzhan 1 alone would justify the title. Its start date was around 750 BC, about the time Homer was writing the *Iliad* and *Odyssey*, making it the oldest known kurgan. Once, it was a huge platform, 110 metres across, with a surrounding wall and a 4-metre-high dome. Almost all kurgans are of wood and earth; this one was covered in stones, which turned it into a giant refrigerator. Over the years, looters mined it, locals used it for their July celebrations, and in the 1960s bulldozers ground across it as part of the Soviet-era campaign to turn steppes into farmland. Even so, when archaeologists arrived in 1971, they found wonders: a wheel-shaped complex of seventy interlocking wooden chambers made from 6,000 larches. A central space held two coffins containing a chief and his wife. Round the tomb were eight hollowed-out logs holding the bones of retainers, killed to accompany their master and mistress into the next world. Nearby lay the remains of six horses, richly decorated with gold.

No expense had been spared: grave-goods included sables, four-colour woollen clothes for the retainers, horse-trappings of bronze and gold in the shapes of snow-leopards and boars, even a golden, coiled panther in the Animal Style that would have been familiar to a Scythian on the Black Sea. In the surrounding chambers were another 160 horse skeletons, plus numerous daggers, arrowheads, a torc (a semi-circular sheet of gold worn around the neck), gold earrings with turquoise inlays, and pendants.

Arzhan 2, made about a century after Arzhan 1, proved even more remarkable, both for its contents, and for the fact that it had been largely untouched. The builders had got smart, as the German and Russian excavation team discovered when they dug it up in 2000–2004. The two central pits were mock graves, which had fooled would-be looters. The main burial was 20 metres off-centre. The archaeologists and their hundred workers found not only the royal couple, but also sixteen murdered attendants, and a trove of treasure: 9,300 objects, of which 5,700 were gold, weighing 20 kilograms, a record for a Siberian grave. The 'king' – that's a guess – aged fifty to fifty-five, wore a golden torc and a jacket decorated with 2,500 small panther figurines, all gold, trousers sewn with golden beads, and gold-cuffed boots. On a belt was a gold-encrusted double-edged dagger. The woman, twenty years younger, wore a red cloak also covered with 2,500 panther figurines in gold. She had an iron dagger with a gilded hilt, a golden comb, and a wooden ladle with a golden handle. Her headdress was a gold pointed cap, decorated with two gold horses, a panther and a bird of prey. The two were buried together, suggesting the woman – wife or concubine – was killed to keep her man company in the afterlife. Nearby were thousands of beads, 431 of them made of amber, traded all the way across Eurasia from the Baltic.

The Arzhan tombs were for royalty. For rank-and-file warriors, there's more information 100 kilometres to the south-west. The cemetery, Aymyrlyg, stretches for 10 kilometres along a tributary of the Yenisei. This is a landscape of rolling hills and high pastures, with mountains lining the horizon, and a foreground now under water, drowned by a reservoir created by a vast hydroelectric dam further down the Yenisei. Here, the Scythians and their descendants had made an ancestral cemetery, burying some 800 bodies mainly in the third and second centuries BC. Buried with the bodies were weapons, Animal Style artefacts, tools, pins, combs, mirrors, belts with bronze buckles, and horse-fittings, all the things commonly found in Scythian tombs.

The bones from 600 individuals, collected between 1968 and 1984 from 200 graves and taken to St Petersburg before the reservoir's waters rose, are an encyclopedia of the pains, diseases and injuries suffered by ordinary Scythians. With the fast-developing sciences of bioarchaeology and palaeo-pathology, scholars can read stories in the remains. Skulls look more European than Mongoloid. Furrows and pits in the teeth, lesions in eye sockets, and the microstructure of bones give clues to diseases, diet, climate change and plant cover. Causes of death are catalogued in bone: murders, domestic violence, executions, ritual sacrifices, battles, accidents. Battleaxe injuries predominate during the early period and sword wounds are more common later.

Eileen Murphy, of Queen's University, Belfast, has made an extensive study of these bones in St Petersburg. She analysed over 3,000 of them. A few skulls show signs of scalping, a few others of being cut open, possibly to remove the brain, 'an aggressive post-combat activity that was part of a war-ritual'. Beyond this, as Murphy says, 'The Aymyrlyg excavations enable us to gain real insight into the lives and lifestyles of the "ordinary" members of these semi-nomadic societies.'[3]

Horse-based cultures are hard on everyone. People fell off horses all the time, mostly without damage; but the healed injuries show that if you fell off you had a 1–2 per cent chance of breaking a bone, though the men were twice as likely as

[3] Eileen M. Murphy, *Iron Age Archaeology and Trauma from Aymyrlyg, South Siberia* (see Bibliography).

women to break something. Fair enough, you would think, in a horse-riding community. But women had it worse in other ways, as their lower backs reveal. They had more than their fair share of hairline fractures in the lumbar region, a condition known as spondylolysis, sometimes called 'clay-shoveller's fracture'. Some 5 per cent have the condition in modern populations; Scythian women suffered over twice that. As Murphy points out, this 'suggests that . . . the women did not spend all their time sitting around in wagons but that they were also engaged in heavy physical labour'.

This tough life was also a violent one. A few of the injuries – bashed-in skulls, facial fractures – seem to have been the result of assaults within the group. Others were war injuries, notably arrow wounds, sword wounds and holes in the skull from battleaxes. There were twenty of those, sixteen of them with no signs of healing: they were death blows. Most victims of course were men, but two were women. Children too were victims, presumably killed when their camps or wagons were attacked. Several of the women had damaged left arm-bones, as if they had held up that arm to ward off blows.

Some bones tell dramatic stories. One woman, between thirty-five and forty-five years of age, had a wound in the thigh, and then lost her head to a single blow from an 'extremely sharp' sword. The attack came from behind, perhaps from horseback. She didn't have a chance. Nor apparently did her assailant. 'The angle of the sword chop . . . indicates that the blow had probably been struck from left to right, with the aggressor positioned posterior to the victim. The skull had been buried with the cadaver, and evidently the head had not been carried away as a trophy.' Perhaps, Murphy speculates, the head was left attached by a strand of flesh, and the attacker had no time to finish the job; or perhaps someone stepped in and dealt with the attacker.

Now come 1,500 kilometres south-west of Tuva, to the mountains east of the Kazakh principal city (not the capital – that's Astana), Almaty. From the northern slopes of the Tian Shan flow rivers that have turned temperate valleys into fine pastures, which now make farmland. Kazakhstan has kurgans by the thousand, about forty of which lie in a pretty valley near a lake called Issyk (Esik in Kazakh, and nothing to do with the huge freshwater lake of Issyk Kul, over the border with Kyrgyzstan to the south).

In the summer of 1969, a farmer ploughing a field near a 6-metre-high kurgan noticed something glinting in the newly turned dark earth behind him. He got down, kicked the soil and found a small piece of patterned gold. Amazingly, he did not pocket his find, but reported it. The Kazakh Institute sent a team to investigate, led by the renowned Soviet archaeologist Kemal Akishev. He was already honoured nationally both for his work and as a fighter in the Second World War. He became the much-revered father of Kazakhstan archaeology, and remained so until his death in 2003, aged seventy-nine.

The kurgan near where the farmer found the plaque was one of those astonishing rarities, an unrobbed tomb. Actually, the central tomb had been robbed, but the robbers had missed a side grave. In it, under piles of dirt, lay a crushed skeleton, quite a small one. Surrounding the bones was treasure.

Overnight a thief made off with some of the gold, but what remained was the most remarkable of all Saka finds. Other than the skeleton, the fifth-century BC burial contained: a jacket decorated with 2,400 arrow-shaped gold plaques edged with more gold plaques in the shape of stylized lions; a belt with thirteen golden deer-heads and three of moose and deer with griffin heads; a golden neck-torc with snow-leopard clasps; a gold-bound whip handle; a silver cup engraved with an unidentified script; a dagger and a metre-long sword, the blades embossed with gold animals and in gold-encrusted scabbards; there were earrings, beads, a gilded bronze mirror, and beaters for churning milk into *kumiss* (mildly fermented mare's milk); and to cap it all, literally, a towering 63-centimetre headdress made of a cone of wood covered with felt.

The skull was too damaged to tell the sex of its owner, but the sword and dagger seemed to leave no doubt. Akishev called the find the Golden Man, fitted him with leather trousers and put him on display. He was adopted as the new nation's symbol when Kazakhstan emerged from the ruins of the Soviet Union in the 1990s.

A Golden *Man*: that was the assumption. Fair enough, at the time. But there were things that didn't quite fit, and they began to bother the American archaeologist Jeannine Davis-Kimball, who had worked on the find: the size of the skeleton, the high hat, the earrings and beads, kumiss-beaters. Her conclusion: the Golden Man was not a man after all. 'This person was actually a young woman . . . a high-ranking warrior priestess.'[4] The truth will probably never be known, because the bones mysteriously vanished around the time it became possible to determine sex from DNA. Kazakhstan's strong man, Nursultan Nazarbayev, had declared himself a big fan. It really wouldn't do to have an ancestral king suddenly

---

[4] Jeannine Davis-Kimball and C. Scott Littleton, 'Warrior Women of the Eurasia Steppes', *Archaeology* (see Bibliography).

turn into a queen. The figure, restored, copied, and constantly reproduced in tourist posters, is likely to remain a flat-chested, trousered youth.

Four hundred kilometres south-west of Tuva and 1,000 metres higher in the Altai Mountains, Mongolia, China, Russia and Kazakhstan very nearly meet. Two thousand five hundred years ago, the local Scythians had no frontiers except their own gorges and pine forests, which locked them into their neighbourhood. They lived in tents and log cabins. Wagons were useless. They used only horses for transport, trapping, hunting and raiding. They lived, fought, died here, and were buried in ancestral cemeteries, where their bodies and possessions remained deep-frozen until discovered by modern archaeologists.

Russians were first on the scene. Sergei Rudenko, arriving in 1924, came up-stream from a long finger lake, Lake Teletskoye, turned left along the Great Ulugan River and found himself in a dry valley called Pazyryk by locals, which is the name given to the people he found and their culture. A long-gone glacier had carved it into a U-shape, which many generations of Scythians had turned into a cemetery. There were fourteen mounds, five of them large, all deep-frozen log chambers. They dated from the fifth to the mid-third centuries BC, with the most recent research placing the five main ones in a sixty-year period, c.300–240 BC. The men wore leather caps with ear-flaps, the women had headdresses up to 90 centimetres high, even higher than the golden person of Issyk. Of the many remaining artefacts – horse-fittings, leather cut-outs, wall hangings, carpets, saddle-blankets – the most surprising is a beautifully made carriage, which when reconstructed has four wheels, each 1.6 metres across, with thirty-four delicate spokes. It was designed for four horses, which had been buried nearby. In these steep-sided valleys, it was entirely useless, and obviously not Scythian. One explanation, suggested by a find of silk in the same grave, is that it had brought a bride from China, and been buried along with her to carry her into the next world.

Another surprise was that some of the people buried here had been tattooed. One man, known as the tattooed chieftain, had animals and bits of animals – legs, tails and bodies of horses, birds, snakes, rams, deer, some sort of winged monster – writhing along both his arms, while a fish lay the length of his shin, flanked by four mountain rams. A lion or griffin with a huge curly tail stood by itself over his heart. These gorgeous designs were probably of soot, pricked into the skin with a needle.

Beside him lay a woman in her forties. As infrared analysis revealed in 2003, she too had been tattooed, with a twisted stag on one shoulder and a contorted mountain sheep on the other. In another mound (No. 5), a woman aged fifty and a man of fifty-five also had tattoos. The woman's arms and hands were covered with intricate, well-planned designs of two striped tigers and a polka-dotted snow leopard attacking two deer with vast sets of antlers.

All of which provides a context for the most dramatic of Pazyryk finds. Two hundred kilometres to the south and 500 metres higher brings us to the drier and harsher Ukok Plateau, almost on the Chinese border. It is a place of waving grass, meandering streams and scattered lakes. Sharp, snowy mountains enclose the horizon in every direction. There's not a tree in sight. Summers range from bitter to blistering;

winters are brutal. But 2,500 years ago, it was much less grim – a popular place for semi-nomadic Scythians of the Pazyryk culture, because summer pastures were rich and in winter winds kept it clear of snow.

Here in 1990 the Russian archaeologist Natalya Polosmak, from the Institute of Archaeology and Ethnography in Novosibirsk, started researching the mounds on the plateau. In May 1993, after a late spring, their truck dumped Polosmak and her team by a mound right next to the barbed-wire fence that marked Russia's edge. Beyond was 8 kilometres of no man's land, then the Chinese border. Spring sunshine freed the lakes and dotted the grass with snowdrops and edelweiss.

Working with a team of six, it took two weeks to remove the cap of rock and earth, dig through a looted grave and reach the original one, untouched, unrobbed. Inside was a block of ice. Once unfrozen, the contents emerged – harnesses, parts of saddles, a table on which had been placed a meal of fatty mutton, frozen after it had started to rot, which now, after 2,000 years, gave off a foul odour in the spring sunshine. Six horses appeared, with the hole of the executioner's pick clear in their foreheads. They still had their last meal in their stomachs: their deaths and burial had been in spring. At last, the retreating ice fell away from a curved larchwood casket. After the removal of four 6-inch bronze nails, the lid came up, revealing nothing but more ice. Melting the ice took many days. It was July, and hot. Every day, team members poured on buckets of hot water, and carted away the meltwater. Mosquitoes pestered. The six dead horses stank. Polosmak's impatience grew.

At last, on Monday 19 July, a jawbone appeared through

the ice, then some sable fur. Polosmak peeled back the fur, to see not bone but flesh, a shoulder and the 'brilliant blue tattoo of a magnificent griffin-like creature'.[5] The body, slowly emerging from the ice, was a mummy, in excellent condition, with much of the skin intact, the brain removed, the muscles scraped away, the rest embalmed with a mix of herbs, grasses and wool. The tattoos were of a distorted mythological animal: a deer, its rear twisted in the Scythian Animal Style, with a griffin's beak and antlers sprouting either griffins' heads or flowers, a shape repeated on the animal's back. Further down the arm was a snow leopard with an extended tail and a head (if it was a head) attacking or consuming a sheep's body with legs at both ends. Next day, a headdress emerged, one-third the length of the coffin. Only then did Polosmak realize this was a woman, aged about twenty-five, the one who would soon be called the Ice Maiden, or the Ukok Princess. The sable fur came away in bits, revealing a long and flowing robe, a striped woollen skirt and a yellow top of silk.

Her looks were important to her. The bag next to her left hip held more than a mirror; it was a cosmetics bag, with a face brush made from horsehair, and a fragment of an 'eyeliner pencil' made of vivianite,[6] a form of iron phosphate which adds a deep blue-green colour to skin. There was some vivianite powder as well, apparently to be applied to the face.

The final surprise, which only emerged when the Ice Maiden was examined close up in Polosmak's Novosibirsk laboratory, was that her head had been completely shaved. She was bald. Her hair was not *her* hair – it was a wig, made

---

[5] Her words, translated in a *National Geographic* article (October 1994).
[6] Named after an eighteenth-century Welsh–Cornish mine owner and mineralogist, John Vivian, of Truro.

with two layers of female hair woven under felt, with a wooden deer covered with gold foil pinned to the front. From the top of the wig rose a spike of felt, 68.5 centimetres long, with a sliver of wood as a core to keep it up. On it were fifteen birds made of leather, each smaller than the last. The device was familiar to archaeologists from Animal Style art in other Scythian graves. It was what they call the Tree of Life, the shamanic symbol of health and status, which was also present on the Golden Man or Woman of Issyk.

There followed a tidal wave of publicity, which inspired much nationalist fervour from the government of the new Altai Republic. They declared Ukok a protected territory, and objected bitterly to the removal of 'their' princess. Since 2012, when the museum in the capital Gorno Altaisk was given the proper facilities, the Ice Maiden has been back in her homeland, resting in air-conditioned peace.

2

INTO ORDOS

By about 500 bc, many Scythian tribes had risen and fallen. Some left long-lasting remains, like those surveyed in the last chapter. Others vanished with hardly a trace, which might have been the fate of two minor tribes living close to what we now call China. They demand our attention, because they were probably the ancestors of the Xiongnu and their homeland was certainly where the Xiongnu were first recorded by the Chinese.

The homeland is a slab of territory defined by the Yellow River as it sweeps north, then east, then south in what is widely known as the Great Bend. It is not a single bend, but – very roughly – three sides of a 1,000-kilometre square defined by mountain ranges. Today, the region is Ordos, an obsolete Mongolian word meaning 'palace tents', which explains why this section of the Yellow River has an alternative name, the Ordos Loop. It is about the size of Scotland or South Carolina, with a historical significance out of proportion to its size, because it is ecologically part of the steppes, but geographically part of China. Throughout history, it has switched between the two many times. In 500 BC it was firmly in the hands of several tribes of nomadic herders,[1] who had no reason to think things would ever change.

Today, much of Ordos is semi-desert, but the climate was better then. Recent archaeological evidence[2] says that some 85 per cent of Ordos was covered by forests and grassland as compared with only about 9 per cent today.[3] Those fine pastures were ideal for horse-riders and herders. Though they must surely have engaged in trade with their Chinese neighbours to the east and south, they looked west and north to the peoples of the grasslands. It was with them that they shared a way of life, and from them they received their cultural influences.

One summer day in 1972, an old herdsman named Wang Shun was tending his flock of sheep in sandy semi-desert west of the region's capital, Ordos City, where pasture merged into desert. A sudden storm caught him out in the open. Rain and wind combined to shift some loose earth from a nearby slope. As the skies cleared, he was astonished to see something glinting in the newly fallen soil. He dug, and found bits and pieces of gold, mixed in with bones. The storm had washed open a tomb, one of two, as later excavations revealed. Among the finds was a golden coronet with a separate golden skullcap topped by an eagle made of turquoise. It has since become the greatest of the Ordos Bronzes, the objects that

---

[1] Notably the Man, Yi, Rong and Di, all later absorbed by the Xiongnu.
[2] Quoted in Joseph Yap, *Wars with the Xiongnu* (see Bibliography).
[3] Ibid.

define not only the culture of Ordos but much of Scythian culture all the way across the continent.

The coronet, the most impressive of 218 golden items found at the tomb-site, is unique. Though almost all the thousands of Ordos's little medallions are of bronze, the golden coronet is treated as the centrepiece of the Ordos Bronzes, and was the inspiration for Ordos City's Bronze Museum, which opened in 2015. The building is circular, as the coronet is, with three storeys, and it has a domed roof, decorated with clouds, which could be both the coronet's skullcap and the Mongolian deity, the Blue Sky.

The museum's curator, Wang Zhihao, who wore one of those sleeveless jackets favoured by archaeologists in the field, introduced me to the collection. He was helped by an English-speaking aide, the Deputy Director of the Education Department, who had adopted a surprising pseudonym. He admired the American basketball player (now retired) and rapper, the vast (104.3-kilogram), towering (2.16-metre) yet remarkably agile Shaquille O'Neal, who shortened his name to Shaq. With a little linguistic licence, my translator, Zhang Ziyang, called himself 'Mr Shark'.

On the way in through the displays, the coronet, of course, had pride of place, well lit and glittering in its glass case. I was thrilled to see this gorgeous object up close. Gold braid forms a circle that links a horse and a goat on opposite sides. Perhaps they symbolize the wealth of the herding community. A braided semicircle accentuates the forehead section, with a pair of tiger heads on either side, looming like a threat above the horse and goat motifs. On the separate little skullcap is a golden eagle with a head of green turquoise. The eagle's head was attached to the body with gold wires, so that it swayed as the wearer moved. The skullcap itself is divided into four embossed sections, each of which – you have to look closely, because it's hard to see the markings – contains a stylized wolf intertwined with a goat or ram. Dating probably from the late Warring States period (403–221 BC), it must surely have proclaimed its owner to be ruler of these grasslands. Nearby the figure of an imperious nomad chief showed how it would have looked in life.

So it was a bit of a let-down when Mr Shark said: 'It's good, isn't? For a replica.'

'*What?*'

'Yes. It's perfect in every way. But the real one is in the museum in Hohhot.' That's Inner Mongolia's capital.

It seemed unfair on the Bronze Museum, since the coronet has become the symbol of Ordos. But Hohhot had it long before the Bronze Museum was built, so no doubt it will stay there.

We moved on to the bronzes. Usually only a few centimetres across, they are typically belt-buckles, but also include tops of tent poles, decorations for horse-harnesses, knives, daggers with decorated handles, arrowheads, bronze mirrors, hooks for hanging things in tents, and buttons. Two intriguing little objects seem to be a pair of weights that were attached to ropes, which were swung and thrown to entangle the legs of fleeing animals – a trick that no other Asian group adopted, but which is widely used in South America.

Belts were important to nomads, signifying status, power, adulthood and identity. In *The Secret History of the Mongols*,[4] the only Mongolian source for the rise of Genghis Khan,

---

[4] There are many editions. The best is Igor de Rachewiltz's (see Bibliography).

Genghis's mother asserts her status by putting on her high hat and belt. When Genghis renews his vows of friendship with his blood-brother (*anda*) Jamukha, he gives him a golden belt. When Genghis punishes his brother Khasar, he seizes his belt.

The designs reveal a fascination with animals – horses, sheep, deer, birds. Some finds have an eagle fighting a tiger for a goat, monsters of various sorts, dogs, and warriors killing captives, any of which may have a face-to-face double. They liked their belt-buckles made of mirror images. Sometimes the maker included an odd mythological creature with a beak-like nose, which seems to have been unique to Ordos. (Other Inner Asian groups liked griffins – half-eagle, half-man – and winged lions, but that fashion did not spread to Ordos.) A favourite motif was the tiger – as the golden coronet showed – often shown eating a sheep or carrying a deer over its shoulder. There were no tigers in north China. The nearest ones were in the forests of eastern Siberia. It seems that to have a tiger on one's belt-buckle was a statement of status and power.

The buckles and plaques could also be used as gifts, which made them a sort of currency to assert equality of status (you see similar behaviour at English middle-class dinner parties today. Guests bring chocolates, wine or flowers as 'house gifts' which may cost more than their meal). Some were in the form of horse-decorations, which were usually discs attached to the reins and bridles. Wagons, too, were decorated, for example with little triangles set around the edges of wheels.

Most of the bronzes come from graves, not just in Ordos but from hundreds of graves scattered across north China and

Inner Asia. Some have even been found in Iran. Specialists try to make sense of the stylistic variants, tracking the trade routes and dating them within their 1,000-year span, between about 800 BC and AD 200, which overlaps the Xiongnu empire. In fact, one cemetery dating from the sixth to the fifth century BC, found in 1979 in Maoqinggou (Liangcheng County, Inner Mongolia, just east of Hohhot), is described by some scholars as the cradle of Xiongnu culture because its contents suggest that the people who used it were changing from farmers to nomads. It had seventy-nine graves, all simple pits, with 229 bronze plaques, fairly evenly distributed between men and women (though elsewhere belt-plaques were mostly used by men). It is tempting to use the motifs – dragons, griffins and other Animal Style images – as evidence for clan or tribal connections. But that's not possible, because the plaques were made and traded too widely. In a system that suggests modern parallels, many were made for the Chinese market, with Chinese characters on them – 'Chinese styles of execution with steppe iconography', as the American scholar Bryan Miller puts it.[5]

Graves were often destroyed by bad weather, as Wang Shun's discovery of the golden coronet showed. In addition, the bronzes were made to be worn and attached to horses and wagons, and must have often been dropped. A century ago in Ordos, these items could be found lying about in the sand. Locals gathered them by the bucketful and sold them for a pittance. No one took much notice of them. In fact, only a few people, mostly foreigners, were interested in Chinese art and antiquities,

[5] Bryan K. Miller, *Power Politics in the Xiongnu Empire* (see Bibliography). See also Ursula Brosseder's long article 'Belt Plaques as an Indicator of East–West Relations' in Brosseder and Miller (eds), *Xiongnu Archaeology*.

which made the early twentieth century a golden age for foreign collectors. Explorers – Aurel Stein from Great Britain, Petr Kozlov from Russia and others – acquired vast quantities of manuscripts for practically nothing. As Mr Shark said ruefully, 'Some people might call this robbery.'

Among the collectors was the remarkable Isabel Ingram. Isabel was the daughter of an American missionary who had good connections with Puyi, the boy-emperor who had been allowed to stay on in the Forbidden City when China became a republic in 1911. At the age of twenty, Isabel graduated from the US, returned to Beijing and became tutor to Puyi's new wife, the sixteen-year-old, missionary-educated, English-speaking Wanrong. A picture of them together shows them looking sweetly beautiful and delicate as porcelain. They enjoyed their similarities, and even swopped clothes to look alike. In her position as royal tutor, Isabel met many visiting scholars and officials. One of them was Horace Jayne, Curator of Oriental Art at the Philadelphia Museum of Art. Another was her future husband, William Mayer, military attaché at the US embassy. In 1924, the emperor and Wanrong were expelled from the palace, Isabel's role as tutor ended and she got a job back in the USA in the Philadelphia Museum. When her boss became director of the Pennsylvania University Museum, she followed, and began to publish scholarly articles on Chinese art. In 1930, she married William Mayer in Beijing, and the two began buying art. Although few people were interested in the bronzes – they did not even have a collective name – there was huge international interest in Scythian art, and she recognized that the Ordos artefacts shared motifs with Scythian ones. Criss-crossing north China and haunting antique shops, she and her husband gathered over 500 'Scythian' bronzes and other items, most of which they sold to the Pennsylvania Museum in 1941.

As experts came to recognize the value of these finds, Europe and the USA built their collections, buying them in small numbers wherever they could. The objects were not just found in Ordos and were made of gold, silver and tin as well as bronze, but from the 1950s they have been referred to as the Ordos Bronzes. Those found locally are now stored in the Ordos Bronze Museum. 'We have a collection of about ten thousand,' said Mr Wang. 'People still find them today.'

'What would one sell for?' I answered my own question online later. Bronzes rarely come up for auction. When they do, they go for £500 and up. In 2015, a bronze of the sixth or fifth century BC sold for 123,000 euros.

'Nothing,' said Mr Wang. 'It is illegal to sell them.'

Which makes one wonder where the sellers got theirs.

Who made them? No one knows. There are no accounts of their manufacture. A few carbon-14 dates suggest that the business was flourishing in 500 BC, which means it must have arisen considerably earlier, when pastoral nomadism and mounted archery began to mature as a way of life. That idea is supported by a reference in about 661 BC to two grassland tribes in what is now Inner Mongolia named Rong and Di, who had a reputation for violence. An adviser to the north-eastern border state of Zhao, Guan Zhong, noted that 'The Di and Rong are like wolves, and can never be satisfied.' Chinese historians often referred to them as *hu*, but this was no more than a generalized term for 'barbarians'. They could have become a real threat, for a coordinated attack by an army of mounted archers could work on infantry like a chainsaw on a tree-trunk. What it took was a leader with a vision. That was what the Rong and Di lacked. The problem for a would-be conqueror was that nomads were famously independent. They were more likely to vanish back to their herds in a cloud of dust rather than do as they were told. Still, there was a threat to be countered.

The first written evidence that a new way of life had emerged survives from Zhao. In 307 BC, a Zhao king named Wu Ling, overcoming opposition from his more conventional uncle, 'decreed that the entire kingdom should adopt the *hu* attire, training his subjects to ride and shoot arrows from horseback'.[6] The kit included a long slit coat for ease of riding (the forerunner of trousers) and no floppy Chinese-style sleeves that might interfere with archery on horseback. It worked. Zhao defended itself from nomadic raiders because it was half-nomad itself, and as a result built a powerful kingdom that lasted almost a century.

No one recorded any further details of the Di and Rong. Sima Qian – a historian of the second century BC who will appear often in this book – also mentions them along with a further ten tribes of 'barbarians': 'These nomadic tribes settled in the riparian valleys and mountainous pastures; each had its respective chieftain and was to each its own.'[7] But from the second half of the fourth century BC, all of them were, it seems, in the process of being conquered, or absorbed, or in some way coming together to create a single tribe: the Xiongnu.

What this new group called themselves in their unwritten

---

[6] Quoted in Yap, *Wars*.
[7] Sima Qian, *Records of the Grand Historian*, translated by Burton Watson (see Bibliography).

language is unknown, but other cultures suggest their name. In 313 BC, a trader from Sogdia (in today's Uzbekistan and neighbouring countries) abandoned some letters – that is, strips of bamboo that were used to write on – in a tower near Dunhuang. One of the letters complains bitterly of the destruction caused by people the writer calls the *Xwn*, Hun. That is the core of their name in both Mongol and Chinese. In the Latin script versions of both languages, they are often simply 'Huns', implying that they were the ancestors of Attila's people who helped bring down the Roman empire in the fifth century AD – a controversial idea to which we will return in the final chapter.

The most common name reflects Chinese usage. To represent foreign names, Chinese chooses syllables that sound vaguely like the original. Since each syllable has many written signs, Chinese commonly selects a character that suggests something suitable. 'Hun' in Chinese is represented by the sign that is transliterated in today's pinyin system as *xiōng*. The sign means 'terrible, horrible, bad, fear-inducing'. Then, for some unknown reason, a Han-dynasty scribe chose to add a second sign – *nú*, with an ascending tone, meaning 'slave'. The two elements together – 'bad slaves' – must have seemed a suitable name for the 'barbaric' northerners. That's what Sima Qian called them, writing in the late second century BC. Since China is the region's dominant culture, the new rulers in Ordos and neighbouring steppes are almost universally known as Xiongnu (pronounced Shiung-noo), in the pinyin transliteration system. In the old Wade-Giles system, now superseded, they are Hsiung-nu.

The first mention of the Xiongnu in Chinese sources refers to a date some time before the mid-third century BC. Sima

Qian says they had been around for 1,000 years before that, 'a vast period during which the tribes split up and scattered into various groups, sometimes expanding, sometimes dwindling in size'. Like all Inner Asian groups, leaders always tried to grow their clans, but if they succeeded their efforts evaporated on their deaths. There were no empires on the steppe before the Xiongnu. Genetic studies suggest that they were 'probably a local development from within Mongolia dating back to at least the Bronze Age slab-grave burials (1200–400 BC).'[8] If so, they migrated into Ordos and somehow by the late third century BC they had become a significant force. We have no idea if the Xiongnu were a separate tribe or the name of a confederacy or what other unmentioned sub-groups they absorbed. The few details given by Sima Qian suggest they resembled the Scythians in their habits. Like the Scythians, they turned the skulls of slain enemies into wine-cups, sewed their scalps into clothes or tied them on to the reins of their horses and mixed wine with the blood of an animal with a sword when swearing an oath. On their origins, Nicola Di Cosmo, of the Institute of Advanced Study, Princeton, summarizes the problem: 'After several decades of debates, questions relating to the ethnic and linguistic identity of the Xiongnu are still unanswered.'[9]

Here's a possible scenario. Imagine the Xiongnu as the Chinese first heard of them – a small group of nomads in the pleasant pastures (as they were then) of Ordos. They are herders, leaving few archaeological records, no large tombs for instance, because their leaders were too poor to amass

[8] Christine Lee and Zhang Linhu, 'Xiongnu Population History', in Brosseder and Miller (eds), *Xiongnu Archaeology*.
[9] Nicola Di Cosmo, *Ancient China and its Enemies* (see Bibliography).

any riches for grave-goods. That would come later, in Mongolia. Life for them is a succession of seasons, herding, horse-raising and occasional raids on their settled neighbours to the south. 'They move about in search of water and pasture, and have no walled cities or fixed dwellings, nor do they engage in any kind of agriculture,' says Sima Qian. 'Their lands however are divided into regions under the control of various leaders.' There is a lot of intermixing and overlap between grasslands and farmlands. Herding, raiding, trading, nomadizing from season to season, intermixing: that was normality, for many unrecorded generations, until the 250s BC.

Now they get their first proper mention, in the records of 244 BC, which look back several years, perhaps as many as fifteen. *The Mirror of Good Governance (Zizhi Tongjian,* the massive 354-volume tenth-century history by Sima Guang, which provides much of the information about the Xiongnu)[10] records the story of the great Zhao general Li Mu, who 'often stayed in the Dai and Yanmen [prefectures on the northern border] to protect them from the Xiongnu . . . he taught his soldiers to shoot arrows and ride horses, and he carefully maintained the beacon towers' (in the Zhao frontier walls, which like those of other states preceded the Great Wall). His plan was to use the Zhao wall not for defence, but for deception. 'He issued a regulation that said: "If the Xiongnu invade the border to plunder, you must quickly enter the fortifications, and unauthorized capturing of enemies will be punished by decapitation." ' This went on for some years. As a result, the Xiongnu concluded that Li Mu was a coward, as did his

[10] This is the basis for Yap's *Wars with the Xiongnu.*

own troops. So did the king himself. He replaced Li Mu with a general who had more aggression but less sense. 'Every time they went into battle, they suffered many setbacks and had many people killed or injured. Therefore they could not cultivate the land or raise animals on the border.' The king saw the error of his judgement, and recalled Li Mu, who accepted only on condition that he could use his former tactics: retreat to safety when threatened. Having re-established his reputation for cowardice, Li Mu prepared a great army of 1,300 charioteers, 13,000 cavalrymen, 50,000 infantry and 100,000 archers. When the Xiongnu, unimpressed by the numbers, attacked next, Li Mu feigned defeat and let them capture 'a few thousand men'. The Xiongnu chief, now certain of victory, sent a larger force, on which Li Mu pounced from two flanks, 'killing hundreds of thousands of men and horses . . . Ten years after this, the Xiongnu still did not dare to come close to the cities on the border of Zhao.'

There is no need to take these figures seriously. The point is the Xiongnu were growing into a formidable force. A few years pass, and they begin to come more sharply into focus. They get their first named leader, Tumen. His title is *chanyu*. This is short for 'Chengli Gutu Chanyu'. The meaning is obscure. Probably *chengli* is the equivalent of Tengri, the Mongol sky god. Chinese sources say that *gutu* means 'son', but more likely, given the Xiongnu's cultural roots, it derives from the Turkic *qut*, meaning 'good fortune'.[11] No one knows

---

[11] *Qut* was part of the nickname of Genghis Khan's foster-brother (or foster-son, accounts vary) and chief official, Shigi Qutuqu, Shigi the Fortunate. The Chinese version of the title is 單于 chán yú, but it is impossible to know if this represents the Xiongnu sounds accurately.

the origin of the word *chanyu*, but the sense is clear: 'Heaven-sent Supreme Leader'.

Not supreme yet. The Xiongnu were subservient both to the Dong in today's north-east China, and to the Yuezhi, a tribe ruling the west, in what is today Gansu. The Yuezhi form an important part of our story, but their origins too are largely a mystery. In a detailed study of them, Craig Benjamin, the Australian-born Professor of History at Grand Valley State University, Michigan, suggests that they migrated from southern Russia, arriving in Gansu around 2000 BC. They established themselves in Xinjiang and Gansu – today's north-west China – and were recorded by surrounding cultures as traders in jade and horses. Their name in Chinese means 'Clan of the Moon', but what they called themselves is unknown. They had a king, and they probably spoke an Iranian language. Some scholars equate them with the Tocharians, who lived in the oasis communities round the great deserts of today's Xinjiang, forming commercial dots on the early versions of the Silk Road. Later, they were expelled by the Xiongnu, undertook a vast migration westward and founded the Kushan empire, which between about 50 BC and AD 200 was a crossroads linking Rome and China (among others). In brief, the Yuezhi formed a wide-ranging, long-lasting, highly significant culture that was virtually unknown to the wider world because it had no narrative history in written sources. The Xiongnu dealt with an eastern sub-section, attracted to them as moths to a flame by their commercial links westward.

Sima Qian tells us a little about Tumen. His clan or family was Luandi (in Chinese), which remained the royal lineage until the Xiongnu fell. He had a son and heir named Modun

(Maodun, Modu and Mao-tun are alternative transliterations), who will soon take centre stage. Tumen became infatuated with a new young wife with whom he had a second son, and decided to replace Modun as his heir with his newborn. What was to be done with Modun? A solution was to hand. To guarantee their security and as a sign of submission, minor tribes often sent princes as hostages to dominant tribes. So Tumen sent Modun off to the Yuezhi, a move that must have left him seething with resentment against his father.

Was this true? It's credible, in part at least. The name Tumen means nothing in Chinese, but in Mongolian and Turkic languages it means 'Ten Thousand', the equivalent of the Chinese *wàn*, with the difference that in Mongol and Turkic it is both a military unit and a common name. There are lots of Tumens in Mongolia today (one being the eminent archaeologist Dashtseveg Tumen). The Tumen River marks North Korea's frontier with Russia.

But only in part credible, for the whole story of Tumen and his son is just too good to be totally true. As Nikolai Kradin (of the Russian Academy of Sciences, Far Eastern Branch, Vladivostok) points out,[12] 'historical events and elements of fantasy are mixed'. It is as if the origins of Xiongnu power had already been turned into an epic by bards, and then told to Sima Qian. Is it really credible that a plot to murder Tumen should unfold in public? That it involves the killing of both a beloved wife and a beloved horse? That events unfold in threes? That a man who murders his way to the throne should be a hero? Perhaps Tumen – Ten Thousand – is no more than

[12] Nikolai N. Kradin, 'Stateless Empire', in Brosseder and Miller (eds), *Xiongnu Archaeology*.

a symbolic character, an Everyman from whom Modun seizes power.

You will see what I mean in Chapter 5, when Modun takes over in dramatic circumstances, and makes the Xiongnu powerful enough to found the first nomadic empire. But that was in response to events unfolding to the south and east, in what would soon become the heart of a unified China.

3

THE GROWING THREAT
OF A UNIFIED CHINA

THE THIRD CENTURY BC, IN WHAT WILL BECOME THE HEART-
land of a unified China: a hundred mini-states and city-states
have whittled themselves down to seven. The seven are at war,
constantly. Unity, a dominant theme for students of Chinese
history, was non-existent. But it was on its way, with many
implications for Ordos and its neighbouring grasslands north
of the Yellow River. For China's unification created pressures
that would soon spill over into the steppes, inspiring the nomads
to match the power of the new China, and confront it. Unity
and pressure on one side led to unity and counter-pressure on
the other.

In the Chinese heartland, unification had deep roots in
preceding periods of rivalry and conflict. Under the influence
of constant warfare, social evolution went into overdrive.
Bronze gave way to iron, tools improved, agriculture became
more productive, trade increased. The obsession with war

had equal and opposite obsessions: with peace, diplomacy, art, philosophy and poetry. Great thinkers struggled with great questions, the greatest thinker being Kong Fuzi, or Confucius to give him his Latinized name. Dismayed by the evils of his world, he devised a system of ethics and government that promoted the good. He taught that people should see clearly their place in a hierarchical universe, from king to commoner. All should fulfil their responsibilities to those above and below, exercising loyalty, piety, filial respect and benevolence. He taught that human beings are part of one big family, governed by family virtues. The advice to rulers from Confucius was: Rule virtuously and peace will follow.

But all too often it didn't. A school of cynics arose, asking a tough question: What is the point of cultivating peace if it does not lead to peace? Their answer was brutally pragmatic: None at all. The only way to peace was through war. In peace, the wise ruler prepared for war; in war, he ensured victory; in victory, he preserved peace by preparing for yet more war. It was this philosophy above all that would, a century later, force the pace of change in Ordos and other nearby steppes.

Warfare inspired another twist in the spiral of social evolution: wall-building. City walls had been a feature of the settled lifestyle for centuries, but now, suddenly, round about 300 BC, *frontier* walls appear. This was possible because, for the first time in Chinese history, states could organize labour on a large scale. These states seemed to need the sort of protection everyone was used to: a city wall, but bigger. So states built walls around themselves, along their frontiers, against each other. The walls, ostensibly for defence, also defined borders and imposed the state's will. Small-scale city-states were becoming nation-states, backed by tough legal systems, huge armies, great irrigation projects, bureaucracies, taxation.

One state, Qin, began to set itself apart. Qin – centred on present-day Shaanxi, the cradle of Chinese civilization – was in those days considered by other states to be an uncouth backwater. But it was very successful. In an age of states dedicated to the rigid rule of law, it was the most dedicated. Every official act had to go towards making the state rich, the army strong and expansion rapid.

This line of thought was given its most forceful expression by an ambitious young scholar named Shang. Lord Shang (Shang Yang), as he became known, was born in the state of Wei, which dominated the middle Yellow River, probably around 400 BC, when the states that would merge as China were at eternal war with each other (hence the name of the age, the Warring States, 480–221 BC). Might is right (he argued), power the only virtue. Human beings are idle, greedy, cowardly, treacherous, foolish, shifty, so Confucius's idea that they respond well to good treatment is simply naïve. The only way to rule is to entice, terrify, reward and punish. This is not arbitrary, but based on the stern rule of law, applied to everyone without distinction, an agenda from which it gets its name: Legalism. The ruler's task is firstly to devise the law, then record it, then ensure that it is applied impartially through officials utterly subservient to the state's institutions.

Wei's prime minister, Gongshu Cuo, was so awed by Shang's abilities that he feared what might happen if the young man took his ideas to a rival king. Sima Qian tells the story. When the prime minister was on his deathbed, he advised the king to keep Shang's loyalty by making him the next prime minister. If not, he said, 'be sure to have him killed. Don't allow him to leave the state!' Claiming that Gongshu was 'quite out of his mind', the king dismissed both ideas, with the result that Gongshu had feared. Shang, unrewarded and very much alive, turned to the neighbouring state of Qin, the state that was emerging as the strongest of the seven warring rivals.

His move to Qin was welcomed by its ruler, Duke Xiao, who seized on Shang's grim policies. In the words of his follower Han Fei: 'Lord Shang taught Duke Xiao of Qin how to organize the people into groups of five or ten families that would spy on each other . . . anyone who failed to report criminal activity would be chopped in two at the waist.' In addition, the duke had three aims: to ensure a professional army; to provide farm-labourers who supplied its food; and to uphold the Law, applied to everyone, except of course the duke himself, for he personified the Law and was above it. For Shang, nothing must rival the prince's laws, not even the cries of the people: 'A weak people means a strong state,' he wrote. 'A strong state means a weak people.'

Shang was not popular. When Duke Xiao died, Shang didn't last long. He was caught, 'tied to two chariots and torn apart'.[1]

But his policies worked. Qin expanded, spreading southwards into Sichuan, then eastwards into neighbouring Zhou. War followed war, and death piled on death, as Qin turned itself into the hardest of the hard.

---

[1] The quotes are from *Han Fei Tzu: Basic Writings*, in Burton Watson's translation (see Bibliography).

Shang's spirit lived on in Han Fei, who set out the Legalist agenda with brilliance. Here are four pieces of his extremely scary advice on how rulers should behave:

- 'It is said: "So still he seems to dwell nowhere at all; so empty no one can seek him out." The enlightened ruler reposes in non-action above, and below his ministers tremble with fear.'

- 'This is the way of the enlightened ruler: Where there are accomplishments, the ruler takes credit for their worth; where there are errors, the ministers are held responsible for the blame; hence the ruler's name never suffers.'

- 'Be empty, still, and idle, and from your place of darkness observe the defects of others. See but do not appear to see; listen but do not seem to listen; know but do not let it be known that you know.'

- 'This is the way to listen to the words of others: be silent as though in a drunken stupor. Say to yourself: Lips! Teeth! Do not be the first to move . . . Let others say their piece – I will gain knowledge thereby.'

The scene is set for the entry of the First Emperor, the man who would confront the 'barbarians' of Ordos and the other northern grasslands, and turn them from rivals into an existential menace. His story, like many in history, mixes character and events entirely at random, yet leads to an end that seems inevitable, in this case unity.

The story starts, as it often does with dictators, in a deep sense of insecurity rooted in childhood.

Our main source is Sima Qian, Grand Historian of Han,

writing a century after the events he describes.[2] As he tells it, the story opens in the next-door state, Zhao, with a rich and ambitious merchant named Lü Buwei meeting a minor Qin prince, Zichu, the son of a junior concubine of the heir to the Qin throne. Zichu, it seems, is never going to amount to much. He is not in line for succession – indeed, there is no line, because the crown prince's official wife, of whom Zichu is very fond, is barren. One of twenty sons by various concubines, Zichu has been sent off to become a hostage in the Zhao court, a common diplomatic ploy to prove Qin's good intentions. But being low in the pecking order, Zichu lives frugally, without a retinue or carriages, and with no future, until Lü spots in him a chance of advancement.

Lü is a novelty in the changing society of the time. Merchants had previously been despised by Confucians as under-educated parasites. But in these Legalistic times, merchants were on the rise. Smart, self-serving, unscrupulous, Lü invites the prince into a back room, and proposes a scheme to lever him on to the Qin throne. The prince has nothing to lose, and agrees.

Lü gives the prince some cash to hire himself a band of followers and buys some 'rare objects, trinkets and toys', which he takes to the Qin capital, Xianyang. He strikes up an acquaintance with an intermediary and has his purchases delivered to the wife of the crown prince along with a message about how much Zichu adores her. Since she has no son, he

---

[2] There are several other sources: Ban Gu's *Han Shu* (finished in the early 100s AD), the *Hou Han Shu* (fifth century) and Jia Yi's *Xin Shu* (second century BC). All are based on lost works, and written a century or more after the events they describe. Sima Qian remains the top source, mainly because of his storytelling skills.

says, she will have no one to look after her when the emperor dies. She had better find a stepson, who will therefore be the crown prince's heir, and second in line to the throne. Eventually, when 'the one whom you call son becomes king, you need never fear any loss of position'. The one she should choose is, of course, Zichu. So it happens. Zichu becomes the crown prince's heir, and Lü becomes his tutor.

Now comes a dramatic incident that may or may not be true. Lü has a very beautiful girlfriend. She becomes pregnant. Zichu sees her, falls in love, and asks for her. Lü, whose whole future is now tied to Zichu, swallows his outrage and hands the poor girl over. In 259 BC, she has a son, named Zheng – the future First Emperor.

In 251 BC, after a couple of royal deaths, Zichu becomes king, the girlfriend his queen, and Lü his prime minister. Five years later Zichu dies, leaving thirteen-year-old Zheng to succeed, under the control of his all-powerful patron.

Lü and the beautiful queen, his former mistress, continue their relationship, but Lü, afraid of discovery, hatches another plot even more complicated and lurid than the previous one. In Sima Qian's words:

> The queen dowager did not cease her wanton behaviour. Lü Buwei began to fear that, if her conduct were ever brought to light, he himself would become involved with the scandal. He therefore searched about in secret until he found a man named Lao Ai who had an unusually large penis, and made him a servant in his household. Then, when an occasion arose, he had suggestive music performed and, instructing Lao Ai to stick his penis through the centre of a wheel made of paulownia wood, had him walk about with

it, making certain that the report of this reached the ears of the queen dowager so as to excite her interest.

Should we believe this extraordinary story? Why *paulownia* wood? Probably because such details add plausibility, of which Sima Qian was a master. But plausibility is not the same as truth. It is, perhaps, no more than a rumour that adds drama to explain the beginning of a long-lasting affair.

Anyway, the queen asked to meet Lao Ai. But there was a problem. The palace system did not allow 'real' men into the dowager empress's quarters. So Lü's plot gets its next twist. He arranges for Lao Ai to be falsely accused of a crime for which the punishment is castration. The official in charge of castration is then bribed to pretend to carry out the procedure, plucking out Lao Ai's beard and eyebrows to make him look like a eunuch. 'In this way,' says Sima Qian, 'he eventually came to wait on the queen, who carried on clandestine relations with him and grew to love him greatly.'

The affair continued for several years. As the queen's top adviser, he was made a marquis and acquired a retinue of 1,000 retainers. The queen bore Lao Ai two sons, who thus became half-brothers and possible heirs of the teenaged King Zheng, who was kept in the dark by his mentor, Lü Buwei, his mother's ex-lover and perhaps his real father. This was a ticking time bomb.

It exploded during the ninth year of his reign (238 BC), when 'someone reported' to King Zheng the truth about his mother's affair with Lao Ai. And Lü Buwei's role. The king ordered an investigation. Lao Ai, panic-stricken, tried to start a revolt in which several hundred died. But his followers deserted him, and he was quickly captured.

So there was the 21-year-old emperor, Zheng, suddenly aware that he was possibly a bastard, or at best the son of a minor prince who came to the throne by trickery, that his mother was an ex-dancer of ill repute obsessed by a well-endowed and treacherous gigolo, all with the participation of the man to whom he owed his throne.

The stakes could hardly be higher. Either he would remain a puppet, controlled by his mother, her lover and his mentor; or he had to assert himself by crushing the lot of them.

He chose suppression. Lao Ai was tied to four chariots, which were then driven off in different directions. His associates and relatives were executed, as were the two boys, his half-brothers and possible future rivals. Lao Ai's 1,000 hangers-on had their estates confiscated and were exiled, as was his mother and Lü Buwei, who committed suicide by drinking poison.

That left King Zheng alone, betrayed, without his closest adviser, surrounded by thousands of clamorous courtiers, any one of whom could turn traitor. What should he do? His first reaction was uncontrolled, foaming-at-the-mouth anger. In the words of the eleventh-century historian Sima Guang, the king issued a decree: 'Whoever even dares to utter a word regarding my mother, I will have him decapitated, quartered and his remains scattered in front of the palace as exhibits.' Twenty-seven people died for daring to utter a solitary remark about the king's mother. An adviser named Mao Jiao, from the kingdom of Qi, was so appalled at the king's unfilial behaviour that he risked death to point out the king's failings. 'Get the giant cauldron ready!' screamed the king. 'I will have him stewed alive!' But Mao Jiao persisted: other kings have been notorious for their abominable cruelty, but Zheng outdid them all. As a result he said, 'I am apprehensive for Your Majesty. No one will dare to come near Qin again.' Saying which, he doffed his hat and prostrated himself, prepared to die. That did it. The king raised him up, spared him and made him an adviser.

What now? Well, he already had the answer, from Li Si, an ambitious Legalist, who had been advising the king throughout his teenage years. His advice, based on Han Fei's, was to withdraw into a world of mystery, guard against all impulses towards mercy, and do only those things that increase power.

At its heart, under King Zheng's iron hand and imperialist vision, were four interdependent elements: efficient agriculture, based on the rich farmlands of the Wei valley, which provided food and excess manpower; a committed bureaucracy which gathered taxes, made lists of recruits, oversaw irrigation and managed the food supply to the army; a large professional army; and, to undermine his rivals, espionage and disinformation.

As all dictators know, nothing secures power at home better than a war abroad. The army was the key, and it worked brilliantly. It had no secret weapon. The same weapons were used by all the warring states – bows and arrows, halberds, swords, armour, even the crossbow, a devastatingly effective weapon, which was far more powerful than an ordinary bow and could be held ready like a loaded rifle. Qin also had repeating crossbows, which had a magazine and could fire ten poisoned bolts in twenty seconds.

On crossbows, the bowstring was caught and held by the trigger. Triggers were wonderful devices. As Joseph Needham puts it in his monumental *Science and Civilisation in China* (Vol. 5, 30), they were 'among the greatest triumphs of ancient metallurgical and engineering practice in any civilisation'. Six pieces of bronze fitted together with the precision of a bolt-action rifle. It made the crossbow into the ancient equivalent of the Kalashnikov: sophisticated but simple, easily made, easily dismantled, easily maintained.

Qin society was a state-sized fighting machine. The men and their commanders trained for years to produce tough, mobile, highly disciplined troops. They could march 50 kilometres a day in leather armour, carrying crossbows, pikes, swords and provisions for three days. The main force was backed up by separate groups of reinforcements, all coordinated by gongs, drums, waving banners and messengers in four-horse chariots.

There was nothing new in any one element. It was the whole coordinated package that set the Qin army apart – the food supply, the recruitment, the vision of conquest and unity, centralized control, communication, training, discipline, weaponry. Thus, for the first time in Chinese history, an army arose dedicated not simply to victory in battle but to the conquest of territory. Once started – with the conquest of Han in 234 BC – the Qin army snowballed inexorably onwards, from strength to strength. If and when Qin turned on the nearby steppes, its tribes would surely stand no chance.

Of the conquests themselves, hardly anything is recorded, except their dates. Campaign followed campaign, details unknown. Han, Zhao, Wei, Chu, Yan and Qi all fell, and in 221 Qin became the core of today's China. Those in the seven states united by the First Emperor had long referred to their lands as the centre, the 'Central Nation' or 'Middle Kingdom' (*zhong guo*), which is what the nation is called by its people today.

But not by foreigners. Now unified from the borders of

Tibet to the Pacific, from the Inner Mongolian escarpment to the South China Sea, this region was gradually equated by outsiders with its dominant power. Thus, as the name passed from language to language across Eurasia, did Qin become China.

Now began a revolution in which the First Emperor seized total control over all aspects of society. It started with a title. How was the king to be addressed? Only the grandest title would suit: Great August (*da huang*) was the title conferred on the legendary founder 2,000 years before. The early emperors were named *di,* a term for the highest supernatural power. Moreover Zheng was to be the first of a long line, the beginning, the *shĭ* 始. So he became Qin Shi Huang Di, the First Qin August Emperor. For the sake of simplicity, he's usually 'the First Emperor'.

According to a popular line of Daoist thought, each historical age was dominated by one of the five elements: earth, wood, metal, fire and water, which overwhelm each other in a fixed cycle. Zhao had ruled through the power of fire. The First Emperor chose water, which extinguishes fire. Water had certain attributes, its colour being black, its number six. So all flags became black, six the preferred unit of length for measuring almost anything, from the height of hats to the width of chariot-axles.

Out went the old kingdoms and their feudal hierarchies, in came three dozen centrally controlled commanderies, subdivided into several hundred prefectures. From all the six defeated states, weapons were collected and melted down to make bells and twelve vast statues of barbarians. Each of the seven states had had different measures of area, widths of cartwheels, coins, weights, measures, styles of clothing and scripts. All were now collated, unified and imposed empire-wide. The revision of the script, various forms of which had been in existence for two millennia, was a major factor in China's cultural unity, because governments could issue edicts that everyone everywhere could read, even if pronunciation varied widely.

Power made the First Emperor a terrifying figure. Sima Qian portrays him as physically unattractive – high pointed nose, slit eyes, pigeon breast, stingy, cringing, graceless. Traditional portraits of him don't conform to this lean and hungry image, showing him as bearded, bulky, and always wearing headgear with tassels dangling down the front to hide his semi-divine features from mortal gaze. It's all totally inauthentic, of course, since there were no contemporary portraits, but – rather like Christ, Genghis Khan and alien abductors – there arose an accepted, iconic version of what he was supposed to look like. Certainly, he was moody, easily angered and unpredictable, traits that he shared with other tyrants. It has been part of accepted history that he burned books, destroyed the records of his predecessors, and buried scholars alive because they opposed him. Whether or not all this is true, national unity was achieved with extremes of character, vision and ruthlessness.

The new society worked brilliantly, if you ignore the extreme brutality with which the laws were applied. Labour became available on an unprecedented scale, not only because of the empire's vastly extended population but because hundreds of thousands of soldiers had been freed for labour by the ending of the wars of conquest. Peasants had always been liable to forced service as soldiers and labourers in their own kingdoms. Now they were called up empire-wide. Every male between fifteen and sixty was eligible for labour on state projects. A population of about 20 million could provide a workforce of several million a year. Infrastructure projects – palaces, canals, the emperor's tomb – dominated the new nation.

One problem remained unsolved, one crucial area untaken: Ordos, with its nomads and their cross-border raids. To tackle them, to get troops into and across Ordos, Qin would need a road, of unprecedented scale, to be constructed at unprecedented speed.

4

MENG TIAN AND THE STRAIGHT ROAD

WHEN I FIRST HEARD OF THE ROAD ACROSS ORDOS, I WAS intrigued. It was an extraordinary idea: apparently Qin had built an 800-kilometre road in order to drive out the Xiongnu, seize control of Ordos and extend Qin's borders all the way to the Yellow River. There are no details in the sources. In my mind's eye, I saw a paved highway, suitable for carriages and battalions of soldiers, cutting across the territory from which the Xiongnu sprang. Perhaps I could explore some of it, and see the reality behind my fantasy.

It became an obsession. Driving along Ordos's express-ways, my mind wandered to the question of the Straight Road, as it is known. I brought up the subject with my com-panion, Alatan. He was very patient. Occasionally, we would be diverted on to earth roads by a new road-construction and I would wonder how many men with spades it would take to match these armies of scrapers and trucks. We had long discussions about how the commander-in-chief, Meng Tian, could have fulfilled his orders. It seemed to me I was on the verge of a great new insight, made possible by today's roads. Surely today's engineers could throw light on the problems and solutions of over 2,200 years ago?

The story starts in 214 BC, seven years after unification and thirty-two years after the First Emperor came to the throne. He was becoming obsessed by the possibility of achieving immortality. Work on his tomb, which had been going on for thirty years, increased. But the First Emperor was also interested in not dying. One of the officers sent to discover the secrets of immortality returned 'claiming that it had come to him from gods and spirits' that 'Qin will be destroyed by Hu' – that is, the barbarians of Ordos.

At this – as Sima Qian says in Chapter 88 of his *Shi Ji (Historical Records)*, the English title of which is *Records of the Grand Historian* – the emperor ordered General Meng Tian to respond. Meng Tian, son of a famous father and brother of one of the emperor's closest advisers, was the greatest general of his day. He was told to 'lead a force of 300,000 men and advance north, expelling the Rong and Di barbarians and taking control of the region south of the bend of the Yellow River'. The Rong and Di were two of several sub-groups coming together to become part of the Xiongnu. In another section, Sima Qian says that 'Meng Tian's might struck terror into the Xiongnu people' (with results that will become clear in the next chapter).

This was going to be a long operation. In his history *Zizhi Tongjian (The Mirror of Good Government)*, Sima Guang adds to Sima Qian's account, saying that Meng Tian 'made successive assaults against the Xiongnu tribes, recovering the territories south of the (Yellow) River ... the armies of the frontier were engaged in a protracted war that lasted for more than a decade', after which 'they held sway in the lands of the Xiongnu'. By that time, Meng Tian was dead, in circumstances we will get to later.

Why this massive invasion? There were several possible reasons. Supposedly, it was to counter the threat of the mounted archers, who would (according to the prophecy that fed the First Emperor's paranoia) bring destruction to Qin. In fact, the idea that they were much of a threat to the whole Qin empire, with its massed armies and ranks of crossbowmen, is ridiculous. They were, however, a constant menace on the borders, and had to be dealt with. That fitted well with the emperor's domestic needs and imperialist ambition. Firstly, armies must be used. Idleness breeds boredom, a decline in morale, insubordination, perhaps even revolution. So, secondly, the First Emperor gave them huge and challenging tasks – take Ordos, and build, build, build. Thirdly, armies must be fed, so Qin needed new lands and new colonists. Ordos, once cleared of its nomads, offered prime new territory. Finally, though this is nowhere stated, it would have seemed vital to extend Qin to its 'natural' western and northern boundary on the Yellow River. It was as much a manifest destiny as young America's urge to expand all the way to the Pacific, except in China's case this would prove just the beginning of expansion.

Invasion of Ordos was secured by the Great Wall, the grandest of several huge infrastructure projects. It supposedly ran from Lanzhou to Liaodong on the Pacific, a distance of 10,000 *li* (about 5,000 kilometres), which conforms with the usual name for the Wall, the Wan Li Chang Cheng (the 10,000-li

Long Wall). Outposts were constructed, says Sima Qian, and convicts were transported to the region to populate the new districts. In fact, Sima Qian is both unclear and self-contradictory. In another chapter, he says the troops numbered 100,000, and the route of the Great Wall is left vague. True, north of the Yellow River, in the Yin Mountains, a low wall winding over the hills has a big sign that names it 'The Great Wall of the Qin Dynasty'. I have been there, and climbed on it. It is no more than waist-high, a metre across, and made of slate. There is nothing great about it, certainly nothing ancient, though it seems to follow the line of a wall built by the state of Zhao in about 300 BC. Decaying bits of the Great Wall run across eastern and southern Ordos, but they were built later and are nothing to do with the Qin wall. Whatever Meng Tian built, it was probably made of a mixture of rammed earth and stones, with beacon towers and lookout platforms of stone. Archaeologists have traced it running across Ordos from the south-west to the north-east, picking up on the other side of the Yellow River to join the old Zhou wall. It was about 1,799 kilometres long. Its purpose seems to have been less defensive, more to seize land – much more fertile than it is today – and then control it. Further east, the Great Wall filled in the gaps between pre-existing walls built by the states conquered by Qin. Not quite as great as its name suggests, but still impressive.

These immense operations secured the whole region by expelling the nomads, an act we would now term 'ethnic cleansing'. But that would have been just the start. If the frontier was to be held, troops had to remain on site, and be relieved regularly, and be supplied with food, clothing, mounts and weapons. Let's say it took a few years of preparation, and that the army needed to be in camp by the autumn of 214 BC, since Qin leaders would not have wished to go on campaigning in the winter. Nomads could cope with temperatures down to minus 20°C, but Qin soldiers would have needed base-camps.

So there had to be a road. And we know it was a good one, because Sima Qian travelled along it a century after it was built. 'I have travelled to the northern border,' he wrote, 'and returned by the Straight Road. As I went along I saw the outposts of the Great Wall which Meng Tian constructed for the Qin. He cut through the mountains and filled up the valleys, opening up a direct road. Truly he made free with the strength of the common people!'

Sima Qian told some dubious stories, but here he claims personal experience. It sounds convincing. So we start with a road that carried armies and construction crews, a road good enough to last over 100 years. The more I learned, the more my admiration grew, the more certain I became that there should be something concrete to see – or at least the Qin equivalent of concrete.

But it was also built very fast. Meng Tian's military orders came through in 214 BC, and thereafter work continued only for another four years, because in 210 BC Meng Tian became a victim of the revolution that, another four years later, brought an end to the Qin dynasty. It sounds very much as if the Straight Road, 740 kilometres of it, from the First Emperor's capital Xianyang to the Yellow River, was built in a maximum of four years. A solid road, with – as I imagined – some sort of a paved surface in four years? Wide enough for carriages to pass? With bridges over the ravines? Was this really possible? And if so, how?

Not far north of Ordos City there is an archaeological site called the Qin Straight Road. This would surely answer my questions. The road led through ridges and over eroded ravines to an entrance that looked like a film set for a Great Wall movie. Inside was a huge car park and a mock fortress with a raised terrace, 6 metres above the ground, on which stood a statue of the First Emperor in his carriage, its four rearing horses about to leap into a void. The place was abandoned. The three of us – me, my guide 'Water' Xu, and the driver – were the only ones there. Weeds poked through the tiled surface. There wasn't even a ticket office. Someone had had a great idea, which had not worked.

It was obvious why not. For tourists, there was nothing to see but waving grass, with no immediate sign of a road. But wait: a few metres from the crenellated wall that fringed the site was a grassy ridge half a metre high heading north. At the edge of the ridge, the grass fell away to reveal eroded, gravelly earth. It was light brown, tinged with red, exactly the same colour as the underlying soil. If this was really the remains of Meng Tian's road, there was no hint of either a foundation or any paved surface. No tiles, no bricks.

In the other direction, a faint path of flattened grass led to a huge white stone, 2 metres high and 4 or 5 metres long, on which three characters, cut into the rock and painted red, proclaimed this was the 'Qin Straight Road'. But there was no sign of it. Beyond the rock, the path led on another 100 metres through the ankle-high grass. It looked like an invitation, so I followed. There was nothing there, except a drop into a ravine, with no sign of a paved descent or road leading on beyond into the afternoon sun.

Well, so much for my fantasies of pavements and bridges.

It looked as if Meng Tian had worked with nothing but coarse earth. And – presumably – tens of thousands of workers to move it.

I needed to rethink. Who better to help than an expert in road-building? What greater expert than the boss of the Oriental Holding Group, which built many of the major roads and expressways across Ordos? His name was Ding Ding, which to my English ears sounded like a delicate and charming bell. In the elegant surroundings of Beijing's Kunlun Hotel, with a discreet orchestral version of Elvis Presley's 'Love Me Tender' to accompany the coffee, I asked him to imagine himself as Meng Tian, commissioned by the First Emperor to conquer and occupy Ordos. It would all depend on building the Straight Road. How would he do it?

Ding Ding certainly had experience to address the problem; not that modern road-building should be compared to Qin road-building. He was virtually born into the business, because his father ran a construction company. Having been to a college for road-construction managers, he took over the business. Almost at once, in 2002, he started work on the road between Dongsheng (part of Ordos City, the local capital) and Kangbashi, the new town to the south. Back then, those 30 kilometres were appalling. I nodded, remembering. That was when I first came here. At one point the rough road vanished into a flooded river, and we crossed only thanks to the foolhardy driver, who accelerated through the muddy waters. The government decided to turn it from two lanes to four lanes, which, said Mr Ding, 'we did in one year'. Two years later, it was too busy, 'so in 2009 the government said, "Let's double it again!" So now it's an eight-lane expressway.'

'You're a modern Meng Tian,' I said.

Not really, he said. 'The technology of building roads across the desert is not very difficult.' But there was one problem I had never considered – to take care of a new road is more difficult than building it, because the sand moves and covers the road. Today, this problem is solved with barriers and by anchoring the sand with plants either side of the road. But Meng Tian would have needed to plan for permanent teams of sweepers in addition to the workers used to make it.

What would that have involved? Mr Ding became thoughtful. Meng Tian would have had to solve another problem even before he started. He would need to know the best route. There were hills to avoid, streams to ford, ravines to fill in, ridges to cut through. He needed surveyors to explore all the possibilities and report back and collate all the information. How long would that take? Could fifty five-man teams survey 15 kilometres each in the course of a summer? Even if that is about right, a whole year has passed without breaking any ground.

Now what? 'The Qin Emperor was the first to standardize measurements, like the width of chariots,' said Mr Ding, 'so Meng Tian would need to ensure the road was wide enough without being too wide, and firm enough without being too slow to build. I think perhaps crushed stones, like gravel, would make a good surface.'

OK, the road has to be completed as fast as possible. We know it was done within four years, from the fact that Meng Tian was commanding in the field for four years before his arrest and suicide. How many men would it take to build 740 kilometres of hard-packed road in four years?

Luckily, I could offer a few thoughts, because I had written a book on the First Emperor's tomb and his army of terra-cotta warriors. I had done a very rough time-and-motion study to see how many men working over what period of time could have dug out, and then created the emperor's tomb. As a rule of thumb, one man with a spade can shift about 5 tonnes per day, but only in conjunction with several two-man teams carrying slings on poles to cart the earth away. Sima Qian suggested a workforce of 700,000, but that is a ludicrous figure, larger than any city then in existence. How would they be housed and fed? In fact, the surprising conclusion is that the tomb could have been dug by 200 diggers shifting 1,000 tonnes a day for about ten months. Considering that work started on the tomb when the emperor came to the throne in 246 BC, there was no shortage of time – though filling it in and creating the tomb-mound after the emperor's death would have been far more demanding.

Now apply these figures to the road. Sima Qian says that Meng Tian's army numbered either 300,000 or 100,000, but this is such a disparity that it cannot be much of a guide. That doesn't matter, because the numbers needed to make the road are much smaller than that.

Let's do the sums in very round figures: 740 kilometres long, 4 metres wide and (say) 0.5 metre deep – that makes about 1.5 million cubic metres of earth to dig up, combine with gravel, and replace. If workers can remove 5 tonnes, or 3.5 cubic metres, per day, and if they can replace it in the same amount of time, the job can be done with 2,400 workers in about two years – not four – even allowing for bad weather, winter and engineering works, like cutting descents into ravines, filling in the gullies at the bottom, and perhaps making a few wooden bridges.

That may make it sound relatively easy, but those 2,400 front-line workers needed a lot of back-up: a two-man team with a sling on a pole to carry earth away. That raises the labour-force to 7,500, operating simultaneously on different sections of the road. They all have to be fed, clothed, housed and defended. Local herders could have supplied meat, but since no rice was grown in Ordos, that would have to be carried in. There would have been horses by the thousand moving to and from Qin, rafts across the Yellow River, defence forces to be recruited and replaced, tents to be ordered and delivered. The back-up army would have numbered several more thousand, beyond the 7,500, though that's still a long way off Sima Qian's figure. Anyway, manpower in Qin's new empire was not a problem; the real challenge would have been to organize it.

Meng Tian's command of the northern frontier was brought to a sudden end by a drama played out in Qin. It involved the emperor's death, a bizarre plot to manage the succession, and the collapse of the dynasty. The tragic consequences of this for Meng Tian explain why his conquest of the Xiongnu and the occupation of Ordos came to an abrupt end.

At the end of 211 BC, the emperor was on a tour of the east with nine ministers and unknown numbers of assistants and families, all in scores of four-horse chariots, with who knows how many troops and herds of replacement horses. Besides the emperor himself, this mass of people included the following main characters:

- Li Si, chancellor. In office for thirty-seven years and now in his early seventies.

- Huhai, one of the emperor's younger sons (eighteenth of twenty). Aged twenty. Ineffectual.

- Zhao Gao, the villain. Transport chief who was responsible for carriages and communications. He doubled as Huhai's law tutor, and was also the most senior of a small group of eunuch attendants.

- Meng Yi, chief minister. Zhao's enemy. He is the brother of Meng Tian, the great general guarding the northern frontier and building the Great Wall.

The villainous eunuch Zhao Gao and Meng Yi loathed each other. Zhao Gao had once been accused of committing a crime, probably corruption of some kind. Chief minister Meng Yi had Zhao tried and condemned. Zhao was a senior official, but as a good Legalist, Meng Yi argued for the death penalty. Zhao, as young Huhai's tutor, was a slippery lawyer, and persuaded the emperor to pardon him. Zhao never forgave, and nursed a bitter resentment against both Meng Yi and Meng Tian.

This immense retinue – a government on wheels – worked its way south-east to the Yangtze, downriver by boat, then cross-country again for 250 kilometres to the sacred mountain of Kuaiji, near Shaoxing, and finally north along the coast for some 700 kilometres. By now it was the summer of 210 BC. The emperor set off for home.

After some 500 kilometres, suddenly, at a place called Sand Hill on the flat and river-rich expanses of southern Hebei, he fell ill with some unspecified disease, and went downhill fast.

Fearing the end was coming, he despatched Meng Yi home, with orders to make life-saving sacrifices along the way. Then he turned to the succession, a matter he had been avoiding and no one else had dared mention because he hated talking about death. He had exiled his eldest son Fusu to the northern frontier under Meng Tian as a punishment for criticizing the execution of 460 Confucian literati, but Fusu was still his heir. The emperor wrote a peremptory letter: 'When mourning is announced, go to the capital Xianyang and arrange the funeral.' Few words, yet a huge order – work on the tomb to be resumed, subsidiary pits dug, horses and concubines and officials designated for suicide or execution, the Terracotta Army to be made ready for burial, all the correct rituals to be organized.

By implication, this confirmed Fusu as the next emperor. There was another implication: having been seconded to Meng Tian, he would have the empire's toughest army at his back.

Soon after handing the letter over to his communications chief and senior eunuch, Zhao Gao, the First Emperor died.

With his death, his top officials faced a problem. So far, not many people knew what had happened. The emperor's hold on his new estates was tenuous. That was why he was making this long journey, to show his restless people that the empire was there for keeps. What might the reaction be when they knew he had died – and died, moreover, far from Xianyang and the mass of his armies? Revolution loomed, perhaps an end to the Qin empire, and back to the bad old days of eternal wars.

This was one of those rare moments when history held her breath. Not even Prince Huhai knew the emperor was dead. The only ones who did were the eunuch chief of carriages, Zhao Gao, the chancellor Li Si, and a few other trusted eunuchs. To tell or not to tell? The high stakes, the few characters involved, their moral dilemmas, their fears, the rising tension of the next few days – once again, we are in the realm of high drama.

As far as I know, there is no film about what happened next. There should be, there could be, because Sima Qian wrote the script, or at least some powerful dialogue. The villain is Zhao Gao, who, as a eunuch in charge of eunuchs, was head of a group suspected through all Chinese history of being malign and self-serving. Real events and outcomes provide a sound historical framework, but it is Sima Qian's invented dialogue and characterization that fill it with life.

It was eminent, trustworthy, elderly Li Si who took the first step, perhaps with the best intentions: to gain time to work out the best policy. He secretly had the body placed in the imperial carriage, which no one could enter without the permission of the attendant eunuch. Imagine Li Si, Zhao Gao and Huhai in adjacent carriages, hemming in the emperor's along the narrow mud roads as the great procession moved slowly westward. Ministers continued to deliver state papers for the emperor's approval, cooks delivered food. Inside, a second eunuch placed the emperor's seal on the papers, and handed them out. For a couple of days – it could hardly have been more given what happens to dead bodies in the height of summer – business continued as usual.

Zhao Gao still had not handed the emperor's last letter to a messenger. He had a motive to delay, because he hated the whole Meng family. If the letter was sent, then Fusu would take over, Fusu who had defended the Confucian scholars and criticized his own father. And what then? Out would go the long-standing chancellor Li Si and minister Zhao Gao, their extensive families and all their retainers. If they were lucky, they would be allowed to commit suicide; if not, their deaths would be very unpleasant. It was Zhao therefore who took the next crucial step in protection of his own interests.

He strode up or down the line to Huhai's carriage and broke the news to him. The emperor's dead, he said, and there are no orders securing the position of any prince, except Fusu. If Fusu becomes emperor, 'you will be without so much as a foot of territory. What will you do?'[1]

Huhai was too young and too distraught to act. It's obvious what I have to do, he said. Nothing. There's nothing I can do, nothing at all.

Not so, said Zhao Gao, and laid out for him the decision before them. 'At this moment the decision of who shall take control of the empire lies with you, me and the chancellor alone. I beg you to think of this! To make others your subjects or to be a subject of others, to rule men or be ruled by them – that is what is at stake.'

Huhai, still the good son, hesitated. An elder brother betrayed, a father's edict ignored by 'a man like me, so lacking in ability' – it is unrighteous, it is unfilial, the empire would never consent, the altars would not accept my sacrifices . . .

Zhao Gao, once the prince's tutor, seized his former pupil, shook him, and snarled sense and treachery together in his face. Other princes have done worse, he said, actually killed their fathers, and no one said they lacked virtue! 'Virtue does not trouble with niceties! Only dare to be decisive and the gods and spirits will step aside! I beg you to see this through!'

---

[1] Here and in later sections, the words in quotes are direct from the original translation, others (not in quotes) are adapted.

Seeing he was on the verge of winning, he changed tack. Look, he said, we have to see the chancellor about this.

But how is that proper, argued querulous Huhai, seeing as how the death is still hidden, the mourning rites not yet performed?

'Now is the time!' shouted Zhao Gao. 'Now is the time!'

And at last Huhai buckled. Zhao Gao locked him into the plot by giving him the emperor's letter. He then sought out Li Si and brought him up to date. Now that Huhai had the letter, 'The choice of an heir apparent depends solely on your say, my lord, and mine. What do you intend to do?'

There followed a series of exchanges in which Zhao Gao convinced the upright Li Si to back his treacherous scheme. My lord, consider, said Zhao. If Fusu were to rule, he would be backed by Meng Tian and his border army. 'Can you compare with Meng Tian in ability, merit, strategic planning, allies, or friendship with the emperor's eldest son?'

Li Si admitted that he was no match for Meng Tian.

Zhao Gao pressed his point. If Fusu became emperor, Meng Tian would be his chancellor, and 'you, my lord, will be impoverished'. Now consider Huhai: kind-hearted, generous, reserved, punctilious, respectful, an ideal emperor. He, not Fusu, should be the heir. 'At this moment,' he concluded, 'the fate of the empire hangs on Huhai, and I am able to have my way with him.'

Li Si was in an agony of indecision. 'There were those who changed heirs, who fought their brothers, who put their kinsmen to death, and the results were turmoil, death, a kingdom turned into a wilderness. Don't talk to me of plots!'

'Listen!' sad Zhao Gao. 'If you permit this chance to slip away, then the disaster that will extend to your sons and grandsons is enough to make the blood run cold. The skilful man turns disaster into blessing. How will you proceed?'

Li Si wept and sighed in distress – 'Alas! That I alone should face such troubled times!' – but at last he too came on board.

And the conspiracy that Sima Qian refers to as the Sand Hill Plot moved forward.

The three destroyed the original letter, concocted an imperial edict making Huhai heir, and faked a letter to Fusu in the name of the emperor, saying: While I have been touring the empire and making sacrifices, Fusu and Meng Tian have been campaigning with several hundred thousand to no purpose. Moreover, Fusu has criticized and slandered me on many occasions. 'Fusu has not acted as a filial son. I present him with a sword so he may settle the matter for himself.'

As for Meng Tian, 'as a subject he has acted disloyally. I present him with the opportunity to take his own life.'

Off went the letter carried by a trusted messenger on horseback, accompanied by a troop of fast horsemen. It was a 500-kilometre gallop to Meng Tian's HQ, which, according to local folklore, was at Suide, almost due north of the capital and just over halfway to the Yellow River, in the middle of Ordos. It would take them a week or so to get there.

Fusu wept on reading the fake letter, but accepted it at face value. He was only prevented from immediate suicide by Meng Tian, who pointed out there was perhaps something fishy going on. They had both been appointed to guard the frontier. This was a 'weighty responsibility'; yet here comes this letter, delivered out of the blue. They should at least get confirmation.

Fusu thought this would show an unfilial lack of trust, and committed suicide.

Meng Tian, however, said he needed to know the order was genuine. Of course, the messenger could not possibly allow such an action – it would delay things by two weeks – so he had the general and his entourage of officers arrested. They were taken to a prison some 60 kilometres south-east of the Great Wall fortress of Jingbian. Only now could a message be sent back to the conspirators that all was well: Fusu dead, Meng Tian in jail.

So Huhai came to the throne as the Second Emperor. His top adviser was, of course, Zhao Gao, the king-maker, the instigator of the Sand Hill Plot. Huhai was weak. 'The chief ministers are unsubmissive,' he complained. 'The various officials still have great power, and the other imperial princes are certain to contest my rule. What can I do?'

Zhao Gao proposed a Stalinist solution: unleash a reign of terror. Make the laws sterner and penalties more severe! See that persons charged with guilt implicate others! Wipe out the chief ministers and sow dissension among your kin! 'By doing so you can strike terror into the empire as a whole, and at the same time do away with those who disapprove of your actions.'

'Excellent!' said the Second Emperor.

Six princes were put to death, and three others, protesting their innocence, chose to fall on their own swords. Sima Qian also mentions ten princesses killed by being torn apart by chariots. This could all be so, because many graves have been discovered in the pits of the Terracotta Army, most of young men and women in their twenties. Fear spread from the imperial family to the population at large.

Zhao Gao, now lord high executioner, was free to turn on his old adversaries, the Meng brothers and their families. Meng Yi, accused of opposing Huhai's accession, was asked to commit suicide. He naturally denied the charge, and delivered one of his own in a long memo that ended, 'One who governs by the Way does not put to death the guiltless.' It did him no good. Zhao Gao ordered his execution.

Meng Tian, still in prison after his arrest on the northern frontier, was confronted by an envoy demanding that he copy Fusu and commit suicide. He too wrote a memo, which the envoy refused to pass on, saying 'I do not dare to report your words to the emperor.'

At this Meng Tian despaired. Sima Qian gives him a tragic death, and a highly imaginative one. How do we know it is imaginative? Because he uses virtually identical words when describing the death of a previous Qin general, Bai Qi, who in 260 BC had killed '450,000' prisoners. In both cases, Sima Qian was using his criticism of the generals and their emperors as an oblique way to criticize his own emperor, Wu, for acts that were (as we will see) comparable in their ruthlessness. In a word, this is history as propaganda.

Still, it's a good story. Like a tragic hero dying on stage, Meng Tian 'heaved a great sigh and said, "What crime have I committed before Heaven? I die without fault!" After a long time he added: "Indeed I have a crime for which to die."' In building the Great Wall, and presumably the Straight Road, 'I have made ramparts and ditches over more than 10,000 li, and in this distance it is impossible that I have not cut through the veins of the earth. This is my crime.'

True, this might be considered a crime, because it ignored the practices of *feng shui*, which would have called for a careful study of the supernatural influences that would have shown whether construction was auspicious or not. But this did not deserve a death sentence.

He deserved to die, Sima Qian goes on, for reasons that had nothing to do with the veins of the earth. His crime was not standing up to the First Emperor: 'He was a noted general, but he did not make powerful remonstrances [to the emperor] at this time.' He allowed himself to be governed by the First Emperor's Legalist agenda. He should have acted like a good Confucian. He did not 'alleviate the distress of the common people, support the aged, care for the orphaned or busy himself with restoring harmony among the masses. [Instead] he gave in to the ideas [of the emperor] and conscripted forced labour. Is it not fitting that he and his younger brother should meet death for this?'

Though hardly a fitting end, Meng Tian committed suicide. In Suide, which locals claim was his HQ, he is considered a hero. A stele standing beneath trees in the town's No. 1 Middle School commemorates him.

II
PEAK

For nomads like the Xiongnu, the horse was an obvious emblem of wealth and identity to attach to one's belt.

Those of higher status favoured the image of a Siberian tiger with its prey – a sheep or gazelle – held in its jaws.

This golden plaque has a complex design of a tiger with a wild boar slung over its back.

THE ORDOS BRONZES

Despite their name, the Ordos Bronzes have been found across all of Inner Asia and many are of other metals. The most common items – and some of the first discovered – are belt buckles and horse accoutrements of bronze. They may represent family or clan emblems. Later finds are of gold, notably the coronet (*below*), found in 1972. It may be a royal symbol.

Horse and chariot decorations included these triangular wheel plaques.

The golden coronet, the prime object in the Ordos Bronze Museum, is topped by an eagle with a turquoise head.

The Great North Road

In 210 BC, the great Qin general Meng Tian was told to claim Ordos for the newly unified Qin empire. To do this, he needed to drive the Xiongnu out of Ordos across the Yellow River and build a road of some 800 kilometres across their territory so that Qin troops could secure the new frontier. The 'Straight Road' would carry not only troops but also chariots, for the delivery of gifts and officials as China struggled to balance war and peace with its northern neighbours. Today there is little evidence of its existence, but it is remembered at a site near Ordos City, where a modern version of the road is due to open for tourists.

The new tourist site (*above*) suggests the original road was a dual carriageway, allowing chariots to pass. A nearby archaeological site shows no signs of the road itself, but is marked by a statue of the First Emperor in his chariot (*above right*) and a stone bearing the sign 'Qin Straight Road' (*right*).

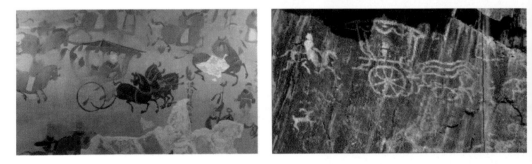

Chinese chariots appear in paintings, like the fresco (*left*), and rock drawings, like this one (*right*) from Khovd, western Mongolia. Drawn by up to four horses, chariots were often sent as gifts to nomadic leaders and buried with them.

WEAPONS: THE EVIDENCE – AND THE LACK OF IT

The Xiongnu owed their success to their supreme skills as mounted archers: no close-quarter fighting, no swords. They liked daggers, though, probably more for status than combat. What were the bows like? Hard to say, because bows rot, leaving only the bone extensions, or 'ears'. Some Xiongnu wore armour, again probably for status, for it would not have withstood Chinese crossbow bolts.

This fine helmet (*above left*) was probably a trade item from China or Greece, of little practical use in a society devoted to bows and arrows, with their dozens of different forms, in bronze (*above right*) and iron (*right*). Lamellar armour was made in bronze (*left*) or leather.

Though the wooden parts of bows rot away, the bone bits often survive – the bones 'ears' (*left and right*) that extended the bow, and the bone plates (*top*) that strengthened the bell. Bronze daggers with ornate handles (*right*) were more a form of personal decoration than weapons.

The 'Princess' Who Linked Cultures

One of the most famous women in Chinese history is Zhaojun, who was given in marriage to the Xiongnu king (chanyu) in 51 BC. She became the best known of many girls married off to many different nomadic rulers, the idea being that they would 'civilize' the barbarians both by introducing Chinese ways of life and by producing children who would, by definition, be part of a Chinese ruling dynasty. The practice was much appreciated by the Xiongnu, but it didn't work. Perhaps for that reason, Zhaojun became a Chinese heroine, one of the four 'Great Beauties'. She is remembered in this park in the south of Hohhot, Inner Mongolia.

A statue (*above*) shows Zhaojun about to leave for the grasslands with her husband, Huhanye. In the background is her tomb-mound, almost certainly not genuine. She is portrayed (*left*) as a traditional Chinese beauty. Mythological animals guard the way to the mound. A view from the top (*below*) shows the park's size, and hints at the respect in which she is held.

To get to sites, set in wooded hills in central Mongolia, you need good 4 x 4s (*above*). Low stone walls (*above right*), restored after excavation, show that the tent-dwelling Xiongnu could have built a city.

GOL MOD: GRAVES FOR NOMAD RULERS

Of the 10,000 or so Xiongnu graves north of the Gobi, several hundred are so-called 'terrace' or 'élite' tombs. Of these, twenty have been excavated, all constructed between 50 BC and AD 50. The most impressive of recent discoveries are the two cemeteries known as Gol Mod 1 and 2, shown here. Revealed by French and Mongolian teams, the tombs are like upside-down pyramids, almost 20 metres deep. Their contents, reduced by tomb-robbers, reveal a rich, artistic society that did well out of its connections with China. Since the only sources are Chinese, many mysteries remain.

Left: Erdenebaatar, discoverer and senior archaeologist of Gol Mod 2.

Below: A volunteer army of diggers parades around Gol Mod 2's Tomb No. 1.

Left: Cutaway of a royal 'terrace tomb'. *Right*: After excavation, the tombs were refilled.

These two figures are part of a group embroidered on a carpet excavated from Noyon Uul in 2006. They are perhaps Indian. The carpet, preserved by permafrost, has been restored by Russian scientists.

The corkscrew-like handle of a bronze dagger is capped by a pair of snow leopards.

TREASURES UNBURIED

The thousands of finds in Xiongnu tombs include textiles, pots, jewellery, bronze mirrors, buttons and golden bas-reliefs with complex designs. In their range and sophistication, these objects show that the Xiongnu had a taste for high-quality art from both China and the west. Textiles were probably locally made, though there is no way to tell whether the weavers were local or foreign. Certainly, the Xiongnu knew how to cast bronze and gold. Several golden medallions and breastplates have a mythological creature with a snarling animal's head, perhaps a snow leopard, and a dragon's body: the *bers*, as it is known in Mongolian, can move from place to place instantaneously. It is also the queen in Mongolian chess.

Below: Bronze cauldrons were probably used for communal feasts. Some scholars point to Xiongnu cauldrons as evidence that the Xiongnu were the ancestors of Attila's Huns.

Above: Wherever the carpets came from, the artists used embroidery to create intricate patterns – suggesting flowers or birds (*left*) – and also portraits, in this case (*right*) of a man with a moustache who could be Indian, or Turkish, or even Xiongnu.

This little glass bowl, just 6 cm high, was made in Rome in *c.* AD 50. Erdenebaatar found it in Gol Mod 2, in a side grave of Tomb No. 1. How it got there is a mystery.

On a jade disc 18 cm across, two cat-like animals hold a circle, their bodies intricately curlicued. Other animals circle 112 knobs.

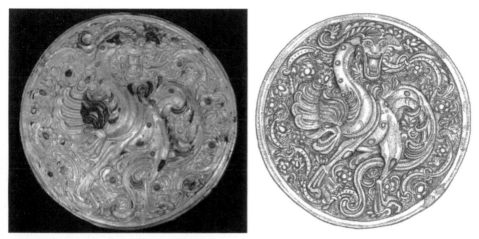

On a plate of embossed gold, a hard-to-see *bers* amidst flowers becomes clear as a drawing.

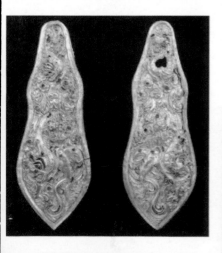

Left: These 17.5 cm breastplates each have a pair of *bers* entwined with flowers. The top creature is part-unicorn. Inlays are of turquoise and chalcedony.

Below: Turquoise buttons, set in gold clasps, with a strip of patterned gold.

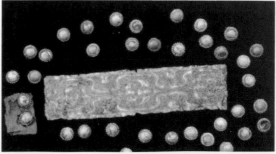

The main tower of Tong Wan Cheng looms over a wall, which links a line of so-called 'horse-face' bulwarks.

Until a few years ago, these caves were homes for families who made their living keeping pigs and farming the abandoned inner city.

Right: Mr Ma describes the layout of one of the entrance gateways.

Holes in one of the towers were left when the scaffolding used in the original construction was removed.

THE ONLY XIONGNU CITY (SO FAR)

Tong Wan Cheng (Ruling Ten Thousand Cities), in southern Ordos, was the capital of the Southern Xiongnu state of Da Xia for a few years in the early fifth century. If there were other Xiongnu cities, they await discovery. Built of pale rammed earth, it is also known as White City. Caves in its walls acted as houses for many families, including the current guide, Ma Junwang.

5

THE FIRST EMPIRE
OF THE STEPPES

In 221 BC, THIS WAS THE APPROXIMATE SITUATION ON THE grasslands (though little is certain, for no one has made sense of all the groups and sub-groups). In Ordos and neighbouring areas the Rong and Di were combining to form the Xiongnu (or were perhaps being taken over by them). In Mongolia, there was a scattering of tribes, none of any distinction. Further east were the Dong, usually known as the Dong Hu, the 'Eastern Barbarians' (though some burial sites suggest that some Xiongnu groups were already adopting new ways, abandoning the old slab burials and rock-pile graves for rings of stone over much deeper pits). The west, today's Gansu and Xinjiang, was dominated by the Turkic group, the Yuezhi. Further west were the Wusun, in today's eastern Kazakhstan. More about these two later.

Then China unified, and so did some of the nomadic tribes. Scholars have argued about the nature of this response. Did they act as a mass, as if driven by some deep historical force, the force being China? That idea was proposed by the great Mongolist Owen Lattimore in the 1940s, and accepted recently by (among others) Thomas Barfield, Professor of Anthropology at Boston University.[1] Lattimore argues that the Xiongnu – indeed *all* nomadic empires centred on Mongolia – were 'shadow empires' that arose 'as secondary phenomena in response to imperial expansion by the Chinese'.[2] It's a hypothesis that has drawn criticism from others, because it is impossible to prove, and because some later nomadic empires arose when China was divided. But in the case of the Xiongnu, it's persuasive.

Perhaps the Xiongnu would have risen anyway. But what actually happened was a matter of luck: they acquired a charismatic leader, a man of drive and vision, a counterpart to the First Emperor, and a forerunner of Genghis Khan, who unified the Mongols almost 1,500 years later. The rise of the two – unified nation and great leader – feeds into an old controversy about revolutionary change. Should we be explaining such changes by looking at great social forces or the characters of great men and women? In this case – both.

Scholars – especially those trained in Marxist interpretations of history – have also argued about what sort of an empire it was. Until recently, empires were defined in terms of conquest, land ownership, wealth and class exploitation. But nomadic empires did not necessarily claim land, since wealth was measured in terms of herders and flocks, which have no fixed territory. Besides, cattle-wealth was hard to accumulate. As a result of severe ice-storms that occurred roughly

[1] Thomas J. Barfield, *The Perilous Frontier* (see Bibliography).
[2] Owen Lattimore, *Inner Asian Frontiers of China* (see Bibliography).

every decade or two, herds were subject to catastrophic losses that affected rich and poor alike. With little or no agriculture to provide surpluses of food, no class system could emerge (at least, not in the early stages of the empire). What emerged in Ordos was something new.

Then in the 220s BC there came the big change detailed in the previous two chapters: wars between the states, from which Qin emerged victorious, then Meng Tian's advance in 214–210 BC, revealing a new agenda: the seizure of territory that had for centuries been the domain of the nomads.

Tumen, still the chanyu of the Xiongnu in Ordos, had no chance against the massed forces of Qin. He led his people across the Yellow River, to safety north of the Gobi, in the grasslands of central Mongolia. To be chased out of one's homeland is a terrible thing. As proud warriors, would they settle down quietly? Not a chance. They responded, and would very soon rise from tribe to empire.

Technology also helped. Finds in Xiongnu tombs suggest that their bows became significantly more effective to counter the threat from Chinese crossbows. Of course, crossbows could have been seized or bought, but they are too cumbersome to use on horseback. For horse-archers, the bow was the ideal weapon. The recurved ends were of bone, bending away from the archer, extending the 'draw' and increasing the power. The lower limb of the bow was shorter, which does not affect the performance, but (say some toxophilites) makes it easier to swing the bow over a horse's neck as you change the direction of fire – vital if, as seems likely, the Xiongnu could shoot both right- and left-handed.

The Xiongnu bow – and the bows of all subsequent nomadic cultures – was an object of remarkable qualities. Almost anyone could have a bow, and most had one. In a 2004 survey of thirty-five Xiongnu graves with bows (or rather the bone bits – the wood, horn and sinew having rotted away), the Mongolian archaeologist Tsagaan Törbat showed that 17 per cent were those of women and 6 per cent were those of children.[3] They would have been relatively lightweight versions. War-bows were on a different scale. To force a really 'heavy' one out of its reverse curve, string it and draw it you needed arms and shoulders strong enough to do a one-arm pull-up, and fingers calloused by years of use (though later archers used a thumb-ring with a hook on it to pull the string).

The power of this weapon was astonishing. At close range, say 50 to 100 metres, arrows from a 'heavy' bow have the penetration of many types of bullet. The right sort of arrow with the right sort of head can slam through half an inch of wood. Through armour, too. The range is equally astonishing, as the earliest inscription in Mongol reveals. It was carved on a metre-high stone, probably in 1226. Found in 1818 in southern Siberia near today's Mongolian border, it was made when Genghis Khan had just returned from a triumphant campaign in the Muslim world. He ordered a celebration during which his nephew Yesunge decided to display his legendary strength and skill. The stone records the extraordinary result: 'While Genghis Khan was holding an assembly of Mongolian dignitaries . . . Yesunge hit a target at 335 *ald*s.' An ald was the distance between a man's fingertips with arms outstretched, about 1.6 metres. So Yesunge's unspecified target – a tree, perhaps, or a tent – was some 500 metres away. In the eighteenth century, English archery experts became fascinated by Turkish bows,

[3] Tsagaan Törbat, *Khunnugiin jiriin irgediin bulsh* (see Bibliography).

because they outperformed English longbows. Longbows may shoot 350 yards. But on 9 July 1794, in a field behind Bedford Square in London, the Turkish ambassador's secretary, Mahmoud, shot 415 yards against a breeze and 482 yards with it. Mahmoud modestly said this was nothing: his master, the sultan in Istanbul, was an even more powerful bowman. Turkish records claim the sultan lived up to his reputation, firing an arrow almost 900 metres.[4]

I have a 'Hun' bow, made by the Hungarian master of horse-archery Lajos Kassai, which looks identical to a Xiongnu bow as reconstructed in Mongolia in a drawing by B. Batsaikhan.[5] It is 1.57 metres long, and the lower limb is 10 centimetres shorter than the upper one. My longest shot is about 200 metres. Pathetic. It's capable of much more, if only I had the strength to draw it fully.

Xiongnu archers carried their arrows in a birch-bark case slung on their backs, and must have reached back over their shoulders to reload. This requires considerable skill, because you have to align the arrow exactly right to fit the nock on to the string, and do it fast, while galloping, using one hand to hold the bow and the other to fit the arrow, while guiding the horse with your knees. Bareback, and almost certainly without stirrups. It took Kassai years to master the technique.

---

[4] These details are from Paul E. Klopsteg, *Turkish Archery and the Composite Bow* (see Bibliography). Shooting for distance, so-called 'flight' archery, is a sub-culture. Today, with modern materials and specially designed arrows, hand-held bows can be made to fire three-quarters of a mile. The world record for a bow drawn purely by muscle-power is 1 mile 268 yards (1.8 kilometres), done by Harry Drake on Ivanpah Dry Lake, California, in 1971. Using his own specially designed bow, he lay on his back, pulling with both hands, with the bow braced by his feet.

[5] In Eregzen (ed.), *Treasures*.

Xiongnu males must have done it from childhood to build both the expertise and (like longbowmen in medieval England) the muscle. Iron arrowheads, too, evolved into a dozen different forms, some with two tines, some with three, with barbs or without. Some had bone inserts with a hole that made the arrow whistle, useful both in deer-hunting, because the sound makes a deer freeze, and for signalling in battle. These became a permanent part of the nomad's bow-case. For close-quarter fighting, the Xiongnu also had double-edged swords, or at least the top people did. All of this must have been serviced by specialist bow-makers, fletchers and blacksmiths who in turn depended on ore-miners, woodcutters and breeders of birds for the right sort of feathers. On all these industries the sources are silent (except a mention of whistling arrows, which we'll get to shortly). Only the graves speak.

Again Sima Qian is the main source for what happened. He does not say where he got his information. Not from direct experience, because he did not speak the Xiongnu language. He says he travelled to the frontier, and his account focuses on the adjoining territory; of the regions further north, in Mongolia and southern Russia, he says virtually nothing. Possibly he heard reports from the many Chinese visitors to the chanyu's court, who would have picked up versions of Xiongnu history, sanctioned no doubt by the imperial founder, Modun, himself (as Genghis Khan and his heirs sanctioned tales about his rise). Possibly, when the earth and the laboratory reveal deeper truths, we will discover that Tumen and Modun were only the latest expression of changes that had been evolving for some time, without dramatic events and characters to focus them. Meanwhile, this is how Modun seized power from his father, in Sima Qian's dramatic – and increasingly incredible – version . . .

Modun, remember, has been sent to the Yuezhi (or demanded by them) as a guarantor of the Xiongnu's good behaviour. His father, Tumen, still determined to keep his second son as heir, attacks the Yuezhi, knowing that they will kill Modun in retaliation. But the prince stages a dramatic escape, stealing a horse to gallop home. His father is impressed by his bravery, gives him a generous reception and bestows upon him his own troops. But he does not reinstate him as heir, and Modun nurses his resentment. Soon he is planning to take revenge on his father. Intending to ensure the loyalty of every one of his soldiers, he drills them into total obedience. 'Shoot wherever you see my whistling arrow strike!' he orders. (This is a rare case of a written source being backed by hard evidence. Several whistling arrowheads have been found in Xiongnu graves.) 'Anyone who fails to shoot will be cut down!' Then he takes his band hunting. Every animal he aims at becomes a target for his men. He takes aim at one of his best horses. The horse dies in a hail of arrows. But some soldiers hesitate, and these are executed.

Next, he takes aim at his 'favourite' wife. Is this credible? The more you think about it, the more it isn't – just one of the many inconsistencies in this story. Anyway, she dies, and so do those who waver. Then Modun shoots at one of his father's finest horses – and somehow the father does not react? Another unlikely element in a tale full of many unlikelihoods. In folklore, things often happen in threes, and this makes a dramatic third. More arrows, another death, and this time there are no waverers. Now Modun knows all his men can be trusted. Finally, 'on a hunting expedition, he shot a whistling arrow at his father and every one of his followers aimed their arrows in the same direction and shot the chief dead', filling him so full of arrows that there was no room for another. Finally – and this may reflect a truth, since other autocrats have committed similar atrocities – Modun secured absolute power by going 'on a bloodletting rampage', killing his step-mother, her son (Tumen's heir and his own half-brother) and all those he suspected of opposing him.

In 209 BC, one year after the death of the First Emperor, Modun became the new chanyu of the Xiongnu, and began to turn himself from a tribal chief into the ruler of an empire. How he achieved this may be folklore dressed up as history, but there seems to be no reason to doubt his emergence, his authority and his impact.

Seeing a threat in Modun's ambitions, the nearby tribe to the east, the Dong, demand a tribute as a sign of submission. They suggest a stallion that belonged to Tumen. Modun's advisers are horrified at the idea of handing over a national treasure, but Modun overrules them: 'The Dong are our neighbours. Why provoke them over a single horse?' Next, the Dong demand one of Modun's wives. Again the advisers are angered: 'This is the greatest insult! Let us show them what we are made of!' Again Modun refuses to break the peace: 'Why bother losing our accord over a woman?' Finally (another triplet of events is emerging) the Dong king – 'his ego being greatly inflated' – demands a bit of wasteland measuring 1,000 li (500 kilometres) from north to south. This time his advisers said, 'Yes, the wasteland is useless to us. Give it to them.' At this, Modun flies into a towering rage: 'Land is the essence of our nation! How could we possibly cede it?'

This was an odd thing to say for a nomad, whose traditions measured power in tribes and herds, not in land-ownership.

If true – and it may have been an assumption by Sima Qian or his unknown source – these words suggest that Modun was already set on building an empire.

Then, mounting his horse, he bellows, 'The last person to mount will be decapitated!' Modun's forces strike like lightning against the Dong, who are sitting on their laurels having concluded the Xiongnu are cowardly. 'With this one battle, the Dong were decimated.'

Now Modun had a problem, common to many other empire-builders. He had a large army, followers hungry for wealth and a court with rituals and ceremonies to be followed. All this was expensive. He was, no doubt, naturally ambitious to extend his rule, but in any event expansion was a necessity. An empire needs to grow to fund more growth. Like a storm-tossed ocean, his growing domain washed up against the frontiers of all his neighbours, the next in line being the new dynasty that had emerged to the south.

He could do this because he revolutionized his society. Somehow, he devised an unknown but persuasive ideology. The obvious comparison is with Genghis Khan, whose empire was built on both a similar way of life and an ideology of world rule. But it didn't start like that (as several scholars have pointed out, notably Igor de Rachewiltz, translator of the *Secret History of the Mongols*). It started with the anarchic conditions of Mongolia in the twelfth century, with clan fighting clan, and the character and skills of Genghis. A father murdered and many threats to his own life implanted a determination to create security, which could only be done by unifying all the feuding clans of Mongolia, and then holding them together with booty from more conquests. At this, Genghis was a genius. As de Rachewiltz put it in an email to me, quoting the sixteenth-century French poet Rabelais: '*L'appétit vient en mangeant*' ('The appetite comes by eating') – conquest inspires more conquest. The result was ever-growing success, and an empire. It was only after his death in 1227 that his son and heir Ogedei devised an ideology to explain past conquests and inspire future ones – the Muslim world, China, and ultimately world rule under the guidance of the Mongol deity, Tengri or Khökh Tenger, Blue Heaven, as it is in Mongolian. As a later ruler, Guyuk, wrote to the Pope when the Mongols were approaching Europe: 'How could we ever have been so successful if God had not been with us?'

Tenger or Tengri (spellings vary) meant both 'sky' and 'heaven' in many Central Asian languages, in both senses, meteorological and divine. In Mongolian, 'the blue sky' is both a cloudless sky and God. English confuses the two as well: God is in his heaven, the heavens opened. Tenger was the overarching deity of the Central Asian form of Animism, which revered countless lesser spirits of the natural world: animals, rocks, rivers, trees, mountains. Tenger was a remote entity, honoured then and now in Mongolia only with little rituals, like placing gifts of old banknotes, empty bottles and bits of silk on piles of stones (ovoos) marking high places, or flicking liquor skywards with the third finger. But it was not worshipped in an established church. The only access to Tenger was through shamans, who could supposedly sense the will of Heaven when in a trance. There was therefore no formal ideology under Modun or his heirs. Apparently, he never claimed that Tenger was on his side. Perhaps the circumstances did not call for divine backing, which was what Genghis's heirs claimed to explain his conquests. Initial stages may have been peaceful: as William Honeychurch, Associate

Professor of Anthropology in the University of Michigan, points out, 'the material record argues for more gradual changes in regional integration grounded in local political precedent as a first step towards the nomadic state'.[6] The sources suggest that Modun had the charisma to unify the clans without violence, and then feed them on enough conquests to keep them happy. His conquests hit a wall, literally, in the south, unlike Genghis, who broke through it and whose heirs took all China. Thereafter, rewards came to Modun from raiding across the border (though under his heirs the empire would expand westwards). On this basis he had the drive, intelligence and leadership skills to create stable rule by forging a system of government that was remarkably sophisticated and effective.

This is how the system worked:

It consisted of the chanyu and an aristocracy of three royal clans that formed a government, with direct rule over heads of local administrators and officials in charge of services, like a 'pony express' for carrying messages and supplies for the military, and festivals that sustained the chanyu's authority. Sons and brothers of the chanyu had the top jobs.

The Xiongnu population was governed by a pair of viceroys who were designated 'left' and 'right'. Both bore an honorific term that Sima Qian says meant 'wise'. There is no way to check, but everyone accepts his word. The Wise Kings of the Left and Right ruled the eastern and western parts, the Left (eastern)[7] King being the chanyu's eldest son and designated heir. The two kings appointed their own officials. Beneath

---

[6] William Honeychurch, 'The Nomad as Statebuilder', in *Journal of World Prehistory* (see Bibliography).

[7] The dominant direction was south, towards the sun. Nomads still pitch their tents facing south. When looking south, left is east.

them were twenty-four 'great chiefs' who were heads of units of ten thousand – a very rough figure, presumably counting just the men. The chiefs' families intermarried with the imperial lineage, thus ensuring that everyone had a stake in the system. Their support for the chanyu was crucial, especially at the time of succession. They were in effect an electoral college. Modun's empire was centralized, but also federal. For instance, if the heir was too young, the chiefs could and did choose a brother of the dead chanyu.

The army was organized on the 'decimal' system, in which the 'ten thousands' were broken down into units of thousands, hundreds and tens, each with its own commander. The structure was extremely flexible, providing anything from a small raiding-party to a full-scale invasion. Since all men were both herders and soldiers, the system guaranteed an army of 240,000, in theory. That fits: assuming that every man had a wife, two children and dependent parents, the population would have been 1–1.5 million, which, as it happens, is the roughly estimated capacity of the Mongolian grasslands. The system may have been taken over from the Persian Achaemenids, whose empire ended only a couple of generations before Modun's birth,[8] with word passing from group to group across Eurasia. Later, this became the usual way for steppe empires to organize themselves (notably the Jin in the twelfth century and the Mongols in the thirteenth).

It is hard to know what to call Modun's creation. Scholars

[8] Herodotus (*Histories*, VII, 83) says that the Persians had a regiment of ten thousand, 'and these Persians were called "Immortals" because, if any of them made the number incomplete, being overcome either by death or disease, another man was chosen in his place, and they were never either more nor fewer than ten thousand'.

debate whether it was some sort of a super-chiefdom or a state. States are often said to be defined by systems of taxation, law and administration, among others. We don't have enough detail to decide. Whatever you call it, the point is that Modun's vision and authority built, from notoriously fickle elements, a confederacy and an empire powerful enough to challenge the new dynasty that had sprung up south of the Gobi.

In newly unified China, the brutality of the First Emperor and his heir had inspired a rebellion, led by a man who had been born a peasant, Liu Bang. Sima Guang, presumably relying on long-lost sources that bridged a millennium, provides a portrait of Liu Bang, with some weird details: he 'had a high nose bridge', a regal aura with a stately stature, and 'it was said that on his left thigh there were seventy-two black moles'. Liu had fled from farm work and become a low-grade patrolman. One day, when escorting prisoners, some escaped. Afraid of punishment, he ran away and joined a band of brigands, eventually taking charge. As their boss, he headed a rebellion against the Qin government, rising to fame and fortune when the rebellion overthrew the Qin empire. There followed a four-year civil war, from which Liu Bang emerged victorious. In 202 BC, he proclaimed himself emperor with the name of Gaozu and established the Han dynasty, with a new capital at Chang'an, today's Xian. Once again, two rival empires confronted each other: grasslands versus cities, nomads versus farmers, Han versus Xiongnu.

Almost immediately[9] – in autumn 201 BC, according to Sima

[9] And aided by the Xiongnu conquest of the Wuhuan, a group living to the east, in present-day Manchuria, forcing them to pay annual tribute, which they did for the next 200 years.

Guang – Modun took on Gaozu. He advanced some 200 kilometres into China, aided by a secret deal with the region's treacherous governor. Advancing via present-day Datong and over the steep Yanmen (Wild Goose) Pass, he reached the provincial capital, Taiyuan, and then, unaccountably, retreated. Apparently his aim was not to take over cities, perhaps because that would mean abandoning his nomadic way of life. A year later, the disloyal governor, faced with a punitive attack from his own emperor, defected to the Xiongnu. Another Xiongnu attack-and-retreat followed in the dead of winter, and 'it was said that two or three [Han] soldiers out of ten lost their fingers through frostbite'. Not a problem for the Xiongnu, in their long-sleeved, fur-side-inwards sheepskin coats and sheepskin mittens.

Come the spring, a new challenge emerged. The Xiongnu were talking to the rebellious state of Hann (nothing to do with Han the ruling dynasty) about a possible alliance. The emperor gathered a huge army (supposedly 320,000 strong) and marched north, through Taiyuan, over the Yanmen Pass to a place called Pingcheng, near today's Datong. Accounts conflict, but it seems that the emperor's spies told him that Modun's army was so weakened it could easily be defeated. In fact, it was a set-up. Modun 'hid his well-fed cattle and horses, only allowing the spies to catch a glimpse of enfeebled soldiers and sick animals'. A general named Liu Jing tried to tell truth to power, only for the emperor to shout him down and imprison him for insubordination. The result: Modun's immense and very fit army surrounded the emperor's, or perhaps cut him off from his main force. For a week, it seemed he was doomed, until his chancellor managed to bribe Modun's queen[10] to have a word with him, advising him to retreat. Sima Qian imagines her saying, 'Even if we are successful in taking over the land from Han, it is ill-suited for your herding purposes.' But the clincher would surely have been the promise of payments on an unprecedented scale – peace in exchange for cash and luxuries. True or not, the Xiongnu relaxed their grip, allowing the emperor to beat a hasty retreat, following which he released Liu Jing, apologized to him, and appointed him his chief adviser.

The catastrophic defeat at Pingcheng showed that the emperor's chariots and crossbows were no match for Modun's horseback archers. That was the lesson drawn by the emperor's advisers, who were not about to blame themselves and him for poor planning. Worried at his inability to stop Modun's predatory habits, Gaozu asked Liu Jing what to do. In reply, the general spouted prejudices that became accepted as truths:

> Our soldiers are tired and exhausted, so we must relinquish the notion of using force against them [the Xiongnu]. Modun committed patricide, usurped his father's throne, taking his stepmothers as wives. He is hideously savage, implacable beyond belief, using sheer brute force to manifest his might. One cannot reason with people like him with compassion and benevolence.

---

[10] What was she doing on campaign? Was this perhaps more of an attempted occupation than an invasion, with families and herds as well as soldiers? Possibly the chanyu decided to pull back having seen that the surroundings were not suitable for herders.

The plain fact was that resistance was useless. Han, the dynasty ruling China, was in no position to bargain. As Liu Jing put it in another memo, the Xiongnu were only 700 li (350 kilometres) away, and the six kingdoms defeated by Qin were unreliable subjects. 'Should they turn against the central government, I am afraid Your Majesty would suffer from recurrent insomnia.' The sensible thing to do 'is to cast our eyes to the future: try to work out a long-term stratagem so that the descendants of Modun will eventually capitulate'.

What would that mean? The only possible answer was to refine the offer made for the emperor to escape with his life after the battle of Pingcheng. Liu Jing outlined a policy of bribery and corruption that would be sure to work. The assumption was that Modun and his male followers, being barbarians, and therefore eager for anything Chinese, were all desperate for social acceptance, diplomatic equality and sex with 'civilized' women: 'If Your Majesty would contemplate betrothing your eldest daughter to Modun as wife . . . accompanied by opulent dowries', he would marry her, and she would produce a son, who would be crown prince. 'During festivals and important dates, we would send them girls from our national surplus,' by which he meant the emperor's harem. Envoys would follow, along with well-spoken officials who 'would educate the chanyu in how to behave as a son-in-law', and in due course 'your grandson would accede to the throne'. And Confucian ideas of filial loyalty meant that the Xiongnu ruler would, by definition, be subservient to Han China, and 'who has ever heard of a grandson being rebellious against his own grandfather?' But why on earth would the Xiongnu know anything about Confucian ethics, let alone put them into practice? In brief, the Xiongnu desire for luxury was their weakness, to be exploited by 'bribes and brides'. It would of course be expensive, but nothing like so expensive as constant warfare.

'Excellent!' said the emperor.

As it happened, the princess's mother objected, wailing and weeping and accusing the emperor of callousness in 'sending my daughter away to the Xiongnu in the wilderness'. Anyway, she was already married, so that obviously excluded her, a fact Liu Jing himself would have known, and which suggests that his speech was one of Sima Qian's inventions.

Never mind: the principles were clear. The result was a treaty between the two empires, signed in 198 BC. It marked the beginning of a new world order in Asia, with the Xiongnu and their chanyu recognized as equal to the Han Chinese and their emperor. Han would send a princess for each new chanyu, along with regular gifts of silk, cloth, grain, chariots, mirrors, jewels and many other luxury items. An unnamed beauty, who may or may not have been of royal blood, chaperoned by Liu Jing, was sent off to the chanyu's tent-HQ, travelling in style in a carriage, with staff and outriders, possibly along the road built by Meng Tian. She, like all the later 'princesses', then vanished from the historical record. This – the so-called *he-qin* (peace-and-kinship) policy – was the basis for a 'peace' (in inverted commas) that would last on and off for some sixty years.

For the first time, but not the last, nomads dominated China by scourging the northern frontier regions. That was the fact, but it was not one the Chinese wished to recognize. It would have been too humiliating. So they put a spin on it. They were not being weak by handing over tribute, but magnanimous by handing over 'gifts', as befitted a superior culture. They lived in hope, for the gifts had a hidden agenda: not just to buy peace, but to undermine the hardy Xiongnu by addicting them to luxuries. As one statesman and scholar, Jia Yi, wrote, 'Our markets beneath the Great Wall will surely swarm with the Xiongnu . . . When the Xiongnu have developed a craving for our rice, stew, barbecues and wine, this will have become their fatal weakness.' Hence the occasional Chinese princess journeying across the Gobi to join the chanyu's court. Every one of them was a germ injected into the body politic of the Xiongnu, intended to multiply and overwhelm its barbarism. Border markets thrived.

But the Xiongnu showed no signs of being infected by Chinese values or corrupted by luxury. Raids continued, perhaps conducted by Xiongnu chiefs independent of the chanyu. Anyway, the Xiongnu remained as tough as ever. 'They scale and descend even the most precipitous mountains with astonishing speed,' reported one envoy. 'They swim the deepest torrents, tolerate wind, hunger and thirst . . . If they ever suffer a setback, they simply disappear without a trace like a cloud.'[11]

Facing a minimal threat from Han and flush with wealth from Han's gifts, Modun turned his army on today's Gansu, China's far north-west, attacking the Yuezhi, who occupied the strategic Hexi or Gansu Corridor and lands to the west, where streams from the Qilian Mountains water oases in the wastes of the Western Regions. This was the tribe with whom he had been lodged as a hostage eight years previously. There

---

[11] In contrast to Sima Guang, Sima Qian downplays the Xiongnu attacks after the 198 BC treaty. His agenda was to show that war was bad and peace good. His account suggests that the treaty worked. In Jonathan Markley's words in *Peace and Peril*, 'Sima Qian created a false impression without ever having actually lied.' (See Bibliography.)

are no details of the campaign, but it was a large-scale invasion, because the Yuezhi were said to have had between 100,000 and 200,000 archers. The invasion must have pitted mounted archers against mounted archers. Modun would surely not have attacked without being confident that his well-coordinated army could shatter the Yuezhi's disunited clans. This was no rout, but he had his revenge, forcing some Yuezhi groups to scatter and seizing their territory. His empire now included the Corridor, with its good grazing grounds and access to the oasis kingdoms of the west – the stepping-stones that we now know as part of the Silk Road. Populations once in awe of the Yuezhi would now be in greater awe of this expansive new power.

Then came the reconquest of Ordos, which was wide open. After Meng Tian's victory, soldiers and colonists had moved in by the thousand. But the First Emperor and Meng Tian were dead, the armies had gone, the Wall's towers were abandoned and the Qin dynasty had collapsed. All that stood in Modun's way were farmers. So, in Sima Qian's words, the Xiongnu under Modun 'again gradually crossed the Yellow River southward into China and set the boundary of their nation at its old limit' – and beyond: sources mention the conquest of smaller tribes which took Xiongnu control south of Ordos.

No one recorded the details of the reconquest, but half a dozen graves hold the evidence that suggests it happened: belt-buckles and other objects are the same as earlier ones. Take one find from Daodunzi, a cemetery in Tongxin County, Ningxia, almost on the borders of Ordos. Twenty-two plaques feature oxen, dragons, gazelles, horses, a dragon wrestling a tortoise, and a camel – all designs common in Ordos for centuries. According to the excavation report, the burial dates from some time in the first century BC. Long before then, the Xiongnu were firmly back in control of Ordos.

And also firmly in control north of the Yellow River. That was where their HQ remained, with Ordos as a sub-region, its local rulers dependent on the chanyu in Mongolia. Now the Xiongnu were only 350 kilometres from Gaozu's new capital, Chang'an. Gaozu could not fail to see the threat, and made preparations for building more walls, a project that would take fifteen years.

Appeasement seldom works for long. It didn't with the Vikings or the Nazis. It certainly didn't with the Xiongnu, for Modun could not stop some of his chiefs indulging in trans-Wall raids, nor was it in his interests to do so. And clearly, as is the way with dictators, he was always on the lookout to increase his power. After the death of Gaozu in 195 BC, China was run by the queen mother, Lü, Gaozu's wife and de facto empress (though technically only a regent). Modun even tried his hand at diplomacy. In 192 BC, he wrote to her in mock-self-deprecating terms. In the letter, part of an exchange recorded in Ban Gu's *Book of Han*, he seemed to be suggesting a marriage alliance:

> I, who am alone but still vigorous, a ruler who was born amidst lowlands and swamps . . . have several times approached the borders, wishing to be friendly with the Central States. You, Your Majesty, sit alone on the throne, and I, alone and restless, have no one beside me. Since we are both bored, and are both bereft of what could console us [or in another more explicit translation 'without pleasures' and 'unable to gratify

ourselves'], it is my hope that we can exchange that which we have for that which we are lacking.[12]

What was he hoping for? Perhaps he was suggesting that Empress Lü herself would be the next princess for his harem? Sima Guang records that in that year 'the Han court was looking for a princess in the royal families to take up a marriage union'. Or perhaps he planned to increase his power by fusing the two nations? If so, he was either misinformed or miscalculated. Empress Lü was an extremely tough-minded lady – 'strong-willed', Sima Qian called her; 'vicious' and 'vindictive' also come to mind – who had gone to great lengths to secure power. When her husband died, she ruled through her teenage son, Hui, a 'weak and soft-hearted' boy. She had a problem: the former emperor's favourite concubine whose son had briefly been favoured as heir by the emperor. She loathed them both, and solved the problem in brutal fashion. First she had the boy killed by forcing poisoned wine down his throat, then dealt with the girl by ordering guards to cut off her hands and feet, put out her eyes, and make her dumb by destroying her larynx with poison. Finally, she had her thrown into the lower part of a toilet, where the pigs were kept, and showed this 'human pig' to her own son, the teenage emperor. When he realized what he was looking at, he was shocked into utter subservience to his mother's will. 'No human being could have done such a deed as this!' he said. 'Since I am your son, I will never be fit to rule the empire!' Later, after Hui's early death in 188 BC, Lü placed two children on the throne, in sequence, the first murdered because he was ill,

[12] Ban Gu, *The History of the Former Han Dynasty* (see Bibliography).

the second murdered later during the struggle for the succession after Lü's death.

When Modun wrote, she was in full control. Sima Guang records her first reaction: 'She was beside herself with mortification and rage.' She called a council, suggested the execution of the poor Xiongnu envoy and wanted to send an army to destroy Modun and his people. Her top general, Fan Kuai, stepped forward. Of humble origins – a former dog-butcher, dogs being raised for their meat in ancient China – he had helped Gaozu establish the dynasty and was also Lü's brother-in-law. He brashly volunteered to lead an army of 100,000 northwards. An unnamed councillor was aghast: 'Fan Kuai should be executed for making such a remark!' He dared point out that Fan Kuai had failed to raise the siege of Taiyuan with 320,000 troops, so what made him think an invasion with an army one-third that size would gain victory? That brought Lü to her senses. Diplomacy trumped outrage. No one recorded the fate of the Xiongnu envoy. Perhaps he was spared to carry her reply, in which she gave Modun the brush-off, in mock-extremes of self-deprecating, grovelling humility:

Chanyu, you have not forgotten our humble kingdom, you have graced us with your missive. It sent our entire nation into a tumultuous commotion with awe. I personally would have gone forth to your court to serve Your Majesty. Unfortunately my blood is thin and weak, my hair and teeth are falling out, and when I walk I stagger. You ought not to sully yourself. I, who stand at the head of an impoverished domain, am not to blame [for refusing you] and should be pardoned. I have two imperial chariots and two teams of four coach horses which I present to you.

That worked. Rebuffed but mollified, Modun saw that his interests were best served by sticking to the 198 BC treaty. He sent an envoy to apologize, and resume the terms agreed six years before, with its lucrative exchanges. 'I am not conversant with Han etiquette, Your Majesty,' he said. 'Please pardon my indecorous behaviour.'

The sources speak of 'letters' and 'missives'. In translation, to English-speakers, the words suggest paper and pen, to Chinese paper and brush. But this was before paper, which – so the Chinese tradition claims – was invented in AD 105. Yet Chinese scripts of many different forms had been used for over 1,000 years. Since about 1500 BC, Chinese had 'written' – drawn, painted, scratched, inscribed, engraved – on many different surfaces: turtle shells (so-called 'oracle bones') to start with, then stone, bronze, clay, pottery, wood, and on countless objects made of these materials. Classics, like the *Yi Jing* (*Book of Changes*) or the works of Confucius, were inscribed in wood or stone, with immense and delicate labour. None of the materials and techniques were suitable for 'letters', such as those between officials and heads of state. Yet Sima Qian and other sources record the contents of letters and the First Emperor is said to have burned subversive 'books'.

What materials could be both carried easily and burned? There were two: silk and strips of wood, usually bamboo. Silk was an equivalent of paper, on which scribes could write, artists could paint, artisans print with woodblocks, and officials make their marks with bronze or wooden stamps. Bamboo breaks neatly into long strips, giving a smooth surface for writing. The strips could then be bound together in the right order to make long messages or scrolls. Many thousands of these strips have survived in graves and in the bone-dry sands of China's deserts. Both silk 'pages' and bamboo strips could be rolled up and transported.

Bamboo strips, being cheap to make, were used for routine communications, like sending orders to border troops manning the Great Wall. Silk was a luxury material available to both courts. Highly prized by the Xiongnu, it was sent north by Han in huge quantities as part of the peace-and-kinship treaty. Having got it, they flaunted it. Sima Guang records that the Han court objected to the Xiongnu habit of using 'oversized scrolls', which they considered a wilful display of arrogance. All of which makes it almost certain that Empress Lü and Modun wrote to each other on silk.

The next question raised by the silk letters is: what language did they use? Since Xiongnu was never written – as far as we yet know – it had to be Chinese. Are we to assume Modun spoke and wrote the language of his enemies? Probably not. (A millennium later, when the Mongols ruled all China, their emperors were notoriously ignorant of Chinese, starting with Genghis's grandson, Kublai Khan.) But there was close contact between the cultures, in terms of trade and diplomacy. Officials came and went. Meng Tian's Straight Road led north across Ordos, and was probably kept in good order, at least in peacetime, to make sure the exchanges were as fast and safe as possible. It is fair to assume that Modun had a team of bilingual secretaries to read and translate the empress's letters, and draft his own replies. In fact, one of them, Xiyuqian, is named in a later exchange.

Other illiterate leaders have had similar arrangements. Attila, the fifth century AD leader of the Huns – possibly a remote descendant of Modun's, as the last chapter explains – had close relations with the Roman empire, trading with and attacking both the eastern, Greek-speaking part and the western, Latin-speaking part. Before he helped destroy it, the Roman empire, like Modun's, exchanged hostages with the Huns. And like the Han and the Xiongnu, the Romans and the Huns also exchanged letters. Attila had his bi- or trilingual secretaries. Same thing with Genghis Khan in the thirteenth century, even more so because he acknowledged his own illiteracy, ordered up a script for Mongolian and had a multilingual secretariat that could read and write in Mongol, Chinese, Khitan, Persian, Tangut and more as the empire grew.

Surely, like all officials, Modun's secretaries kept copies? After all, they would have supervised not only the correspondence but the terms of the many-times-renewed peace-and-kinship treaties. Somewhere, perhaps, in some undiscovered grave, lies a collection of silks that will bring alive the inner workings of Modun's government.

Modun recognized that wealth flowed from China only because war and peace remained in precarious balance. China followed the path of appeasement only because the Xiongnu were seen to be unstable, uncontrollable barbarians. To get gifts, Modun had to act the wild man; to avoid retaliation, he had to act the diplomat. It was a tricky balancing act, but if it could be managed he would have his cake and eat it. So raids continued, recorded in 188, 183, 182 and 181 BC. These last three marked a new phase in their attacks. They came in the far west, from Ordos, now firmly under Xiongnu control. They struck today's Lintao, the extreme western point of the

Great Wall. A successful breakthrough here could have opened the way to the Wei Valley, to a road that was a predecessor of the Silk Road, and, some 500 kilometres downstream, to Chang'an. Han cavalry stopped them, but the threat remained.

The Empress Dowager Lü's death in 180 BC led to a bitter dispute over the succession, resolved with the accession of Wen, aged twenty-two, another of Gaozu's descendants. Wen was a well-meaning man, determined to do his best for his people. Not ruthless enough for the times, but – uniquely – famously frugal, and therefore popular, or at least that is how Sima Qian presents him. During his twenty-three-year reign he built no new palaces, added no new carriages, and ordered hardly any new clothes. Sima Qian, critical of his own emperor's ruinous expenditure, approved of Wen's frugality:

> The emperor always dressed in thick, coarse silk. He would not allow his favourite, Lady Tian, to wear gowns that trailed on the ground, nor would he have curtains or hangings with embroidered patterns on them. Thus he set an example for the empire in the simplicity of his way of life.

Wen was not the man to stand up to Modun. The peace-and-kinship deal remained in place, which, in Sima Qian's view, was a lot better than declaring all-out, risky, self-destructive war as his own Emperor Wu would do (a subject that forms a major theme in the next chapter).

Well financed by Chinese 'gifts', Modun secured his authority and his empire. He was even able to turn an apparent lack of authority to his advantage.

In 177 BC, his third-in-command, the Wise King of the

Right, launched a not-so-wise attack east of Ordos, where his troops 'plundered, slaughtered, pillaged and dispensed all atrocities imaginable'. When Han mobilized in retaliation, the Xiongnu beat a hasty retreat. Perhaps the attack had Modun's sanction, perhaps not, but in any event Modun followed up by sending the Wise King of the Right westwards into present-day Gansu to drive out the remaining inhabitants, the Yuezhi. He had attacked them once already, but this was on a different scale.

The same campaign seized the small kingdom of Loulan, which is now a sand-blasted site in the middle of the Desert of Lop by a dried-up lake, Lop Nor, where China conducts its nuclear research. Back then it was a thriving city on an earlier version of the Silk Road. It lay at the mouth of a river, now the dried-up Kuruk, which was once part of a river system flowing from the Tian Shan Mountains. Later, Loulan fell into ruin when its river shifted course and Lop Nor became a 'wandering lake', before both river and lake vanished. Loulan, too, vanished. Its ruins were rediscovered by the Swedish explorer Sven Hedin in 1900. But in 176 BC it became the western outpost of the Xiongnu empire, and remained so for seventy-five years.

Modun knew that the original assault could threaten the arrangement he had with Han China, so once again he played the diplomat. He wrote to Emperor Wen a letter that was part mock-contrite, part threatening. Sorry about the invasion, which 'indubitably unravelled the harmony between us', (or 'cut off our fraternal friendship', in another translation). But it was not his fault. In part it was the emperor's, because he, Modun, had sent an envoy who had vanished – detained? Defected? Who knew? – and had received no envoy in return.

In part, it was the fault of the Wise King of the Right for reacting without 'seeking prior approval'. He had been reprimanded, and – as if it were a punishment – sent off westward, to attack the Yuezhi, where . . .

> . . . praise to the benevolence of Heaven, having endowed our warriors with great spirits and making our warhorses robust, we have completely vanquished the Kingdom of Yuezhi. Their tribal members have either surrendered or been killed; the kingdom is now completely under my control . . . and their neighbouring states, Loulan, Wusun, Hijie and twenty-six others[13] have all been subjugated to us, the mighty Kingdom of Xiongnu. All the warriors of the various tribes ['all the people who draw the bow', in another translation] are now under my control and unified into one grand entity.

He overstated: the Yuezhi may have been defeated, but they were still a force to be reckoned with, and would not be totally destroyed for another fourteen years. The letter makes clear that the Xiongnu were not now an ethnic or racial group – perhaps they never had been – but a political entity, an empire. The implication was obvious: if Modun chose to turn his armies on Han, it would be a walkover. But Modun was (he implied) a reasonable man. As reasonable as any other ruthlessly ambitious empire-builder in need of cash. Also (he claimed) a lover of peace. He would rather 'repudiate wars to allow our warriors and horses respite'. The best thing would be to 'return to the old treaty . . . and let our young people reach adulthood and our old people live

---

[13] And more in due course. Sources list up to 36.

peacefully'. To show goodwill, he was sending 'my Gentleman-of-the-Palace Xiyuqian to present my wishes in writing, and to present one camel, two riding horses, and two carriages with teams of four horses'. Please keep your people under control, he urged, 'if Your Majesty does not wish to see the Xiongnu near the frontier'. Then, as a final, peremptory PS: 'When my envoy arrives, send him back immediately.'[14]

Emperor Wen was in a quandary: attack or placate? His advisers were in no doubt: 'Since the chanyu has just conquered the Yuezhi and is riding on a wave of victory, he cannot be attacked.' So the emperor replied with soothing words, delivered by two emissaries. If Modun really intended not to dwell on past malice, his proposal of renewed peace was welcome, because 'Han and Xiongnu are sworn brothers.' There is no mention of the Xiongnu envoy who had mysteriously disappeared. Perhaps peace could be ensured with the gifts that came with the letter – an embroidered and lined silk jacket, a brocade-lined gown, a decorative comb, a sash and a belt both adorned with gold, 30 pieces of brocade, 40 pieces of thick, red silk and 40 pieces of green silk. He was happy to forget the problem with the Wise King of the Right. 'Please order your officers not to break our treaty.'

Would that have worked? Probably not, because Modun was a ruthless, devious, self-made dictator and Wen was a pushover. We will never know because later that year, 174 BC, Modun died, probably in his sixties, after ruling for thirty-five years. Had he been merely ruthless, devious and dictatorial, his empire might have collapsed into a struggle for the

---

[14] These quotations combine versions from Markley (*Peace and Peril*) and Yap (*Wars*).

succession. But, like Genghis Khan and very few other great leaders, he had a long-term vision, which meant appointing a successor and setting up a system that guaranteed the appointment. Under his system, his authority passed seamlessly to his eldest son, Laoshang, and then on for the next ten generations and 150 years, ensuring the rule of his family and the stability of his empire.

Postscript

Did the chanyus and emperors really write to each other on silk? A find by French archaeologists suggests another possibility. The evidence comes from a chariot buried in a Xiongnu élite grave (Gol Mod 1, tomb T20, which we will get to in Chapter 11). Like others, the chariot had a parasol held up by flexible wooden struts, which ended in bronze tips with hooks to hold the canopy. One of the bronze tips had some sort of fibrous material around it, as if the driver had used it to jam the tip on to its strut. Under microscopic analysis, the fibres turned out to be hemp. The archaeologists, Guilhem André and his colleagues, suggest that this is the remains of a bit of paper.[15] A lacquered bowl in the same grave has an inscription dating it to 16–13 BC. Tradition says that paper was invented in AD 105, but this find suggests the Chinese were making paper over a century before. If true, perhaps those royal letters were not on long-lasting silk but on fragile paper, which would explain why none have been found.

[15] Guilhem André et al., 'L'un des plus anciens papiers du monde exhumé récemment en Mongolie', *Arts Asiatiques* (see Bibliography).

6

THE GRAND HISTORIAN'S HIDDEN AGENDA

ALMOST ALL WE THINK WE KNOW ABOUT THE XIONGNU comes from one man, the historian Sima Qian and his monumental *Shi Ji*. The book covers the whole history of China down to Sima Qian's own day in 130 chapters. A brilliant synthesis of oral and written sources, it is to China what the histories of Herodotus or Thucydides are to western culture: original in structure, content and style; fundamental; judicious; and full of anecdote, dialogue, character and colour. And it is based on records and real events. In the words of his translator and biographer, Burton Watson:

Undoubtedly he heard the speeches of many of the men he described, listened to the deliberations of the courtiers, consulted files of official documents kept in the palace, and observed the effects of various government policies when he accompanied the Emperor on tours through the provinces.

He had personally visited some of the barbarian lands that were being brought under Han rule by the Emperor Wu's foreign conquests, and in other cases he no doubt heard from the generals themselves the accounts of their wars and hardships.

His history is obviously important, and it remains as popular as ever, as does the man himself. His tomb lies in the grounds of a temple dedicated to him in Hancheng, 150 kilometres north-east of Xian. A fifty-eight-part TV series on his boss, Emperor Wu, started transmission in 2005, which was the 2,150[th] anniversary of Sima Qian's birth. The series was mostly based on the Grand Historian's work. Given its virtues, it is – as Jonathan Markley[1] puts it – traditionally considered to be 'objective truth simply because Sima Qian said it'.

But it's not. Can the writing of history ever be objective? The Grand Historian's history certainly isn't. Judged by modern standards, he lacks rigour. On the other hand, he's all we have, so it's important to try to understand his distortions, in the hope that historical facts will emerge from his absorbing fictions. Luckily, the other great historian of this age, Ban Gu (AD 32–92), whose work overlaps Sima Qian's, did not share his predecessor's agenda and provides different material that allows a better understanding both of events and Sima Qian's biases.

To assess Sima Qian – to read between his lines – scholars point out five ways in which his reporting is distorted:

- He had an agenda, which can only be understood with an unchronological step into the future. Sima Qian was

[1] Associate Professor of History, California State University, Fullerton.

writing during the reign of the brilliant, empire-building Emperor Wu (141–87 BC), the 'Martial Emperor', who gave up on peace and tried to solve the Xiongnu problem with war. We shall see the outcome in due course, but it threatened to undermine China's economy. Throughout history, writers, when wishing to criticize their own bosses, have directed their venom at substitute targets. So it was in the case of Sima Qian. His aim was to show up the faults of his own emperor by emphasizing similar faults and contrasting virtues of previous ones. Often, he fixed the evidence to suit the theory.

- He used sources that he did not list. He had access to countless documents stored over many centuries, but he does not tell us what they were. When he quotes the advice of ministers, he may be quoting directly, or he may be putting his own words to their brushes. When he quotes 'letters', we have no idea whether he does so accurately, or whether the quotes are a way of adding spurious authenticity. The only way to check up on him is to use other sources, of which there are very few, while some apparent sources actually relied on him, with further additions of their own – distortion upon distortion.

- He used his imagination to bring his narrative alive. In particular, he is shameless in his use of dialogue. He gives his characters long speeches that could not have been recorded. He may have captured the spirit of an utterance, but the only truly authentic ones are in his own voice, as commentator on events or as autobiographer.

- His history is not a single narrative, but an encyclopaedia of articles and topics. Each of the 130 chapters is a mini-history, many going over the same ground, each with its quotes, character assessments and anecdotes, often with alternative facts. He was not too concerned if he contradicted himself.

- To cap it all, Sima Qian had deeply personal reasons to write as he did. Much of his history is very much 'his story', his tragedy.

All of which make him a most unreliable narrator. Sima Qian himself pointed this out, obliquely, quoting Confucius, who 'in his writings about the current age, and in his criticisms and praise, had to avoid certain matters'. To tell the truth about the present, it had to be mirrored in a well-spun, vivid version of the past.

Sima Qian, probably born around 145 BC, possibly up to 10 years later, owed his inspiration to his father, who among other roles looked after the archives and started the *Records*. When his father died in 110 BC, his son took over. As Grand Historian[2] at court, all went well, until disaster struck.

One of his themes was the threat posed by the Xiongnu, which he knew something about, because when he was a boy, they had penetrated to the heart of China. They were kept in check by handouts of cash and silk. But no emperor of a unified China could claim the Mandate of Heaven and at the same time tolerate 'barbarian' rulers who drained the Chinese economy and were liable to launch raids whenever they felt like it. The man who grasped this nettle was Sima Qian's

---

[2] Tài Shi 太史. His actual position was Grand Astrologer. Because of his life's work, he later became known as the Grand Historian.

emperor, Wu (141–87 BC). Wu was a monarch of genius – autocrat, statesman, strategist, artist – with a reign long enough to follow through on his long-term strategy. His fifty-four years on the throne was unmatched for 1,800 years. His despotic ways mirrored those of the First Emperor, and his achievements – his laws, institutions and conquests – would mark China from then on. His answer to the Xiongnu menace was to set the boundaries of China wider, and to do that he decided to escalate the rumbling rivalry into a full-scale war.

From this decision flowed many consequences – for the Xiongnu, for China, and for Sima Qian.

As we see in a later chapter, the war was catastrophic for both sides. Repeatedly, the opposing armies thrust into each other's territory. A dozen times – almost every year – the Xiongnu went on the offensive. Eventually, Wu would come to see that conquering the Xiongnu with direct assaults was impossible. The only way to win was to outflank them. But that decision, so significant for China's future, was slow in coming.

Meanwhile, war continued. In 99 BC another campaign ended in total catastrophe. An army of 5,000 men with wagonloads of food and arrows struck northward under a general named Li Ling, an acquaintance of Sima Qian. 'We never so much as drank a cup of wine together,' he wrote. 'But I observed that he was clearly a man of superior ability . . . I believed him to be truly one of the finest men of the nation.' This was the man who was soon to become the focus of the historian's attention, and the unwitting cause of his tragedy. His story is told in a later chapter.

In brief: Li Ling led his force for a month across the Gobi and the Mongolian heartland. It was not a big force. Perhaps

Li Ling was confident that his repeating crossbows would win the day. But these terrifyingly effective weapons were no match for the Xiongnu horsemen. Li Ling staged a fighting retreat over grasslands and the Gobi's gravel plains to the mountains where he and his wagons were trapped. The surviving Chinese – only half of the number that had set out – fled through a narrow valley, while the Xiongnu tossed rocks down on them, blocking escape until night fell. That night, Li Ling took ten men and galloped clear, only to be hunted down and forced to surrender, later opting to work with his captors. Just 400 of his men, armed with clubs made from the spokes of their wagons, made it back home.

Emperor Wu was so furious at Li Ling's defeat that 'he could find no flavour in his food and no delight in the deliberations of the court'. His officials responded to his mood by accusing the general of treachery for not committing suicide and by punishing his family. Only later did the emperor relent, blame himself for not sending another brigade of archers as a back-up, and reward the survivors.

For Sima Qian, however, Li Ling's treatment was scandalous. He was unaware, of course, that Li Ling had actually committed himself to the Xiongnu, and would never return home. His defence of the general, with its dire aftermath for him personally, is included in one of the strongest, most heartfelt and moving pieces of writing in Chinese literature.[3]

True, Sima Qian and Li Ling were not close, but, he said, Li Ling was a man of superior ability, filial (that great Confucian virtue), trustworthy and modest. His behaviour had

---

[3] It is preserved in Ban Gu's *Han Shu* (ch. 62) and included as an appendix in Burton Watson's fine translation, *Records of the Grand Historian*.

been exemplary. He had led his small force deep into Xiongnu lands, where he had been ambushed and captured (the story is told in detail in Chapter 8). Though a captive, he was surely awaiting an opportunity to fight again for the emperor (not so, but Sima Qian had no way of knowing that):

> His constant care was to sacrifice himself for his country . . . A subject who will go forth to face ten thousand deaths, giving not the slightest thought for his own life but hurrying only to the rescue of his lord – such a man is rare indeed! Now . . . officials who think only of saving themselves . . . vie with each other in magnifying his shortcomings. Truly it makes me sick at heart!

Unfortunately for Sima Qian, Li Ling's superior was the eldest brother of the emperor's favourite concubine. To exculpate the No. 2 would be to blame the No. 1, which was inconceivable, since he was still in office at the behest of the emperor himself. Sima Qian was summoned to explain his opinions, and spoke again in Li Ling's defence. He had always shared hardships with his officers and men, always commanded loyalty, always served his emperor to the best of his abilities. 'But I could not make myself fully understood,' Sima Qian wrote, with outward humility and bitter irony. 'Our enlightened ruler did not wholly perceive my meaning.'

There was no money to buy his freedom; no one spoke up for him. He was charged with attempting to deceive the emperor, arrested, tried, condemned and sentenced to castration.

He wrote of his experience to an old friend who was at the time accused of some unspecified offence and was under threat of execution. In his memorial, he equates himself with the lowest of the low. The least a man can achieve is to bring no shame on his ancestors, or himself. Below such a person, he writes, is one who is bound with ropes, and below him, in a descending sequence of degradation, is the prisoner, the fettered, the beaten, the shaven-headed, the manacled, and the mutilated. Finally, lowest of all, is the eunuch. 'Alas! Alas! A man like myself – what can he say? What can he say?'

He might have committed suicide to avoid the humiliation, as others did, but chose to endure castration, because – he said – if he died he would soon be forgotten. His death would 'make no more difference to most people than one hair off nine oxen'. They would just assume 'my wisdom was exhausted and my crime great'. A gentleman would surely settle the affair in accordance with what is right. 'Even if the lowest slave and scullion maid can bear to commit suicide, why shouldn't one like myself be able to do what has to be done?' he asks, and then answers his own question. 'The reason I have ... continued to live, dwelling in vileness and disgrace without taking leave, is that I grieve that I have things in my heart that I have not been able to express fully.' Yes, castration was the grossest humiliation, but there was worse: 'I am ashamed to think that after I am gone my writings will not be known to posterity.'

I wished to examine all that concerns heaven and humankind, to penetrate the changes of the past and present, putting forth my views as one school of interpretation. But before I had finished my rough manuscript, I met with this calamity. It is because I regretted that it had not been completed that I submitted to the extreme penalty ... if it may be handed down to those who will appreciate it and penetrate to the villages and great cities, then though I should suffer a thousand humiliations, what regret would I have?

His higher purpose demanded telling the truth (as he saw it) about his emperor and the imperial excesses, not simply the military campaigns, but the ruthless commandeering of men to build and guard the Great Wall, the burdens of taxation, overspending on vast palaces, and an obsession with death that led to a lunatic hunt for the 'elixir of immortality' and to decades-long labour to build a tomb that would outdo the First Emperor's.

But, having received his punishment, Sima Qian still had his position as a court official. He could not be direct in his criticism. So he was indirect, attacking the First Emperor and the rulers of the next dynasty instead of Wu. In the case of the First Emperor, the result was an overblown portrait, which, in Burton Watson's words, skilfully set 'examples of the grandiose rhetoric employed by the monarch to celebrate his achievements' against 'grim accounts of the cruelty, folly and oppression of the populace'. Sima Qian also had a go at the First Emperor's officials for 'bowing too readily to the will of the ruler, for accommodating themselves too readily to the trend of the times, instead of endeavouring to reform it'. The same criticism applies to the Han rulers after the collapse of the Qin. He was at pains to emphasize their attempts to deal with the Xiongnu peacefully, as a contrast to Emperor Wu's pursuit of all-out war, with its appalling losses in men and cash.

That part of his history was a small part of the very ambitious whole – a complete history of the world as he knew it, namely China, from its beginning to his own time. The structure of the *Shi Ji* is totally original. It is an encyclopaedia in 130 'chapters', comprising articles on dynastic annals, chronologies, topics (rites, music, astronomy and others), noble families, individual biographies and accounts of foreign lands (including the Xiongnu). A century after his death in 86 BC, the *Shi Ji* was copied, revised and extended by Ban Gu and by his brilliant sister Ban Zhao, China's first woman historian and one of its greatest scholars. Both works, the *Han Shu* (*Book of Han*, sometimes called the *Book of the Former Han*, as opposed to the *Hou Han Shu*, the *Book of the Later Han*) and the *Shi Ji* were copied many times, with many errors and interpolations. Sorting fact from fiction and error is a considerable academic industry, let alone the ongoing work of translating the various texts, which demands another level of expertise and explanation.

Sima Qian's fate was more than a personal tragedy. He was certain that his emperor was on the wrong track, wasting the nation's resources on a hopeless quest for victory. His views were powerfully reinforced by the way he was treated, so that his account is infused with prejudice, against war and against his emperor. It is almost everything that a history should be – vast in scale, comprehensive, colourful, persuasive, and often (surely) as true as can be, since he experienced much of what he reports. The problem is to sort fact from prejudice and fiction, which is difficult, because he influenced every history that came after him, including this one.

7

A PHONEY PEACE,
A PHONEY WAR

MODUN WAS DEAD, AND THE PEACE MIGHT HAVE DIED WITH him. But his heir, Jizhu (usually referred to by his Chinese title, Laoshang, Vencrable-Supreme), followed the letter of the deal cut by his father, as did Emperor Wen. The emperor's first recorded act after Modun's death was to choose a 'noble princess' for the new chanyu, an unnamed daughter of the royal family. She would have been sent off in some style, in a carriage, guarded by outriders, and accompanied by a eunuch, one of a notoriously recalcitrant, influential and self-serving group of officials. This eunuch, Zhonghang Yue, came from the state of Yan, one of those taken over by the First Emperor almost fifty years before and then crushed again by Han. In fact, Yan's crown prince had fled to the Xiongnu. The eunuch, having found new employment with the Han government, was very unhappy with the idea of leaving the comforts of Chang'an for northern wastelands, but had to follow orders.

Old resentments surfaced. 'If the court insist that I go,' he said, 'it will be a great calamity for Han.' His reluctance and his threat were ignored by his superiors. He departed determined on revenge.

Before we get further into this story, with its colourful quotations, it's worth re-remembering that the details are invented. It was Sima Qian's style to bring his narrative alive with fictional dialogue, a technique followed by Sima Guang over a thousand years later. No doubt there is a core of truth to the events and people involved and their characters, because reports travelled between the courts, but what follows is at best a 'faction' – a melding of fact and fiction – not verbatim drama. Moreover, it is so carefully argued that it is surely a device by which Sima Qian can express his own critical views of his society. 'The Zhonghang Yue dialogue recalls a classical use of the wisdom of foreigners to indirectly critique the self, especially during times of political decadence.'[1]

After about two months of travel – some 2,000 kilometres at an average of 25 kilometres a day – Zhonghang Yue would have been happy to arrive at the Xiongnu capital. Which looked like what? We have no idea, because no one left a description of it. Chinese sources refer to a place called Long Cheng (Dragon City), but the Xiongnu would not have given their base a Chinese name, and anyway no such site has been identified. For that very reason – the lack of physical evidence – all we can do is make a guess at what Yue saw, based on Sima

---

[1] Tamara Chin, 'Defamiliarizing the Foreigner', in *Harvard Journal of Asiatic Studies* (see Bibliography).

Qian's notes and on the even greater nomadic empire built by Genghis Khan and his heir Ogedei some 1,200 years later.

The two empires were comparable in many ways – clans, tribes and vassals united to form a nation and an empire by a charismatic leader, a lifestyle based on herding, a tradition of riding and horseback archery, big round tents of felt, the same foods (mainly meat and kumiss), a lack of luxuries and a desire to get them from the major source, China, either by trade or robbery. These elements were common to those who lived on Mongolia's grasslands for 2,000 years. Some still underpin countryside living today (ignoring others that make life easier, like satellite dishes, TVs, mobile phones and motorbikes).

But conquests, tributes and trade created new wealth, and also stability. To rule an empire, you need administrators, who need payment of some kind, whether herds, slaves or luxuries, anything to enhance status. That leads to a desire for permanence, and an interest in building. Before Genghis started on the creation of his empire, he was based at a little place – more village than town – called Avraga, on the Kherlen River in the homeland of the Mongols in central Mongolia. With nearby mountains to hide in, it was a good spot from which to raid or trade with China, which lay a few days' gallop away across the Gobi. Here, as Japanese archaeologists have revealed, were a line of stone houses, a paved temple and a stone base for a palace-tent. It was, in effect, a capital-in-waiting. But it was no place to rule a new nation, certainly no place to rule an empire, because it was too far east – not central enough. Previous rulers, preceding the Mongols, had discovered that, and made their HQs further west, in the valley of the Orkhon River. That's where Genghis decided to place the seat of his government. He died before work got under way, leaving it to Ogedei, his heir and third son, to build the Mongol capital, Karakorum (of which there is nothing left except an archaeological site, with its stones forming the walls of a nearby monastery). By western standards, it wasn't much of a place: a palace, a wall with four gates, a dozen temples, two mosques and a Christian church (the Nestorians, an orthodox sect, were well established in Asia). To one of the few western visitors, the monk William of Rubruck, it was no more than a village, its Chinese-style palace vastly inferior to countless buildings in Europe. But there was much more to it than its buildings, for it had a semi-permanent penumbra of tents and on special occasions many hundreds more, housing traders, officials, officers and envoys.

The Xiongnu had similar needs, and could have built a similar capital. They certainly had the ability to build, or use Chinese artisans and slave labour to do so. Prisoners and defectors, living in settled communities of farmers, provided a core of foreign labour. The results have been excavated from many graves (which we will look at later in this chapter) and about twenty fortified settlements, some earth-walled, some with stone walls. I was at one of the earth-walled sites a few years ago – Dövölzhin on the Terelzh River, in the southern foothills of the Khentii Mountains, and a few kilometres from the broad valley of the Kherlen, which would later become the heartland of the Mongols. It is a square of 200 metres per side, made by a ditch and a low rampart, a not-very-impressive barrier no more than 3 metres high. Today, you can drive over the grassy ridges and hardly notice them. The wall surrounded a central building – beams, clay walls and a roof of locally made tiles, some of which were stamped with a Chinese character.[2]

The most impressive of the stone-built sites is Ivolga, in southern Siberia, south-east of Lake Baikal. Ivolga was a fortified village facing the Selenge River, walled on the other three sides, with over fifty stone buildings, most of them half buried, some with stone heating ducts. It had a population of 2,500–3,000, many working as farmers and fishermen, but also including potters and metal-workers. A cemetery held 244 individuals, buried in little 'shaft-pits', without any of the large burials that are common further south. It was not, apparently, used as a capital. Today, it is open for tourists, signposted in Russian, Mongolian and English: 'Hun City' (suggesting once again that the Xiongnu were the forefathers of Attila's Huns, a subject for the last chapter).

But the Xiongnu were traditionally nomads, and proud of it. You can administer an empire from tents. The chanyu could summon his people to the gathering place known as Long Cheng in Chinese sources, which became a centre for annual celebrations and sports. It must have been all tents, horses and wagons, because there's no trace of it. So why build at all? Not, surely, for the Xiongnu themselves. Perhaps to house officials – like scribes and translators – and labourers and farmers unused to nomadic lifestyles, who could make tools and weapons and grow crops to feed themselves and their masters. Such communities might have felt the need for Chinese-style walls for defence, though none match the Terelzh 'fortress', which looks more like a caravanserai than a

---

[2] Sergei V. Danilov and Natalya V. Tsydenova, 'Ceramic Roof Tiles from Terelzhin Dövölzhin', in Brosseder and Miller (eds), *Xiongnu Archaeology*.

fortress. There are half a dozen such places in Mongolia. Perhaps the chanyu had special campsites built where he could spend time as he toured his empire.[3]

So, to summarize, they could have built a capital. But they didn't. Or rather, there is as yet no evidence that they did. There is no Xiongnu equivalent of Avraga or Karakorum, or at least not one big and solid enough to be found. Yet, as the graves of the Xiongnu élite suggest, the focal point of the empire was in northern central Mongolia. A great empire, yet no capital. It's a puzzle.

One possible explanation is that to build in this area would create a target for Chinese armies, whereas a capital of tents remained mobile. It seems likely that the stone-built settlements were subsidiary, with the biggest, Ivolga, way to the north, almost certainly beyond the reach of Chinese armies, leaving the capital as a city of tents, impressive to look at but still quickly moved in case of an invasion. And also movable in response to the weather and the season, in the tradition of nomads. Perhaps, when we know more, the lack of stone buildings will not be a puzzle after all but a consequence of political realities and a long-established way of life.

So, placing yourself in Zhonghang Yue's boots, imagine dozens of family tents, all with their horses tethered to lines strung between two poles. From a few tents come the slop-slop sounds of women churning milk with paddles to make curds. Someone is rubbing a goatskin against a sheep's scapula wedged into a wooden pole, turning a stiff hide into soft,

---

[3] A millennium later, Kublai Khan had about 20 overnight places built for his spring and autumn journeys between Beijing and his summer capital, Xanadu.

oil-tanned chamois leather.[4] Ahead are larger tents and one huge palace-tent, 30 metres across, supported internally by two circles of posts, carpets decorated with mythical animals, a throne for the chanyu, warriors in leather armour acting as guards, officials and interpreters in silks and furs, dogs kept to fight off wolves held back by leashes – all very threatening in Chinese eyes, for these are traditional enemies notorious for their violence.

But, to this embittered newcomer from south of the Gobi, the place was a sanctuary. On arrival at the chanyu's court with the princess, Zhonghang Yue defected. Perhaps he found support from the descendants of the Yan heir who had sought Xiongnu protection during the wars of conquest. Anyway, Zhonghang ingratiated himself by muttering dire warnings about the dangers of dealing with the Han. Word soon got back to Chang'an, where officials took note, and as a result the eunuch's treachery found its way into the later histories. Here is Sima Guang's version of what Zhonghang said:

The entire population of the Xiongnu empire is no more than one prefecture in the Central States. Hitherto you have been invincible and robust. Do you know why? Because your eating and dressing habits are vastly different from the people of Han, you have never been dependent on them and have the least admiration for their way of life. But now you are changing your culture and lifestyle and starting to indulge in things from Han. The Han people have only to

[4] Denis Ramseyer and Marquita Volken, 'The Staking Tools from the Xiongnu Settlement of Boroo Gol', in Brosseder and Miller (eds), *Xiongnu Archaeology*. Oil-tanned leather, with the fur left on, made superb cold-weather undergarments.

spend one-fifth of their national expenditures[5] to have the entire Xiongnu empire under their domination.

Sima Qian had more. 'Ride quickly through the grass and brambles,' says the eunuch, 'and you will see that their clothing will be ripped to pieces and is not as good as felt and fur garments.' The same with Han foodstuffs, which 'are not as convenient nor as excellent as milk or kumiss!'

Having abandoned all hope of returning, Zhonghang Yue was eager to see the Xiongnu as the embodiments of noble savagery and his own people as softened by luxury. When Han envoys made disparaging remarks about Xiongnu habits and manners, Zhonghang Yue countered by saying that the Xiongnu were strong because they stuck together. When a man dies, his brother marries the widow. Chinese might find the practice barbarous, but it kept the clan name intact. A junior wife might marry her stepson – the son of the senior wife – for the same reason. For the royal family, the succession from father to son or brother kept things simple, so that 'governing the nation is like governing a single person'.

How different from life in China, where 'families become increasingly distant from one another and consequently murder each other'. In China . . .

. . . ruler and people look at one another with hatred, and the extensive building of houses exhausts the strength of the people . . . when the people face disturbance they are not used to fighting, and when the crisis is over they are too

[5] The actual estimated figure was 7 per cent of the Han national income – one-fourteenth – but that was not nearly enough to win control of the Xiongnu.

fatigued to work. Pfui! The Han people who live in houses built of earth chatter and dress up to no avail. What is the use of wearing an official cap?

Why would Sima Qian be so eager to put such words into the eunuch's mouth? Perhaps to show how virile and self-sufficient the Xiongnu were, and how impossible it was to defeat them, as Emperor Wu was set on doing. The only way to solve the problem (he implies) was to deal peaceably with these sturdy, independent people.

Whether or not he said the words attributed to him, Zhonghang Yue talked himself into a job as a top royal adviser, with one important result mentioned by Sima Guang: he 'convinced the chanyu's attendants to keep records, in order to levy taxes on all the domestic animals of the people'. Since no evidence exists that these records were in Xiongnu, this backs up the conclusion suggested by Modun's letters that the court had teams of officials making records in Chinese, presumably on silk.

This all makes a great story. But, like so much of Sima Qian's work, it has an ulterior purpose to do with the strange fact that Sima Qian's account misses out eight years (174–166 BC). Other sources partially fill the gap. For instance, the *Han Shu* records another Xiongnu attack across the far western Wall in 169 BC. But the main reason for the gap seems to be that Sima Qian wished to suppress two long memos from two scholars, Jia Yi and Chao Cuo, suggesting that the way forward was to subvert the Xiongnu – undermine them with good food and luxuries, seduce their allies away from them, and turn them into Han with kindness. This would cause the Xiongnu to defect in ever-increasing numbers. In effect, the two were refining the policy recommended by Liu Jing when the peace-and-kinship treaty was negotiated about thirty years previously.

Chao Cuo was one of the great men of his age – severe, outspoken, austere and inflexible, according to the sources, but with a formidable intellect. He was so well read and his advice so solid that he was nicknamed 'the Wisdom Bag', a reference to the sealed bundle of secret instructions that generals carried with them on campaign. He would come to a bad end fifteen years later, when the emperor blamed him for unrest looming in seven semi-autonomous kingdoms and had Chao Cuo cut in two at the waist. But at the time he was riding high, and his proposals would eventually, after a delay of nearly thirty years, be put into effect.

The peace-and-kinship treaty, Chao argued, was not working. The army was a disaster. Generals were inept, soldiers undisciplined, war-drum signals meaningless and weapons so ineffective that 'one might as well fight with one's bare hands'.[6] Out on the open plains, of course, Han armies had an advantage, with fast chariots and crossbows and tight formations in which crossbowmen could advance and retreat behind the shields of the vanguard. But the Xiongnu, being barbarians, did not fight like this.

When trudging over craggy mountains and fording rapids Han warhorses are no match for Xiongnu horses. At defiles and strategic passes, Han cavalrymen are no match against the Xiongnu, as they are most proficient with their riding and archery skills. During thunderous storms and torrential

[6] Sima Guang, quoted in Yap, *Wars*.

rain, the Xiongnu warriors persevere and continue to fight on in the most adverse conditions despite hunger and thirst.

What was to be done? Qin had failed because of its brutality. To raise his army, the First Emperor had scraped many barrels, employing 'convict conscription', first conscripting small-time criminals, then in turn bonded servants, criminal merchants, former criminals who had served their sentences, idlers, the sons and grandsons of criminals, and finally the neighbours of criminals. Moreover, troops were unused to the extreme conditions on the frontier: 'When they were conscripted it was no different from sending them to be executed.' And they were unpaid, and when they died their families received no compensation. No wonder that when Liu Bang revolted, 'the people under heaven followed him like a tidal wave bursting open a floodgate'.

Current strategy was not working. Small armies were useless, large armies hard to control. Troops sent to garrison border fortresses were replaced every year, so they never had a chance to get properly trained. If it went on like this, China would end up broke and 'our people will live in total misery and abject poverty'.

Han needed a new strategy. The answer Chao proposed was two-fold:

Firstly, to 'use barbarians to fight barbarians'. There were several groups in the Han empire who lived and fought like the Xiongnu. They should be enlisted, armed and used as border guards.

Secondly, in a recommendation that sounds like a draft for modern China's policy in Tibet and Xinjiang, he said that the government should send civilians to colonize the border regions, providing them with protected settlements: 'We should proceed to encourage people to migrate.' This would be a massive operation – settlers by the million, state-funded, over decades. They should receive official titles, tax relief, clothing allowances, and food until they can look after themselves. If state-owned cattle were stolen, settlers should be encouraged to seize them back by being given half of what they recover. His proposal was a blueprint of how to organize the colonies, in terms of size, leadership, location and defence. 'This policy of resettling immigrants is far superior to deploying troops from remote places,' Chao Cuo concluded. 'This is a lasting strategy and the benefits will be enduring.'

None of this finds a place in Sima Qian's history. The 'missing' years during which Jia Yi and Chao Cuo made their well-reasoned arguments were taken up with the story of the embittered eunuch. Why would such a great historian wish to suppress the proposals of two of the greatest scholars of the age? Because – as Jonathan Markley argues – the unfortunate truth was that the Xiongnu were as active as ever. And that undermined Sima Qian's thesis that under the Emperor Wen the empire was at peace and growing in wealth, as opposed to the disastrous state of affairs under Sima Qian's war-loving Emperor Wu.

Chao Cuo urged instant action, because he was sure that the Xiongnu would attack as soon as there was a hint that the peace-and-kinship treaty was at risk. So it proved. In the winter of 166 BC they invaded, with 140,000 horsemen.[7] A Xiongnu detachment galloped to within 80 kilometres of the

---

[7] A campaign in winter was unusual. Possibly they were driven by bad weather, which for a decade in the 160s BC brought droughts and famines to China.

capital, Chang'an, spreading panic inside the city walls. The emperor declared a state of emergency, called up 1,000 chariots and 100,000 infantry, made an inspection of the camps outside the capital, and announced that he would personally lead an expedition against the Xiongnu. His cabinet and his mother were so appalled at this rash idea that he dropped it, giving the task to three generals. All this took a month. Meanwhile the Xiongnu army camped 'within the passes', the phrase for 'inside Chinese territory'. As usual, when they saw the Han army coming, they retreated with their loot. By the time the Han got to the border, the Xiongnu were long gone.

So it went on, every year for four years, with the Xiongnu going from strength to strength. In 162 BC they turned again upon the Yuezhi, already broken by previous assaults in 207 BC and 176 BC. Under Jizhu (often called 'old' because he was in his forties when he succeeded Modun), they probably advanced across the Gobi, past a thriving city, Edsen – later known as Khara Khot, the Black City – and south along the Edsen River. The invasion was intended as a death blow to their old enemies, and so it proved. Sima Qian records: 'The "old" chanyu killed the king of the Yuezhi and made his skull into a drinking cup,' a common way for steppe-dwellers to publicize victory over a rival. No source names the dead king, and none records his successor, but some hint that it may have been a woman, perhaps his consort who acted as regent for an underage prince.

Whoever was in control authorized a momentous decision: get out, or die. The Yuezhi, cut off on three sides, had only one line of retreat: north-west. Jizhu's victory pushed the Yuezhi into a wholesale, year-long migration – imagine several hundred thousand with their herds and a myriad of horses, most of them moving almost 2,000 kilometres north of the Taklamakan Desert and then west to the valley of the Ili River in today's south-eastern Kazakhstan (with a smaller splinter group going south into Tibet). These moves affected other groups, turning Central Asia into a sub-continental game of skittles over the coming decades. In this case, the Yuezhi forced out the local Scythian group, known as Saka; decades later, they would end up in Kashmir. The Yuezhi, seeking only to put a safe distance between themselves and the Xiongnu, had no idea that they were starting on something far greater, a migration that would take them another 1,500 kilometres to the borderlands of India. They will play a further role in this story forty years later.

In the same year, the emperor, greatly depressed by China's losses and Xiongnu gains, sent an envoy with a peace proposal to the chanyu, who responded by sending an envoy of his own to Chang'an. The result: yet another treaty, yet another princess despatched. The emperor announced the news full of self-doubt. He had failed to bring peace, and 'my virtue is insufficient'. At one point, frustration drove him to belligerence. According to the *Han Shu*, quoted by Joseph Yap, he put on military dress, practised horseback archery and studied strategy. But fighting was not the answer. What was? He was at a loss. Rising early and retiring late, concern for his people had filled his days with unrest:

Therefore I have despatched envoys in such profusion that their caps and cart covers are within sight of each other on the road, and their wheel tracks are joined, in order to explain my intentions to the chanyu, the ruler of the

Xiongnu. At last the chanyu has returned to the wise ways of earlier times . . . Together we have cast aside our petty faults and together we will walk the higher road of virtue. We have united ourselves in bonds of brotherhood.

If only. The chanyu, Jizhu (a.k.a, Laoshang, Modun's son) died in 160 or 161 BC. Another (Gunchen in Mongolian, Junchen in Chinese) took his place. Nothing changed. It happened again in 158 BC: 30,000 Xiongnu here, another 30,000 there, smoke signals sent along the Great Wall from beacon tower to beacon tower, the capital 'reverberating with shock', generals appointed, imperial inspections made, armies mobilized and sent to the frontier, only to find the Xiongnu long gone.

To cap it all, the Xiongnu showed no sign of being undermined by their new-found wealth. With gifts from China and tributes in people and cattle from vassal tribes, the ruling class had built a rich and varied life for themselves in northern Mongolia and southern Siberia. To the west, beyond the Great Wall, the Xiongnu, having expelled the Yuezhi, controlled thirty-six little kingdoms in the Western Regions.

Things could not go on like this. As Jia Yi said in his advice to the emperor, the Xiongnu are arrogant, insolent plunderers, 'yet each year Han provides them with money, silks and fabrics'. The natural order of things – the emperor at the top, the vassals below – had been turned on its head. 'Hanging upside down like this is something beyond comprehension.'

Someone had to do something. Not Emperor Wen, because he died in 157 BC, aged only forty-five, carrying depression and self-abnegation into his grave. 'I am deficient in moral character and have contributed little to my people,' he said in his will. Do not mourn for me, he went on, spare the funeral expenses. No carriages or troops. Sweltering summers and shuddering winters are enough of a burden for my people without undue mourning. Mourn for three days only, don't stop eating and drinking, and a note to family members: only fourteen days in mourning clothes, please, not the usual ninety.

Thus ended a reign portrayed by Sima Qian as one of peace and amity with the Xiongnu – but this picture could only be maintained (in Markley's words) 'by suppression of information and distorted general summaries'. Luckily, the survival of the memorials by Jia Yi and Chao Cuo allow scholars to see that his reign was just as violent as ever.

A new emperor, Jing, succeeded. A student of Daoism, he ruled with a light hand, made heavy by a year-long civil war (154 BC), when the rebellion of seven states threatened Han's very existence. Also he was obsessed with the notion that he could make himself immortal, and paid much attention to a guru who claimed he could invoke the Kitchen Deity 'to ward off the ageing process' and other gods to transform cinnabar into gold. The guru died, but the emperor's faith remained intact. He said it was only the guru's body that had died, while his spirit had surely obtained immortality. 'Bizarre occultists,' says Sima Guang, 'travelled to the capital in droves.'

Domestic troubles and esoteric obsessions left the new emperor no inclination in his sixteen-year reign to solve the Xiongnu problem. One thing he did do: he made an order to raise more horses and control the horse trade. Over time, thirty-six new stud farms were opened, which could hold an estimated 300,000 horses. In theory, this was a sensible policy: cavalry would be met by cavalry, a significant change given that in 148 BC it seems that the peace-and-kinship treaty fell into abeyance, with no records of carriage-loads of gifts heading north. And in 147 BC, seven Xiongnu princes defected to Han, possibly driven by greed, and, since their entourages would have been expected to join the Han cavalry, they would have needed horses. But all those horses would prove a target for the Xiongnu. Meanwhile, raids continued. Details are lacking, but one general, Li Guang, was said to be in 'almost daily skirmishes with the Xiongnu'. A government official even asked for him to be transferred from his frontier HQ in Ordos because he 'repeatedly engages the enemy in battle. I am afraid that one day we will lose him!'

Li Guang is worth a diversion, because he will play a significant role in Han–Xiongnu relations in a later chapter and because there is a good story told about him. He was the most famous general of his day, tall, strong, 'with arms like an orang-outang', and a noted archer. Also the most popular, because he 'disseminated rewards to his followers, and while his army was on the move, he lived in their quarters, ate their food and shared their congenial and arduous moments'. Controversial, too, because of his relaxed style of leadership, as Sima Qian knew, because 'I met the general in person. He had a mild manner and was most approachable. He was like a commoner, not particularly proficient with words.'[8] Li Guang 'never placed too much emphasis on the discipline of his troops and their marching formation was pell-mell at best'. Like a nomad, he camped wherever the pastures and

[8] Sima Qian's account was a major source for Sima Guang in the eleventh century. Here, both sources are used.

water supplies were good, dispensing with nightwatchmen and the gongs sounding the all-clear. Instead, he allowed his men their rest and relied on scouts to scour the country-side. He never bothered much with records, keeping them 'simple and rudimentary'. His methods contrasted starkly with his colleague General Cheng Bushi, a martinet who made his men march in step and was up all night writing meticulous notes. Both were equally effective leaders, both successful commanders. The contrast reflects an enduring debate among military strategists about how best to sustain morale: discipline is vital, but so is motivation and initiative. As Cheng Bushi himself conceded, Li Guang's style worked just as well as his own 'tedious and niggling' approach. '[Li Guang's] men are relaxed and contented, and they would die for him' – just as well, considering how the following incident played out.

The sources record Li Guang at his most effective in the summer of 144 BC:

The Xiongnu enter through the Yanmen Pass, the main entry through a section of the Great Wall that runs through north Shanxi. Surrounded by the towering Heng and Wutai Mountains, it gives way 150 kilometres further south to the rich plains of central China.

I was there once, on a drab autumn day with a Mongolian–Chinese friend, Jorigt. We drove uphill on a back road, hemmed in by coal-trucks keen to avoid motorway tolls, through a village guarded by beacon towers, and up past a baffling maze of walls and terraces and fields towards misty hills. A wild area of ravines and boulders and dripping trees led to a dead-end at a stream. An abandoned bridge had been turned into a drying floor for a shaggy mat of corn stalks.

Beyond lay a rough track. Up we went, through slowly swirling mist, into a stone-built village. It seemed abandoned, until two damp camels with drooping humps proved it wasn't. Further on a small house turned out to be a guide hut, with – to my astonishment – a guide, Miss She Yifeng. It turned out that this was a major tourist attraction in summer, the most important pass in Shanxi. Two hundred people a day came here, she said. We had missed the summer season, but she was still on duty. She led the way steeply upwards into deepening fog, until a wall loomed up, damming the head of the valley. An arch at its base carried the path onwards. This being the only way over the mountains, the Xiongnu must have come here, making short work of the Wild Goose's predecessor fortress. Today's pass, with a well-restored pagoda on top of the wall, was once commanded by a great general named Yang Ye, who kept the 'barbarians' – Jurchens from Manchuria – at bay in the time of the Song Dynasty (AD 960–1127). 'Invincible Yang', they called him. Two stone lions and a slender pillar formed a memorial to him.

'What were the Jurchens doing attacking up here?' I asked. 'Surely it would have been easier to attack down on the plain?'

'No,' said Miss She. 'Down there we could see them coming, and the wall was strong. If they could break through here, the way was open,' avoiding the forces arrayed below.

The landscape and the strategic purpose of the fortress had not changed for 1,000 years. Back in 144 BC, though, there had been no equivalent of General Yang to stop the marauders. The story continues. The Xiongnu gallop on for another 140 kilometres to the Yellow River, through low hills where farmers have been making terraces and cutting cave-houses from the hillsides for millennia, and make off with all the horses they can find. This may well have been the purpose of the raid, because some of the emperor's new stud farms had been in existence for ten years, with a capacity of, on average, some 8,000 each. Not that they would have needed horses for themselves, but the loss would severely weaken the Han cavalry. The Xiongnu are said to have killed over 2,000 government soldiers, which is possible given that the farms employed an average of 800 each. These ballpark figures point to a huge operation. It takes about 10 hectares to feed a horse, so each farm would have been about 8 square kilometres in size. Imagine tens of thousands of horsemen rounding up between 10,000 and 20,000 horses, which would then have to be herded back several hundred kilometres into Mongolia – at a speed of 30 to 40 kilometres a day – with the bulk of the force guarding the retreat.

A few days later, a eunuch from a contingent commanded by General Li Guang is out in the countryside with two dozen horsemen when they are spotted by three Xiongnu riders. The three Xiongnu start to circle the eunuch's force, firing arrows, picking the Chinese off one by one – proof of their supreme ability as horseback archers – until the eunuch is the sole survivor. Wounded, he barely makes it back to base with the news. At this Li Guang says, 'They must be Eagle Hunters!' – hunters who use eagles, not who shoot them – gathers 100 cavalrymen and heads out to track down the three Xiongnu.

Suddenly Li Guang and his little contingent come face to face with the main force of several thousand Xiongnu on horseback. The Xiongnu, experts in ambushes and feigned retreats, hold back, suspecting a trap. Li Guang's men are extremely nervous, 'their faces turning a deadly pallor, eager to make a run for their lives'. But Li Guang keeps his nerve. We're far from home, he says, and we have only 100 men. If they see us flee, they'll come after us, and we're doomed. If we stay cool, they will fear an ambush, and not attack. So he orders 'resume normal marching formation'. When they get closer to the curious but suspicious Xiongnu, he tells his men, 'Dismount and undo your saddles!'

'But there are too many of them, and they are almost on top of us!' his men protest. 'What will we do if they attack?'

'They expect us to run away,' Li Guang replies. 'But now if we undo our saddles, and show them we have no intention of fleeing, they will be more convinced than ever that there is something afoot.'

A Xiongnu scout on a white horse separates from the main force, presumably hoping to see if there is a hidden Chinese army somewhere. Li Guang takes ten men, gallops after the scout and shoots him dead. By now, night is coming on. Li calmly returns to his men, and orders them to settle down to rest. The Xiongnu warriors are in a quandary: they should attack, but dare not, because they fear a Han army is waiting for a chance to ambush them. They blink. By dawn, the Xiongnu are gone, and Li Guang leads his men safely home.

Two years later, the Xiongnu invaded again through Yanmen, and this time managed to kill the region's commander, an incident that Sima Qian fails to mention, giving the impression that all was peaceful on the frontier for fifteen years.

His message is that peace worked. Han China was not in constant panic-stricken disarray. Things were improving across the land. Despite 'minor' disasters – floods, sandstorms, locust-plagues, droughts, famines, the occasional revolt – basically, as Sima Guang said in a review of the first sixty years of the new dynasty, 'the average citizen was able to live a comfortable life'. Indeed, there was so much grain stored for so long in the state granaries that it began to putrefy, and so many strings of cash in the treasury that the strings which held the coins began to rot. And 'the populace had become so affluent that they began to keep horses'.

But whatever impression Sima Qian gives, the Xiongnu and their raiding was a major problem, to which no one had an answer.

8

THE WAR, THE WALL AND THE WAY WEST

FOR 150 YEARS, UNTIL THE MIDDLE OF THE FIRST CENTURY BC, the Xiongnu dominated the steppe. Nothing like their empire had existed before, and nothing like it would again until Genghis Khan's empire 1,000 years later.

This is how they managed it:

The secret – the economic foundation for their empire – was the exploitation of China. The Xiongnu had worked out how to run a national protection racket. They were master predators. They had to be, because in steppe societies there was no other way to accumulate wealth. In China, power depended on grain surpluses and taxation and an enduring bureaucracy; on the steppe, wealth depended on animals, which might vanish overnight in a blizzard or a raid, and loyal chiefs who might suddenly become disloyal and vanish over the horizon. Lasting success meant extracting wealth from China by raiding or trading or receiving 'gifts'. That was the chanyu's purpose in life. He was the *capo di tutti capi*, the one who negotiated a new deal with Chang'an. How he did it – whether he made unrefuseable offers, like demanding a princess in exchange for restraining his violent underlings, or whether he insisted on high-status receptions for his envoys – wasn't important. The point was that he did whatever it took to lever wealth from China.

For this to happen and go on happening, the chanyus needed stability, which was ensured by the two principal elements introduced by Modun: the power structure and the laws of succession.

The chanyu, with a staff of 'marquises', acted as an autocrat in dealing with vassal tribes and other foreign powers, principally China, but internally it was a confederacy, based on duality: the two commanders, the Wise Kings of the Right and Left, with their twenty-four 'Leaders of Ten Thousand', each of whom was responsible for military commanders of thousands, hundreds and tens, matched by political officials who looked after administration. The system stopped the chanyu becoming oppressive, and stopped those below him turning into warlords. An ambitious local leader – a tribal chief, say – had three unattractive options: to flee westwards (available only to those in the west), rebel (with little chance of success), or defect to China (an easier life, but as an inferior). Most chose to remain, choice being the key element in the relationship, as events in 60 BC proved. A lesser noble tried to seize the throne by executing the rightful heir and imposing family members to rule all the twenty-four 'Ten Thousands'. That inspired a two-year civil war, revealing what happened if any chanyu tried to seize more power than tradition allowed. Local autonomy, national autocracy – that was what worked.

Secondly, stability was guaranteed by the system of succession, which worked well from Modun's time for 150 years and ten heirs. Each chanyu chose his heir, a son (usually the eldest) who was made the Wise King of the Left. If he was too young or incompetent, he could be replaced by the chanyu and his commanders. This system avoided the possibility of a child-king, always a problem in China, where a young heir was under the control of his mother or a top adviser, opening the way to power struggles and civil war. To start with, sons succeeded fathers, and later brothers succeeded brothers. Subsidiary families, intermarrying with the chanyus, had a vested interest in preserving the status quo. The system had only one major hiccup. In 126 BC, Ichise took power, probably because he was an established warrior, and forced the official heir, the younger, less experienced Yutan, to flee to China. Even so, there was no civil war. Other disputes also ended peacefully. In 85 BC, for instance, a queen acting for her son had a junior wife's son assassinated. To heal the ensuing rift, the chanyu named his brother as heir, but on his death, the queen, ignoring her husband's death-bed instructions, persuaded the sub-commanders to name her son as heir. From then on, the rival half-brother never came to court, but at least did not rebel, for the system and the need for a chanyu who would deal with China trumped everything else.

What did success mean, exactly? Not enough for everyone to get a share, but enough to fund a lavish lifestyle for the top people. The grain sent from China would have fed about 140 people for a year, or 700 people if it was an addition to the normal Xiongnu diet.[1] They had food enough anyway, as

---

[1] These details are estimates by Barfield, *The Perilous Frontier*.

Mongolia does today, because the steppes produce meat way beyond what the population can eat. Drink, though, was a different matter. They had their kumiss, but Chinese grain-based 'wine' gets you drunker quicker, as anyone wandering the streets of Ulaanbaatar can testify. The Chinese sent the Xiongnu about 200,000 litres of the stuff every year, enough for 1,000 feasts of 200 guests each. The aim, as Nikolai Kradin says, was to turn the nomads into drunkards.[2] Then there was the real wealth, silk, which was used as currency. Coming in approximately 17-metre rolls or 'bolts', the Xiongnu received almost 170 kilometres of it every year (10,000 bolts, each weighing about 2.4 kilos). It sounds a lot, but China produced silk in prodigious amounts: in AD 301, the court recorded that the treasury stored 4 million bolts (almost 10,000 tonnes, about 70,000 kilometres).

These gifts were not, as the Chinese court seemed to believe, to feed the chanyus' greed. Most went to subordinates in displays of generosity that bought their loyalty. Far from undermining the Xiongnu, the luxuries in fact strengthened the political system, guaranteeing that when the gifts ran low, there would be more raids followed by more demands. Not much of it would have trickled down to ordinary herdsmen; hence the need for frontier markets, where the Xiongnu and their vassals could trade camel hair and Siberian furs for rice, pottery and other Chinese-made goods. This was a way for the Xiongnu to get their hands on iron, which was

[2] Kradin, 'Stateless Empire', in Brosseder and Miller (eds), *Xiongnu Archaeology*. As Kradin adds, 'A similar phenomenon happened time and again in history ... ending wih the developing of the New World by American pioneers.'

officially banned because it could be turned into arrow-points and swords, but was available on the black market.

For over a century, the Chinese response to the demands of their insatiable, aggressive neighbours had been bribery and despair. Now, at last, came a new policy: bribery and all-out war.

The man who took on the Xiongnu was Emperor Wu (reigned 141–87 BC): a brilliant mind, autocrat, strategist, visionary, and with almost enough time in his fifty-four-year reign to make his vision a reality. His conquests would define China from then on, especially in the north-west. Five decades of war would not quite break the Xiongnu, but they would prepare the ground for victory.

It took Wu a while to find his feet, because he was only fifteen when he succeeded to the throne. Then he focused on the realm's most urgent matter: finding a final solution to the Xiongnu problem. His first thought was to find allies – tribes to the west, beyond the Xiongnu, so that he could open a war on two fronts. No one had yet penetrated the expanses of Central Asia, but there was at least one tribe which would surely hate the Xiongnu: the Yuezhi, expelled by the Xiongnu from Gansu three decades previously and now somewhere deep in the heart of Asia. Where exactly no one knew, but once contacted the tribe would surely make a valuable ally.

In 138 BC Wu sent off a 100-strong expedition headed by a leader noted for his strength, generosity and charismatic leadership, Zhang Qian, who was to become one of the nation's most romantic figures, a hero of exploration. He set out with instructions to persuade the Yuezhi to return, become allies of the Han empire and help destroy the Xiongnu.

This highly dubious venture foundered almost at once

when Zhang was captured by the Xiongnu. This event began a series of adventures which turned him into a sort of Chinese version of Lewis and Clark, the explorers who crossed North America in the early nineteenth century. As an eminent official with no hostile intent, he was treated well by the Xiongnu – perhaps also because he had a Xiongnu companion, Ganfu – and he stayed with them for ten years, taking a local wife. Then he escaped, with his wife and Xiongnu companion, and resumed his journey westward. Two thousand kilometres further on, he found the Yuezhi, who were in today's Uzbekistan on a long migration to north-west India,[3] and had no interest in going to war with their old enemies, the Xiongnu; it would mean returning over the Pamir and Tian Shan Mountains, not to mention the Taklamakan desert and the Desert of Lop. Instead of going home with this bad news, Zhang continued his explorations, visiting many of the great cities of Central Asia, even picking up information about India and the eastern Roman empire, before finally returning home after an absence of twelve years – having lost all his entourage except his Xiongnu wife and the faithful Ganfu.

After Zhang Qian vanished into the wilderness, and without any barbarian allies, Emperor Wu tried diplomacy. The peace-and-kinship treaty having fallen out of use for many years, Wu and the Xiongnu signed a new one.

And instantly the Xiongnu broke the terms with another invasion.

Wu called a cabinet meeting to discuss how best to respond. A huge row between pro- and anti-war ministers broke out.

---

[3] Craig G. R. Benjamin, *The Yuezhi* (see Bibliography).

War would be a disaster, said one: the Xiongnu 'move around like a multitude of birds' and can never be defeated, so best stick to bribery. No, countered another, Han had the strength now and the Xiongnu are 'like an abscess which must be burst', not by invasion but by trickery – draw the chanyu to the border and capture him there. The debate ended with the young emperor's decision: it would be war. Except that it wouldn't be, not yet, because war was expensive, high-risk and above all ineffective unless the total destruction of the Xiongnu could be guaranteed. It would take a few years before Wu could find the strength of mind and the resources to commit to all-out war. Meanwhile, raids continued. In the spring of 133 BC Emperor Wu issued an outraged proclamation: Despite having sent a princess for the chanyu and given him gold, silk and ornamental embroidery, the chanyu had responded with disrespect, 'he has invaded and plundered . . . If now we wish to raise troops and attack him, how would that be?' He'd tried peace; he'd tried war; he'd tried a bit of both; and still he didn't know how best to proceed.

He proceeded not with a head-on assault, but with the plot suggested by his pro-war adviser – a plot so complicated that an experienced tactician should have told the emperor it was doomed to fail. An official named as Old Nie Yi was 'fired', a ruse that allowed him to 'defect' to the Xiongnu and claim he would murder the top men in Mayi, 100 kilometres south of the Great Wall. This (he claimed) would allow the Xiongnu to pillage with impunity. Old Nie Yi returned, killed some condemned prisoners, hung their heads outside the city wall, and sent a message saying that one of them was the governor's. It was, of course, a trap. The Chinese army lined the hills on either side of a valley that was the obvious invasion route, ready to pounce. But the Xiongnu realized what was up 50 kilometres from the town, as Sima Qian relates with his usual flair for the dramatic (and flagging up our usual suspicions about his agenda and how he could possibly have known the details, like the chanyu's exact words – in what language, one wonders).

The chanyu, leading 100,000 troops, noticed that, although the fields were full of animals, there was not a single person in sight. Growing suspicious, he attacked one of the Great Wall's beacon towers, perhaps to see if it was manned or not. By chance, an official who knew of the planned ambush had taken refuge there.

> When the chanyu captured him and was about to kill him, he told the chanyu where the Han forces were. The chanyu was very alarmed and said, 'Just as I thought!' And so he led his troops back. When he had gone beyond the border he said, 'I captured a military official. It was Heaven, yes Heaven, that sent him to warn me.'

Since in Chinese philosophy Heaven is on the side of the virtuous, Sima Qian was putting the chanyu forward as morally superior – to whom? The implication is that it was the emperor – Sima Qian's own emperor. Men had been executed for such treasonable words. But he had a point. Someone had to take the blame, someone who had advised the emperor to back a disastrous strategy. The imperial finger pointed at Wang Hui, leader of the pro-war faction at court and the commander of the force that failed to engage. He committed suicide.

The peace faction sensed victory. Three scholars wrote

memos to the emperor pointing out the disadvantages of war: its expense, the sorrow, the hardship, the despair, the dangers of rebellion.

Still the emperor vacillated. It took him another four years to decide, with roads being built as if to prepare the infrastructure for all-out military action, but with the border markets still open for trade, as if peace was everlasting.

Then, finally, the events of 129–8 BC began to undermine the log-jam in his mind. In a series of tit-for-tat campaigns, the violence slowly escalated. A raid on Shanggu (in the northeast) drove Emperor Wu to order an attack by four battalions of 10,000. The first was victorious, capturing or killing 700. The second failed to make contact. The third was defeated. The fourth, under the famous Li Guang, the so-called 'Flying General' with the long arms who shared his men's hardships, was also defeated, and Li Guang himself briefly captured, until he managed to escape. The next year the pattern repeated itself: an attack, a response, a few defections from leading Xiongnu and a mass defection by one of the Xiongnu's vassal tribes.

In 127 BC, a campaign into Shuofang (to the north-west of Ordos, just outside the Great Bend of the Yellow River) and Ordos retook lands once conquered, and then lost, by Qin, thus 're-establishing the old border that Meng Tian had created in Qin times, and the river was fixed as the border'. It was in this context that Sima Qian placed his criticisms of Meng Tian, saying that he had cut through the 'veins of the earth', ignored the suffering of the common people, and failed to stand up to the emperor. All of this was a backhanded way of criticizing Wu's imperialist agenda, pushed forward by his general Wei Qing – invasion, the building of fortifications, road-building – a mirror image of what the First Emperor and Meng Tian did in the same area.

By this time, Emperor Wu had given up on the Yuezhi. But the information about peoples and established trade routes that Zhang brought back in 126 BC would change his country's history, turning attention westward to cultures of which the Chinese had had no previous inkling – thirty-six in the Western Regions alone – all leading like stepping-stones along what would eventually be called the Silk Road, to India. Wu was happy to learn that, in military terms, these powers were 'feeble at best'. So, given a decent army, 'all the lands within the realms of the four seas and all the people therein would be under the beneficence of Han'. In particular, Zhang told of wonderful horses raised in Ferghana, the fertile valley of what is now eastern Uzbekistan. Tall, standing at 16 hands, these 'celestial horses' – or 'blood-sweating' horses, as they were known, from the pin-prick wounds caused by local parasites – were just what Wu needed to strengthen his cavalry. Such tempting prospects would inspire China's conquest of Central Asia and in effect determine its modern borders. From the seeds planted by Zhang sprang both the great trade routes joining China and the West, and their defence: the future Silk Road and the Great Wall's western extension.

In the year of Zhang's return came a swift response from the Xiongnu, despite a troubled succession – Gunchen's death, a power grab by his younger brother Ichise (Yizhixie in Chinese) – and despite the defection of the true heir and two Xiongnu princes. That year saw a catalogue of assaults: a provincial boss killed and 1,000 captives taken in one raid; another 1,000 in a second; more thousands in a third, fourth and fifth; a full-scale invasion across the Gobi that took 15,000 prisoners (well, a lot anyway); a counter-attack; a counter-counter-attack, with many more prisoners taken and unlikely numbers killed on both sides. This all happened in 126 BC.

This was not the kind of stability Wu could tolerate, with its occasional raids, expensive appeasements, and the eating of much humble pie. No emperor of a unified China could put up with a 'barbarian' neighbour who was liable to launch raids whenever he felt like it. The only answer was to set the boundaries of China ever wider. In the words of Owen Lattimore, Mongolist, linguist, traveller and historian, who was forced to leave his native America for Britain during the McCarthy anti-Communist witch-hunt of the 1950s, Wu needed 'a closed economy, a self-sufficient world, and an absolute Frontier'.[4] It was in pursuit of this absolute that Wu finally escalated the rumbling rivalry into full-scale war.

He had to grapple with two problems. The first was the grasslands of Mongolia, which started just north of the Yellow River and ran eastwards and northwards, fading in the wastelands of the Gobi and picking up again to the north. The other problem was the oasis states – the thirty-six mini-kingdoms ruled by the Xiongnu – of the Central Asian badlands, which lay westwards. The difference between them was this: the Gobi and the steppe could not be conquered and held; the oasis kingdoms could. Once the Chinese had taken them, they could run them like their own cities, whereas nomads could benefit from them only by giving up nomadism. The war aim that Wu adopted, therefore, was to 'cut off

[4] Lattimore, *Inner Asian Frontiers*.

the right arm' of the nomads (the west, since the dominant direction for nomads was southward) – i.e. to pick off the tribal kingdoms one by one and garrison them in order to deny them to the Xiongnu. With the Western Regions in Chinese hands, it would be possible to isolate, invade and destroy the Xiongnu.

There were two keys to success in this venture. The first was Ordos, reoccupied a few years before in 127 BC. The second, starting only 150 kilometres west of Ordos, was the narrow stretch of land running westward through what would later be known as Gansu. The Gansu Corridor, also known as the Hexi (*hé xī* 河西, 'river-west', i.e. west of the Yellow River) Corridor, is another geopolitical keystone, crucial to understanding China's relations with Inner Asia. The Corridor is hemmed in by the Qilian Mountains to the south and deserts to the north, with icy rivers from the Qilian's snowy heights forming fine pastures down the middle. It was this bottleneck, only some 25 kilometres across at its narrowest point, through which nomads galloped to invade north China from the west. From now on, Chinese emperors imbibed a great truth with their mothers' milk: Whoever wishes to rule China must rule the Gansu Corridor.

To close off this open frontier, Wu had only one option: total, all-or-nothing commitment to a range of tactics, all interlinked, all leading step by inevitable and very expensive step to an extension of the Great Wall. He had the manpower (a population of 60 million, a million-strong conscript army, some 10–13 million available for forced labour). He had the firepower. He needed horses by the tens of thousands, and these would have to be raised in China, or bought. There had to be an enduring relationship with the oasis kingdoms to the west, which meant great expenditure on gifts, especially silk. There had to be invasions of Xiongnu lands, and a conquest. Trade goods had to flow. There could, perhaps, be an invasion of the steppes, but that would be of no use unless the border-lands were secured. This meant garrisons, which would have to be fed, which meant sending in colonists to grow grain. And there would have to be fortresses, and overnight places, and houses, and lookout points, and an administrative appar-atus to supervise the whole thing. This was the iron logic that drove Wu's decision to conquer the west.

In 121 BC, Han attacked in the far west and the centre (Dingxiang, the region adjoining the Yellow River where it turns south near Hohhot), two vast invasions, each with 50,000 cavalrymen and 'several hundred thousand' infantry com-plete with baggage trains and fodder. Commander-in-chief and commander of the central force was Wei Qing. In com-mand of the western force was Huo Qubing. The two need an introduction, because they, and especially the young Huo, are about to play vital roles in the story of the Xiongnu wars.

The most remarkable thing about Huo was that he was just nineteen, all the more remarkable because of his unusual origins, to understand which means looking into events in the palace of the Princess Pingyang, elder sister of the emperor. It is an extraordinary sequence of random events, strong evi-dence for those who think history is all about luck.

This is the story in brief, without names:

A servant girl in the princess's palace had a baby girl. The husband died. The mother had two more affairs and pro-duced two more children, a boy and a girl. The first-born girl became a song-and-dance entertainer, the other two grew up as servants. Eventually, the princess put on a show for her brother the emperor, who was unhappy with his empress, a woman eight years his senior and childless, which to his embarrassment was blamed on *his* impotence – bad news for him, given that he was young and politically weak. During the show, the first-born girl caught his eye, and then his heart. He took her into his palace, along with her half-brother to act as a stable boy. The empress was bitterly jealous, made the girl's life a misery, and ensured she was employed as a maid, not a concubine. A year later, depressed, the girl applied to leave the palace. By chance, the emperor saw her tearfully waiting her turn to leave. By now, he had gained in authority. Re-smitten, he told her to stay, took her to bed, made her pregnant, and thus proved his virility. The bitter empress sought revenge by kidnapping the pregnant girl's half-brother, who was saved by friends. When the emperor heard of the incident, he demoted the empress, made the girl his No. 1 consort and the half-brother his chief-of-staff. What meanwhile of the other girl, the half-sister? Another palace affair, another illegitimate child, a boy.

Now to summarize where we stand, and add the names. All the main characters belonged to a single family, named Wei. The emperor's pregnant concubine, Wei Zifu, became Empress Zifu, and remained the emperor's consort for the next forty-nine years. The ex-stable-boy half-brother, Wei Qing, became one of the two most famous generals of his generation. The son of the other sister, Wei Shaoer, was named Huo Qubing, who as a teenager was taken under the wing of his uncle General Wei Qing. At the age of seventeen this 'exemplary horseman and archer'[5] made a name for

---

[5] Yap, *Wars.*

himself fighting the Xiongnu, capturing the chancellor and two relatives of the chanyu, which is why, two years later, he was leading an army on his own account with the poetic rank of Agile Cavalry General, and on his way to match his uncle in fame. Not that he was a popular figure, because he was noted for his lack of care for his men. Once when his soldiers needed rest, he ordered them to make a field where he could watch them play *taju*, a game with a leather ball stuffed with feathers. Sources do not record the rules, but it sounds like a sort of football.

The 121 BC campaign westward marked a turning point, because Huo Qubing was aiming to clear the way through the Gansu Corridor. He left Ordos by its far north-west corner, where the Yellow River is deflected by mountains into a right-angle bend. It is a region of lowlands and meandering streams, as if the river hasn't quite made up its mind to head east. He made his exit through the Gaoque Pass, guarded by a mountainside fortress, the ruins of which can still be seen today. He 'trampled five Xiongnu vassal kingdoms', marched on for 500 kilometres, captured a Xiongnu chancellor and several commanders, and killed or enslaved 32,000 Xiongnu (as usual an unbelievable figure from Sima Guang that simply suggests victory). He returned with his prisoners to rich rewards and a towering reputation that, two years later, would win him a special place in the history of the Xiongnu wars.

His victory had quite an impact. Five more Xiongnu princes defected, all being granted the title of marquis, along with 'several tens of thousands' of ordinary Xiongnu, who were rewarded with cash, transported to the capital in 20,000 carriages (not really: that's two *wan*, short for 'many') and supplied with horses requisitioned from local Chinese. One of the defecting princes, Hunye, settled down near Chang'an and went into business, to the fury of a top official named Ji An. In summary, he said: We're draining our coffers to service Hunye, just because he surrendered! We're honouring him as if he's the Son of Heaven! We should be using his wealth to repay ourselves for the Xiongnu attacks! The Emperor disagreed. Ji An was 'babbling nonsense'. It was better to honour enemies to encourage others to defect.

And to protect conquests with the Wall. It was not that the Wall itself would stop the Xiongnu – it never had in the past – but its soldiers and settlers might. Besides, the Wall was a mighty project that would allow him to control his own population. Hence the 1,000 kilometres plus of rammed earth that ran westwards from the Yellow River. In Wu's day, this was a frontier marked by hard-packed, whitewashed earthworks (yes, whitewashed – that's why Mongolians call it 'the White Wall'). Today, from car or train, the weathered, saw-toothed remnants mark nothing but itself.

Several years ago, I had a chance to get close to the Han–Xiongnu war. My guide, Xu Zhaoyu, or Michael, as he called himself, was the best guide in Gansu. He told me so, several times, and I was inclined to believe this was more than a boast, because he had a knowledge of history that was astonishing.

We headed north-west out of Zhangye, which guards the Gansu bottleneck, to a site that Michael said was important in the struggle between the two empires. Autumnal corn lay drying in the fields and the radio blared pop songs – number one at the time was 'Ta bu jidao', 'She doesn't know (I love her)'. We turned down a farm track, and parked by a field of chilli peppers. Michael led the way through the peppers and another field of corn stalks awaiting harvest.

Ahead loomed a sand dune, dotted with camel thorn and red willow bushes, above which rose an earthen wall. This, Michael explained, was once a Xiongnu fortress-city, their advance base, dominating the Gansu Corridor. We climbed, and the full thing came into view: eroded walls making a huge square, 250 of my paces on each side, with the stub of a guard-tower in the north-east corner. This was a revelation to me. I had known of the fortified town of Ivolga, but that was way north, in southern Siberia. I had no idea that they had for-tresses on the border, of which several others have since been revealed by archaeologists. All (like this one) were built close to springs or rivers. They were probably maintained by pris-oners and defectors used to a settled lifestyle and able to grow food enough for themselves and their Xiongnu garrisons.

In this case, Michael explained, the river was the Black Water (Hei Shui), which flowed from the heights of the Qilian Mountains, and still does, though with a different course. The Xiongnu must have thought they were there for keeps: fine farmland, their own river, a stranglehold on trade through the Corridor. But they had reckoned without Emperor Wu and his brilliant young general Huo Qubing.

It was Huo who assaulted the Black Water fortress. He at once saw the weakness of the Xiongnu position: there were no defences right across the Corridor, and the fortress was utterly dependent on its water supply. So he diverted the river – easily said, but an immense engineering achievement of which nothing is known – isolated the fortress, destroyed it, and moved on into territory once occupied by the Wusun, before the Xiongnu kicked them out.

Emperor Wu was so delighted with the victory that he sent Huo a huge flagon of wine, which caught up with him 150 kilometres further on, in the town now known as Jiuquan. Huo said that it was his soldiers, not he himself, who deserved the wine, so he poured it into a spring to share it with all his men. Though he was noted for his utter contempt for the lives of ordinary soldiers, this gesture entered folklore. Jiuquan means 'Wine Spring', recalling his act for today's residents and tourists.

Huo went on to follow the Black Water northwards to what was then Lake Juyan, part of a vast and well-watered delta where the river vanished into the desert. It has all changed now. Lake Juyan has been a dusty plain since the mid-twentieth century, though the lake's last remnant still appears on maps as Lake Gaxun. In Huo's day, the lake lapped another of the Xiongnu's border fortresses, which bore the same name as the lake, Juyan, where he besieged a Xiongnu force under the Xiongnu general Xiutu (or something similar in Xiongnu). Somewhere nearby was the chanyu, because Huo seized a golden statue that had been central to the worship of Tengri, the Xiongnu's highest deity. So Sima Guang tells us, though this is the only mention of a focal point for the religion and the details of ceremonies are unknown. A dispute between Xiutu and another Xiongnu general, Hanye, ended with Hanye killing Xiutu and surrendering with both their armies. Sources claim Huo's army killed tens of thousands, figures that are beyond literal belief, being as always shorthand for 'lots and lots'. The chanyu, down but by no means out, escaped, returning to his tent-city 750 kilometres to the north, beyond the Gobi, in the heart of Mongolia. As a result, wrote Sima Guang, the whole region from the Gansu Corridor into the

Taklamakan Desert 'had become a no man's land, in which there were no Xiongnu to be seen'.

Wu offered Huo Qubing a mansion to settle down in, to which Huo replied: 'The Xiongnu have not yet been wiped out. How can I settle and start a family?' He died on his return in 117 BC, aged just twenty-three, supposedly after drinking water from wells the Xiongnu had poisoned by dumping dead animals in them.

His grave, 50 kilometres west of today's Xian (Chang'an), honours him in a fascinating way. Emperor Wu had his tomb-mound raised close by his own, itself a considerable accolade. In addition, the tomb became the focus for something entirely new in Chinese art: monumental rock sculpture. Set out in the pavilions and arcades around Huo's 40-metre tomb-mound are seventeen lumps of roughly carved boulders weighing many tonnes each, all made of granite quarried from the Qilian Mountains some 500 kilometres away. The mound is swathed in firs today, but originally the statues were scattered over the bare flanks. Mostly of animals – fish, tiger, elephant, boar, frog, ox, horse – they seem unfinished, as if each subject was suggested by the shape of the boulder and is struggling to escape from its rocky embrace. Three seem to be magical carvings: a monster holding a goat in its jaws, a masked figure hugging a small bear, a human head with a hand raised as if to say 'Stop!'

One statue is of particular importance. Usually described as 'a horse trampling a barbarian', it seems to be an obvious symbol of Huo's achievement. But that idea comes from the man who first described the statue in 1914, the French ethnographer and art historian Victor Segalen. In fact, there is no trampling going on. This superb composition in 3.8 tonnes of granite portrays a horse simply straddling a heavily bearded 'barbarian', recognizable from the bow in his left hand and an arrow in the other. It is as if the horse and barbarian are in some sort of formal relationship, superior and inferior, a static portrayal of an ideal, now that the Qilian Mountains and the 'barbarian' inhabitants of the Western Regions had been brought inside the empire. In any event, as the historian of Chinese carving Ann Paludan points out,[6] this is the first example of stone animals of the kind that line the approaches to later imperial tombs.

The ruins of the Black Water fortress would make an equally good memorial to Huo Qubing's victory, for it was the very image of desolation. Sand had piled up against the walls and flowed down the inside. At the south-east corner, a dune had risen higher than the walls. I climbed it, and saw that someone in authority had made an attempt to recall the significance of the place with a little pavilion and a plaque: 'Ancient Ruined City of Black Water'. But it was not its history that was recalled. 'This is the most mysterious sand dune in history,' it announced in Chinese and poetic English. 'It is shaped like a big whale. No matter how the wind blows, it has not moved in 2,000 years. It is as if it is waiting for something. Who can solve the problem, and say why it is still here?'

So much for the western campaign. What of the other one, in the centre, north of the Yellow River? It had had its successes, mixed with disasters.

It was plagued by disputes, because the eminent, elderly, feisty loose cannon Li Guang, veteran of seventy battles against

---

[6] In Ann Paludan, *Chinese Sculpture* (see Bibliography).

the Xiongnu, demanded a chance to finish them off once and for all. But because of his age and perceived unreliability he was granted only a sideshow, leading his own contingent apart from the main force. That one, the main force, was under the command of Wei Qing, who in 119 BC headed north, across the Gobi – a three-week march, easily long enough for Xiongnu scouts to see them coming – and ran directly into the chanyu Ichise and his army. Wei Qing formed a laager with armoured wagons, Wild West fashion, making an effective defence against Xiongnu arrows. There were charges, and counter-charges, 'carnage and slaughtering' (in Sima Guang's words) until late afternoon, when a dust-storm struck, one of those so-called 'black storms' that can shred tents and strip the paint off cars: 'sand, gravel, pebbles and stones were sucked into the sky, pelting against the faces of the warriors ... it became almost pitch black, so that the warriors could not distinguish friend from foe'. Then, as the storm passed, Wei Qing ordered a two-pronged assault, so astonishing Ichise with the size of the Chinese forces that he 'clambered into a carriage drawn by six mules' – mules rather than horses because they have greater endurance – and escaped to his tent-city capital several hundred kilometres to the north-west. 'Shocked to the core,' the Xiongnu scattered, while Wei Qing led a task force in a night-time pursuit of the chanyu.

Come the dawn, 'they looked to the horizon. It was a desolate wilderness with no Xiongnu in sight.' Arriving at a fortress built by a Xiongnu chief who had defected to the Han then defected back again, Wei Qing's men fed themselves from the stores, trashed the place so completely its ruins have never been found, and returned to Chang'an.

Li Guang, meanwhile, had lost his way, and on returning, was arraigned before a military court. He was a model of decorum. Getting lost was all his own fault, he said, 'my subordinates are not guilty of any blunder'. He was over sixty now, he went on, and 'simply could not bear to face these petty bureaucrats'. Saying which, 'he drew his sword and slit his own throat'. All his men 'wept bitterly' at the news, as did civilians young and old, whether they had known him or not.

Military victory was not enough. Something had to fix the frontier, define what was China and what wasn't. That something was, of course, the Wall. So Wu picked up where the First Emperor had left off. In the centre and east, old walls were repaired, and sections linked. In the west, new bits of the Wall arose, running from Lanzhou northward then west over the border of what is now Xinjiang. To build and man it, four new administrative areas sprang up, with two, Gan and Su, straddling the narrow mid-section. Eventually, these two gave their joint names to the province, Gansu. Its origins explain Gansu's odd thigh-bone shape, 1,500 kilometres long, fat at either end with the extremely narrow waist of the Gansu Corridor.

Wu's push west went into overdrive. In theory, it all fitted together beautifully. The borderlands would be colonized. The colonists would make deserts bloom, and feed themselves, and provide labour for an extension of the Great Wall, which would protect the soldiers, the traders, the farmers, the administrators. The far western oasis kingdoms would fall into line, as China proved itself the dominant power. Silks would be sent, and horses received. China would not only be unified; she would be secure at last and eventually, surely, richer than ever. What greater legacy could an emperor leave?

This, the influx of 119 BC and afterwards, was the real beginning of the modern Wall as the defining symbol of China, the one running all the way from the western deserts to the Pacific. It became a sub-culture, a 'long city', which is the alternative meaning of its Chinese name, indeed several 'long cities', given its many branches and doublings. Soldier-farmers began to arrive by the hundred thousand, supplementing volunteers, conscripts and convicts. Families followed, making an estimated 1.5–2 million settlers – roughly equal to the whole Xiongnu population – all being provided with land, animals and seeds. Villages and farms arose where there was water.

Silk began to flow westward in prodigious amounts to buy the loyalty of the oasis kingdoms – the beginning of the trade network we now know as the Silk Road, an exercise in empire-building that would reach out far beyond the Great Wall, driven by the need to outflank the Xiongnu. This was an empire inspired by strategic need, founded by force, underpinned by bribery, secured by colonists and traders, and guaranteed by government. And there could be no turning back. Princesses could not be abandoned and treaties broken, or the Xiongnu would be back in an instant.

By 111 BC, ten vast caravans a year, each the size of a small city on the move, were rolling west, the beginning of an economic offensive that by 50–40 BC would carry westwards every year anything up to 18,000 rolls of silk and some 3–4 *billion* coins, about 30 per cent of the national cash income, perhaps 7 per cent of the empire's total revenue. In Chang'an, the opening of the west turned into a gravy train for adventurers, all claiming they would be ideal ambassadors, once they had received imperial backing. Many simply took the money and vanished. Others did go west, but ran out of supplies and imposed themselves on unwilling hosts, who, when their patience ran out, 'harassed and robbed the envoys'. More troops followed to sort out the mess. In 105 BC, another princess was despatched to be wife to the chief of the Wusun, 2,000 kilometres westward in the Ili Valley, in present-day Kazakhstan (a move countered by the Xiongnu sending one of their own princesses, though what happened to her was not recorded). Other tribes were knocked into line with military expeditions.

Could the Xiongnu respond? Only further east, where attacks and counter-attacks across the Great Wall preserved a Western Front balance of military power. To the west, a Chinese force drove into the Ferghana Valley, over 2,000 kilometres from Chang'an. The idea was to capture enough of the 'blood-sweating horses' to start a breeding programme, and to shock vacillating states into submission. Two centuries before, this kingdom, known as Great Yuan (Dayuan), was home to the Greeks left behind by Alexander the Great in the fourth century BC. Now it was probably a mix of Greeks and Scythians. This was another epic, for in the first approach all the Han envoys were killed, leaving Emperor Wu 'seething with rage too fearful to behold'. His response was: more of the same. Under Li Guangli (not to be confused with the Flying General, Li Guang), an army of 60,000 – with conscripts including petty criminals – gathered in Dunhuang, backed by volunteers. This turned into both an invasion and a migration: 100,000 cattle, 30,000 warhorses and 180,000 settlers started to arrive to build new farming communities along the Gansu

Corridor and up the Black Water (the Edsen Gol, the Lord's River, as it is in Mongolian). That was how the army would be supplied.

Even so, it took a regiment of Xiongnu defectors, two campaigns and two more years to assert the royal will on Dayuan. A 40-day siege of the capital ended after Li Guangli had his engineers divert the river on which the city depended. 'In a state of complete bedlam', the inhabitants of the capital revolted, killed their king, sued for peace and handed over 'a few score' of the blood-sweating horses. The effort, the cost and the losses achieved Wu's aim: Dayuan cowed (though not conquered), the Western Region kingdoms stunned into compliance, the Xiongnu held in check, potential allies bribed and scared into allegiance, blood-sweating horses delivered – though without much effect, because no one heard of them again. Perhaps in the end there was nothing special about them.

This immense effort, which drained both the Han economy and its army, took some time to take effect. War and peace with the Xiongnu continued, envoys came and sometimes went (one Chinese at least was detained by the chanyu in retaliation for a Xiongnu envoy who defected), a Xiongnu prince defected, and three chiefs of Xiongnu vassal states came over to Han.

In 110 BC, the two empires had started to talk seriously about renewing the peace-and-kinship treaty, perhaps because the Xiongnu had a new chanyu, Ichise having died. His son and heir, Wuwei (Uvei in Mongolian) even suggested a face-to-face meeting with the emperor, but withdrew when in 107 BC a Xiongnu envoy died of natural causes while he was in

Chang'an. So it all came to nothing. Wuwei died, a plot to murder the next chanyu failed, he died anyway, as did the next after only a year on the throne, and – perhaps to paper over the cracks of so many suspiciously premature deaths – the raids restarted, worse than ever.

Wu could do nothing except keep on fighting. He wrote a letter to the new chanyu, Chedihou, warning him of the risks. Almost a century before, Wu said, his great-great-grandfather had been humiliated by the Xiongnu. Now that humiliation had been reversed, with more to come, he implied, if these provocations continued. Chedihou was in no position to act belligerent. 'I am but Your Majesty's junior in ranking,' he replied. 'I do not have the audacity to affront Your Majesty.' To show his goodwill he released several Han officials who had been held captive for the last few years. In the hope of re-opening civilized diplomacy, Wu reciprocated, and sent back some Xiongnu prisoners, under the command of an envoy, Su Wu, an assistant Zhang Sheng, and a secretary. Su Wu is the hero of this story (told in lurid detail by Sima Guang) and has remained so down the centuries.

By the time they arrived, the mood in the Xiongnu court had changed. Chedihou had gained in confidence, and treated the Chinese as if they had come to pay homage. Zhang Sheng took offence and, as word of his anger spread, he became embroiled in a plot to topple the chanyu, kidnap his mother and murder his top adviser, Wei Lu, a defector from Han whose father was a Xiongnu. The idea behind this plot was that the emperor would be so delighted that he would reward the plotters and their families back in Chang'an. A turncoat leaked the scheme to the chanyu, who arrested most of the plotters and held them, pending their trial. This threw the leader of the Chinese delegation, Su Wu, into a panic. They will torture them! he said in a conversation with Zhang Sheng, his aide and also one of the plotters who was still free, and: 'They will trace the whole affair to me!' It would look as if he'd betrayed his country! He was on the point of committing suicide, but Zhang Sheng persuaded him to put down his sword, with more drama to follow: the captured plotters indeed revealed all, and the chanyu demanded Su Wu's surrender in a message delivered by the royal aide Wei Lu, the intended victim of the plot. And this time Su Wu, determined to avoid humiliation, 'drew his sword and ran it through his body'.

> Wei Lu was aghast at Su Wu's action. He clasped hold of Su Wu and sent for a physician instantly. The doctor dug a trench, lit a simmering fire and placed Su Wu face down above the warmth of the fire and massaged his back to release the clotted blood and ease his circulation. Su Wu was in a coma for several hours before he regained consciousness.

When he came to, his colleagues 'broke down and wept', and carried him back to their camp. Chedihou was so moved – or perhaps just plain astonished – by Su Wu's act that he sent messengers every few hours to learn the details of his recovery, but had his colleagues arrested as accomplices in the plot. One was executed; the other chose to join the Xiongnu. When Su Wu had recovered, Wei Lu, the one-time defector and now royal aide, tried to get him to defect also. Surrender, he said, or go to prison. But, countered Su Wu, I am entirely innocent, so 'why should I be incarcerated?'

There followed another piece of high drama:

Wei Lu thrusts a sword at Su Wu, and says (in this pared-down version of Sima Guang's account): 'I turned my back on the Han court. My lord the chanyu has been most benevolent. I preside over several tens of thousands of men. I own thousands upon thousands of cattle, horses and sheep that cover the entire landscape. If only you will give me just a nod, you will receive similar treatment tomorrow. On the other hand, if we execute you and expose your corpse to the elements, who will know or care?'

Su Wu remains silent.

Wei Lu tries again: 'Consider – if you surrender, we will be the best of friends, like brothers. If you don't accept my offer, you won't be given a second chance.'

At last Su Wu responds: 'You, who were once a subject of His Majesty, are but a slave of the Xiongnu. You have no shame. Why should I want to see you again? The chanyu may allow you to preside over life and death, but you do so with injustice. You incite two kingdoms to engage in warfare.' He goes on to quote several instances of what happens when Han envoys are killed – war and annihilation for the perpetrators. 'However,' he finishes, 'if you are bent on eternal war, please start with me.'

Wei Lu gives up his attempt at conversion and retreats to tell the chanyu what happened. The chanyu, while admiring Su Wu's fortitude and loyalty, is even more determined to break him. He has Su Wu shut up in a cave, deprived of food and water, with a wall separating him from the bitter snows outside. After a few days, Su Wu eats the wool from his leather jacket and reaches through the window for ice and snow to make water. 'Totally astounded' at his survival, the chanyu grants him his life, but banishes him and a few servants to the shores of Lake Baikal with a herd of rams and a back-handed promise: 'On the day your male sheep produce milk, you will be set free.' For that to happen, of course, he has to be kept alive, so the chanyu promises to send food to him and his entourage.

How do we know all this? Because nineteen years later he returned, in circumstances we will get to shortly.

In 99 BC, another campaign ended in a total and very famous catastrophe. One army, attacking westwards, killed 10,000 Xiongnu – meaning 'many' – yet lost 70 per cent of its men. But the greater catastrophe involved the second force, 5,000 men with wagonloads of food and arrows, which struck northwards along the Black Water River, across the Gobi and into the Mongolian heartland, aiming perhaps to entice the Xiongnu into a frontal assault against Han's repeating crossbows. It was led by the general Li Ling, grandson of the late and much-lamented Li Guang, with all his forebear's bravado. It was not a big force, but Li Ling was confident: his warriors, armed with crossbows, with 500,000 arrows in their wagons, were 'great fighters, specialists and swordsmen. Their strength is so great they could kill a tiger bare-handed, and when they shoot they never miss.' He was short of horses, but said it didn't matter, because his infantrymen were supreme. Besides, it was autumn, the best weather for marching. He planned to be back before winter, stopping off at a Han border fortress in the south Gobi to rest his soon-to-be-victorious troops.[7]

---

[7] Alexei A. Kovalev et al., 'The Shouxiangcheng Fortress', in Brosseder and Miller (eds), *Xiongnu Archaeology*.

The fortress, called Shouxiang in Chinese and Bayan Bulag (Rich Spring) in Mongolian, was near the present-day town of Nomgon. It still has a rich spring, which produces 12,500 litres an hour, though its surroundings are much grimmer now than they were 2,000 years ago, when the guards could grow their own crops. Russian and Mongolian archaeologists, who excavated it in 2009, identified the fortress from bronze crossbow triggers and halberds, which the Chinese used but the Xiongnu did not. This confirmed the written accounts that mentioned the crossbows, and also confirmed that the Han had fortresses on the border. There is another, revealed in 2005, 180 kilometres to the east – due east, exactly, the same latitude to within 0.03 of a degree. It was a great location, for back then it was on an island in a river. The Han must have had some top-class surveyors. Its local name is Mangasyn Khuree, the Ogre's Circle, an insulting reference, perhaps, to the Han soldiers who manned this square base, about 150 metres per side, guarded by a circular wall, 3.7 kilometres around. This was home territory for the Xiongnu, the back of beyond for the Han.[8]

What happened next turned into one of the best-known incidents in Chinese military history, a sort of Custer's Last Stand, with tragedy for some, especially for the major source, Sima Qian, embarrassment for the emperor, and his even greater determination to end the menace of the Xiongnu for ever.

A month's march and 250 kilometres later, halfway across the Gobi, Li Ling's force was in the mountains – probably the

[8] Chunag Amartüvshin et al., 'On the Walled Site of Mangasyn Khuree', in Brosseder and Miller (eds), *Xiongnu Archaeology*. You can see both places on Google Earth (42.36/105.10.5 and 42.33.45/107.24.14).

Gurvan Saikhan (Three Beauties) range – when they found themselves surrounded by 30,000 Xiongnu horsemen. Li Ling laagered his wagons, held off the attackers with halberds, then retreated behind the crossbows. That held off the Xiongnu a second time, allowing Li Ling to retreat to a hilltop. Stunned by his losses, the Xiongnu commander sent for reinforcements, another 80,000 according to Sima Guang. Outnumbered twenty to one, Li Ling staged a fighting retreat into a valley. 'The enemy was lodged in the hills, surrounding him on all sides and shooting arrows like drops of rain,' according to the *Han Shu*. With only half their number still alive, the surviving Chinese, with few arrows left, fled towards a narrow defile, while the Xiongnu fired down on them and rolled boulders to block their path. Days passed, arrows ran out, death for all seemed the only outcome. In Sima Qian's florid words: 'Li Ling with one cry gave courage to his army, so that every man raised himself up and wept. Washed in blood and choked with tears, they stretched out their empty bows and warded off the bare blades of the foe.' Finally, one night, Li Ling ordered his men to disperse in small groups, each with some food and a chunk of ice for water. They were 50 kilometres from the border. Perhaps a few would make it. Li Ling himself galloped clear, only to be hunted down and forced to surrender. Just 400 of his men made it back over the Gobi's coarse gravel and tussocky dunes, finding refuge perhaps in the Han fortresses on the border.

The disaster has several sequels, one being the appalling fate of the Grand Historian Sima Qian, detailed in Chapter 6. Another was the result for Li Ling's family.

The consequence of Li Ling's defeat and defection is another long story, tying up with the famous non-defector Su Wu. A high-status hostage with the Xiongnu, Li Ling lived on with them for another twenty-five years. Two years after his capture, an attempt to rescue him failed, because, according to the general in command of the operation, Li Ling was working with the Xiongnu, a report that again infuriated the emperor, driving him to order the execution of Li Ling's family. It turned out the report was wrong. There *was* a Chinese officer helping the Xiongnu, but it was not Li Ling, who had the man assassinated. Li Ling, too ashamed to return home, accepted his privileged position and joined the Xiongnu as a commander. The chanyu Hulugu (reigned 97–85 BC) gave a daughter to him in marriage. So the false report became right, as did the emperor: Li Ling turned traitor after all.

So there were the two generals, Su Wu, the high-minded loyalist, minding flocks in the far north, and Li Ling, the traitor, living in luxury, honoured by his Xiongnu master, but forever in misery at his betrayal.

Now for the final chapter in this saga. Su Wu and Li Ling knew each other. They had been friends, both serving the emperor as 'palace attendants'. A few years after Su Wu's banishment to the shores of Lake Baikal, word filtered back to the chanyu that he was in a bad way, 'reduced to digging up grassroots and catching rodents for food'. The chanyu told Li Ling to pay him a visit and persuade him to defect. Inviting Su Wu to a lavish reception, Li Ling did his best in a long speech of which this is a summary:

So many years, all this suffering, he mused, what was it for? Your two brothers have committed suicide, your mother died, your wife remarried, you had two sisters, two granddaughters and a grandson, but that was ten years ago, so who knew if they were still alive? Life is like the morning dew that dissipates when the sun rises. I know how hard betrayal is. But the emperor is old and driven mad by rumours of revolt and witchcraft, and life and death at court is at His Majesty's whim. Why keep on tormenting yourself?

It was useless. Su Wu said he owed everything to the emperor. He was like a father. You could hack me in pieces or stew me alive, he said in Sima Guang's version, it would make no difference. 'When a son dies for his father there is no regret. Please do not continue to pester me.'

' "Alas!" said Li Ling. "Such chivalry and righteousness!" He broke down and wept, tears rolling down his face and drenching his lapels.' Leaving a few sheep and goats for his friend, he left.

More years passed. Back in Chang'an, the ageing emperor slipped into the grip of paranoia, imagining a plague of shamanic curses and 'hexed mannequins'. He wracked the palace with accusations, inquisitions, bisections-at-the-waist and decapitations. Of the many themes in Chinese history worth an epic film, the Madness of Emperor Wu ranks high. An uprising, the suicide of the crown prince and too many Xiongnu raids to list reduced the empire to chaos.

In 87 BC, Li Ling came again to Su Wu with the news that the emperor had died aged seventy after his fifty-four-year reign, leaving a dangerously unstable government under a regent and a seven-year-old successor. Su Wu 'wailed until he drew blood', but refused to come home.

Two years later, a new chanyu, Huandi, still uncertain on his throne after a disputed succession, suggested renewing the peace-and-kinship treaty with the successor regime in Chang'an.

Envoys came. They asked about Su Wu. The chanyu claimed he must be dead. But Su Wu's one-time secretary, a defector to the Xiongnu, told them that Su Wu was still alive, and concocted an unlikely story to 'prove' it. He said the young Han emperor had been hunting in the royal park when he shot a goose which, marvellous to relate, had a message tied to its leg – from Su Wu, would you believe, asking for help for himself and some hostages. Embarrassed, the chanyu had Su Wu and the others brought to his court, where they were given a send-off banquet, with fulsome praise from Li Ling: of all the great men recorded in chronicles and paintings, no one was Su Wu's equal. How he regretted being unable to return with him. So in 81 BC Su Wu made it home, after nineteen years, along with many others released as a goodwill gesture, being received with high honours, high office, high pay and a mansion.

Li Ling, having rebutted an offer of reconciliation from the Han court, died in 74 BC of natural causes. Su Wu, despite the grey hair he had acquired in his wilderness years, outlived his friend by fourteen years, dying at eighty, a symbol then and now of loyalty and courage.

A thousand years later (for immortal tales a millennium is an eye-blink), all of China fell to the Mongols, whom both cultures considered descendants of the Xiongnu. So imagine the humiliation for the Chinese – after all this time, the 'barbarians' were victorious, ruling as the Yuan dynasty under the Mongol Emperor, Kublai Khan.

And this, for those few Chinese subjects who had any freedom of choice, was a problem, the age-old problem of conquered peoples: whether to oppose the invaders forever, until death, a fate embraced by hundreds who committed suicide; or to choose *disloyalty* – the accusation marked the accused like a plague-spot – accept, kow-tow, collaborate, live and prosper?

There was no easy answer, of course. Today's intransigence will seem pig-headed tomorrow; this year's disloyalty may seem like next year's good sense. Even though Kublai proclaimed a Chinese dynasty, even though China accepted and still accepts that fact, the conquest injected a virus of bitterness that would a century later overwhelm Kublai's inadequate heirs.

Look now at one man who struggled to find a way through this moral maze. He is not typical, because he was a master painter; some say a genius. His name was Zhao Mengfu. A distant relative of the Song royal family, Zhao was starting a career as a minor official, aged twenty-five, when in 1279 his world was shattered by the Mongol invasion of southern China. Like many other scholar-officials, he was appalled by the new regime and its crude class structure which put southerners at the bottom of the heap, and by his own helplessness. No longer did examinations offer the educated the chance of a career. All hope gone, he became one of the 'leftovers', those who preferred obscurity to collaboration. He retreated to his home town, then Wuxing, now Huzhou, which then and now was famous for its glorious countryside – the huge Taihu Lake to the north, the bamboo forests of the Tianmu Mountains to the west. In a country retreat, the Gull-Wave Pavilion, he buried himself in classical studies, and discovered prodigious talents.

He wasn't the only one. Wuxing's lake and green mountains inspired a loose confederation of masters: the 'Eight Talents of Wuxing' as they became known. Over the course of the next seven years, Zhao won fame as a master of three genres, painting, calligraphy and poetry (later to become, many think, the greatest of his age in all three).

In 1286 an imperial official arrived in Wuxing, scouting for talent in the name of Kublai. He heard of the Eight, sought them out, and made them all offers of employment in the imperial service. Zhao accepted. Some who refused turned against him – a descendant of the first Song emperor serving the Mongols! – and from then the reek of disloyalty hung about him. It was no easy decision, and there was no escape from its consequences. Zhao achieved eminence, in government – as an official in the Ministry of War and a provincial administrator – as a scholar, as an artist. But regret for his lost world of lakes and mountains, where he had been his own master, gnawed at him for the rest of his life. As he wrote in one poem:

> Before I was as a seagull,
> Now I am a bird inside a cage,
> No one cares about my sad weeping,
> My feathers are falling off every day.

His distress also permeates one of his paintings, portraying a sleek sheep and a miserable-looking goat: simple enough at first glance, less so the deeper you look. In traditional fashion, it includes some of Zhao's beautiful calligraphy, which hints at hidden meanings. 'I have often painted horses, but never before painted sheep or goats,' he notes, as if to say he had painted subjects dear to his horse-loving masters, but not those closer to the people they ruled. 'So when Zhongxin [a friend] requested a painting, I playfully drew these for him from life.' One commentator, Chu-tsing Li, of Kansas University's Department of Art History, has argued that there is a hidden message here. The sheep and the goat are the two most significant Han generals captured by the Xiongnu, Su Wu and Li Ling. Both had a chance to collaborate. One, Su Wu, refused, and was sent off to mind his flock of sheep for twenty years. The other, Li Ling, accepted collaboration and became rich. Which was the better off? Here is a haughty sheep, fat and healthy, but ripe for the pot, and here a scraggy goat, dejected, but at least alive. It seems, reader, that Zhao Mengfu couldn't decide which was which, and which the wiser choice. Can you?

Today, the landscape out west is semi-desert, but back then it was wetter, with pastures and reed-beds. By 100 BC the lines of the western Wall were established pretty much as they remain to this day, stretching from Wuwei to Yumenguan. Much of it is still there today, eroded into saw-teeth and cut through by roads, but easily traced. A few summers ago, I drove past the final fortress, Yumenguan, the Jade Gate Pass, a stark block of baked earth. A couple of kilometres beyond, the Wall sinks to its end in a 2-metre-high bank of mud and straw, piled up in layers. Two thousand years of wind-blown sand have scooped away the hard-packed soil, leaving the dried reeds sticking out like the hairs of a caterpillar. The reeds could have been harvested yesterday. I picked up a few strands from the dusty ground, tossed them to the oven-hot wind, and looked to the horizons. To the east, it was 1,400 kilometres to Wu's capital, Chang'an. Westwards lay another

1,400 kilometres to China's edge, all of it desert, dotted with oasis communities linked by camel-trails. That was where Wu's armies went to outflank the Xiongnu, building outposts all the way to Kucha, almost 1,000 kilometres from the end of the Wall.

There was also another line of the Wall that broke away, running northwards for 250 kilometres from the Qilian Mountains with the Black Water River (the Edsen Gol), following it until it ended in Lake Juyan. Although this counts as part of the Wall, it was in fact a line of 156 watch-towers and ten forts, ending in the back of beyond on the edge of the Gobi. It was colonized by the Chinese in 107–102 BC to grow food for the Wall garrisons, deny pastures to the Xiongnu, defend traders, control (i.e. count, tax and recruit) the scattered locals and catch fleeing convicts.

For the 800 or so officers and men charged with manning this line of towers, the bone-dry climate made life harsh, especially in the bitter winters. For modern archaeologists, it has been a godsend, because the sand preserved thousands of bamboo strips as the only written evidence of life in these distant parts. Ten thousand strips – a minute fraction of those that were produced – were gathered in 1927–34 by a Sino-Swedish expedition led by the great Swedish explorer Sven Hedin. Via Beijing and Hong Kong, they ended up in the Library of Congress in Washington, DC, where they were examined by the eminent Cambridge Sinologist Michael Loewe in the mid-1960s. Thousands of others were also recovered from Dunhuang and Wuwei, a trove of information it will take decades to assess.

'Wooden stationery' was made of many different woods, in many sizes, but overwhelmingly it consisted of 30-centimetre strips of bamboo, which could be joined by thread to form scrolls. These strips and scrolls, on which clerks wrote vertically, bound the Wall's officers, men and families to higher authorities. Most were written to officers down the line in the next sector, a few to or from seniors in Dunhuang, or even the national capital. Besides strips used as labels and travel documents, there are reports, statutes, accounts, lists of food, numbers of men coming and going, charge sheets, and all the other routine items of documentation that armies generate. The strips would be bound, tied, put in a leather container, addressed and despatched, with instructions for either first- or second-class delivery, i.e. either by horse or by runner. All mail was logged in and out, and the actual time taken for the journey compared to the official time. A runner was supposed to cover 11 li (about 5.5 kilometres) per hour for short distances, a little less – hardly more than walking pace – for longer stretches.

Overwhelmingly, the content of the strips is what you would expect from junior bureaucrats: tedious in the extreme. But it is possible to use the strips to paint a composite portrait of life on the frontier.

Take, for example, young Xu Zong, twenty, section commander. He is a volunteer from somewhere in central China, fifty days' march away, and has been well rewarded. He needs to be, because he already has a considerable family to support: a wife, four children, two brothers and two sisters, all of whom help on his 5-acre plantation. He is a low-grade official, paid partly in cash, partly in grain. Not long before this, cash would have been highly suspect. Coins varied; counterfeiters were everywhere. But Emperor Wu had introduced new coinage, which had won universal acceptance.

You knew what you could get for one of the new 3-kilo strings of 1,000 coins.

Young Xu fields a stream of directives, for this is a time when the Han dynasty is imposing itself with tough laws. One of his tasks is to catch criminals and deserters. If a deserter is caught, Xu has to report the deserter's name, age, height, colouring, clothing, equipment and baggage, along with the date. He has to make sure local troublemakers are duly caught and punished – as happened with two who got into a swordfight. One was injured near the right eye, the other in two places on the fingers of the right hand. Both were 'detained in manacles'. He also checks on travellers, like Cui Zidang, who 'states that he is engaged in domestic and private marketing ... I beg to state that Cui Zidang has not been subject to official judicial proceedings, and is qualified to receive a passport.' Cui would then be given his numbered passport, written on wood split into two parts, one of which is held locally, so that on his return he will be allowed on his way only when an official, like Xu, has matched the two.

Xu's job includes looking after contingents of three types: convicts, conscripts and volunteers like himself. They arrive in squads, exhausted by their march from the farmlands, ignorant of conditions here, illiterate, resentful, but cowed. They must all be listed, provided with clothing, equipment and food, and allocated to a group, with specific duties: guardsman, pioneer, farmworker. You couldn't trust the convicts and conscripts, of course. Given a chance, they will sell what the state provides and be off to join the Xiongnu. Then he has to get his clerk to write up what he has done: 'Issued: barley, [1,740 kilos] as rations for 66 pioneers engaged in hard labour for the 5th–8th months inclusive.'[9] Their tasks include digging earth for the body of the Wall and clay for baked bricks (each man to make eighty bricks of standard size, 41 × 18 × 14 centimetres, per day). Meanwhile, others are preparing the horse-dung plaster or splashing on yet another coat of whitewash. Reed-gathering, tree-cutting (yes, there were plantations then, though there are none now), tending orchards and vegetable gardens, guarding them against pilferers – the tasks were never-ending, and all subject to checking by seniors. 'One large flag on the tower old and damaged; wall unswept and unplastered,' a carping officer wrote. 'One dog absent.'

Then there were the camels and horses to be fed, and their fodder to be accounted for. As in most guard duty, boredom must have been the greatest enemy, followed by carelessness. The twenty-six watch-towers in Xu's 40-kilometre section did not have staircases, only handholds and ropes. You could easily lose your footing, as one of the officers did. One hot August evening, runs his report, 'I fell off the tower accidentally and injured my back. After recovery I resumed duties this day, August 31.' Imagine him climbing the towers, inspecting heavy crossbows on their mountings – one in reasonable condition had a range of 255 metres – making sure they were well greased, counting the helmets and armour and pots of grease, and wishing himself and his family back south, where there were no bitter winds in winter, where there were trees to lie under, and fruit, and cool streams.

One of Xu's duties is organizing the roster of patrols along the outer sandbank, hunting for the footprints of would-be

[9] This composite portrait is drawn from Michael Loewe, *Records of Han Administration* (see Bibliography).

intruders. For ten mornings in succession a private would take the dogs out, scanning a few kilometres of sand, almost always returning with the same report: 'No traces of illegal passage by men or horses.'

Then there was archery practice (with crossbows: twelve arrows to be fired, six hits for a pass) and signal practice (with flags and smoke-baskets by day, torches and fires by night). You had to remember your flag-and-fire codes and use the right one, depending on the numbers of attackers and what they were doing. 'For penetration by 1–10 men: by daylight – one wood-pile and two flags raised; by night – two torches to be lit. 500 enemy sighted: one wood-pile and three flags by day, or three torches by night.' Each signal was carefully logged: 'Officers in command of posts shall record in writing the date and time of arrival of signals,' so that the signal could be sent on down the line and then back again as confirmation that it had been received. Sometimes, someone would arrive from HQ with the records to check how long the whole operation had taken.

And supposing he couldn't stand it any longer – the boredom, the bureaucracy, the attacks – would he dream of defecting to the Xiongnu? Some did, criminals mainly. Not Xu and others like him, though, knowing the punishment. 'As to those who abscond . . . these are to be cut in half at the waist. Their wives and children should be shaven and made hard-labour convicts.'

There were carrots as well as sticks. If you captured a Xiongnu spy alive, your reward was 70,000 'cash' – 70 strings of 1,000 copper coins, equal to about 2.8 kilos of silver. If you tipped off the authorities about a Xiongnu spy and they caught him, the reward was 50,000 coins. If you killed a Xiongnu commander, it was 70,000.

Did Xu or his fellow-officers ever have to signal an attack? Did they get their instructions right? Did they survive? Did they and their families ever return to central China? Perhaps buried somewhere in the sands of Edsen Gol there are strips of bamboo that will tell of their fate in this, the most northerly outpost in Han China.

III
COLLAPSE

9

DECLINE AND FALL

THIS CHAPTER STARTS THE STORY OF THE XIONGNU EMPIRE'S collapse. It involves a series of tribal migrations that remade Central Asia like well-struck balls on a snooker table. On this vast carpet of baize, with its rough edge of mountains and deserts, tribes ricocheted off each other under the impact of war and migration. Nothing was fixed, nothing predictable, nothing explicable except by hindsight. There were no borders other than the Great Wall (as in Mongolia today, where you can drive wherever you like over fenceless steppes).

For the Xiongnu, their descent from greatness shattered their self-image. For two centuries, they had taken what they wanted. They had become rich. What happened to all the wealth – the silks, the carriages, the ceramics? Scattered, given away, wasted, buried. They might have invested it in cities, roads, and institutions as grand as those of their Chinese enemies. Instead, there is almost nothing, hardly one stone standing upon another. There are graves, but there was nothing much in them – until, suddenly, late in Xiongnu history, they increased in size and wealth. That is the essential mystery at the heart of Xiongnu studies. Something changed. To explain what and how, we have to look at why the Xiongnu collapsed and what the effects were.

It was the loss of the Western Regions that undermined the Xiongnu. From the settled oasis communities, they had derived grain, iron weapons, taxes and manpower. When the empire was at its height, the chanyu had delegated authority to subsidiary kingdoms, and their rulers now worked at making themselves independent. The chanyu Huandi tried to retain leverage by invading China in 80–79 BC, with no success. Envoys came and went, talking about talks about reviving the peace-and-kinship treaty. But with the Xiongnu on the back foot, and with no hope of them regaining the crucial Gansu Corridor, Han could afford to ignore the pressure. The Great Wall was doing its job: any attack anywhere along it was reported by fire-and-smoke signals within three days. From the early 70s BC, former Xiongnu vassals turned against them. Wuhuan, in the north-east of present-day China, was shattered by a Han invasion. To have a vassal destroyed by Han might once have galvanized the Xiongnu. Now it stunned them into inaction. The once great empire was in a slow but steady decline.

Lucky for Han China, because it was riven by intrigue and in no shape to reinforce Emperor Wu's warrior policies. His young heir died in 74 BC, aged twenty, leaving as empress dowager and nominal head of state a fifteen-year-old wife, Shangguan – the youngest empress dowager in Chinese history and also the granddaughter of the regent Huo Guang. Under the guidance of the regent, the throne went to Wu's grandson, Liu He, who proved to be 'totally debauched, a hedonist, given to a life of utter and excessive dissipation' (Sima Guang). Liu arrived from his estate with 'young women concealed in the baggage carriages for his sensual pleasure'. When they were discovered, he said he knew nothing about them and had those who had hidden them executed. Moreover, he refused to undertake the rituals of mourning, saying he had a sore throat and could not weep. In brief, he would obviously be a disaster.

A month after the coronation, the regent Huo Guang summoned the ministers, announced that Liu was wantonly debauched, and proposed that he should be impeached instantly. With the ready cooperation of his granddaughter the young empress dowager, he had Liu He locked in his apartment. She – wearing her imperial tiara, enthroned in state and flanked by hundreds of guards – summoned Liu He, accused him of ignoring rituals, using the Treasury as his personal cash-box, organizing fights between wild boars and tigers, using the empress dowager's carriage without her consent, having an affair with one of the dead emperor's concubines, threatening any informants thereof with bisection, et cetera, et cetera. He was then deposed and banished to his former estates, becoming the only emperor in Chinese history to be fired, and the one with the shortest reign. His replacement was a virtually unknown great-grandson of Emperor Wu, a seventeen-year-old named Liu Bingyi, who was reportedly erudite, austere, parsimonious, gentle, benevolent, and in all ways thoroughly filial. He was crowned with the ruling name of Xuan.

In 71 BC, now re-stabilized, Han joined with the Wusun to attack the Xiongnu again, capturing '40,000' people and '700,000' animals, all in quotes to inject scepticism, but there was no denying that the blow was devastating. A revenge attack by the Xiongnu that winter ran into a blizzard that killed 90 per cent of their force. Their weakness inspired further uprisings by vassal states. More deaths in battle, more livestock lost, yet more deaths through famine, chaos, anarchy, and in response only frantic, hopeless efforts by the Xiongnu to re-establish the peace-and-kinship treaty.

As the Xiongnu declined, Han rose. An attempt at independence by the ruler of Shache, an oasis kingdom on the trade route south of the Taklamakan Desert, was crushed by a Han force, the king's decapitated head being pony-expressed to Chang'an for display over the city gate as an example for visiting dignitaries. 'As a result, all the nations of the North and South Passages [i.e. north and south of the Taklamakan] were restored to the sway of the Han kingdom.' (Sima Guang.) Indeed, the King of Dayuan gave the victorious general a special 'blood-sweating horse' named Elephant Dragon, which was taken back to Chang'an and presented to the emperor. To stamp his authority on the region, the emperor ordered the construction of a new fortress-city just north of the Taklamakan, declared the whole Western Region a protectorate embracing all thirty-six mini-kingdoms, and proclaimed 'that the entire region was again open to travellers heading west'.

Not that peace was guaranteed. Take the Wusun, who had been forced to follow in the tracks of the Yuezhi by the Xiongnu some seventy years before; they had displaced the Yuezhi from the Ili Valley and settled there on the border of

present-day Kazakhstan and China. They were supposedly
bound by a peace-and-kinship treaty, by which a Han princess had been sent to the ruler, Nimi. But he was known as
the Mad King for his 'ferocious and petulant' behaviour.
Complaints from the princess led in sequence to a planned
assassination of the king, its failure, his escape, a revenge
attack by the king's son, his assertion that the Xiongnu were
about to come to his aid, the murder of the Mad King, and too
many other consequences to mention here. It was all sorted
out by a remarkable woman called Feng Liao, the companion
of the abused princess.[1] Lady Feng was a brilliant diplomat
who, on no basis but her own skill, negotiated with local
chiefs and the Han government. Summoned to report directly to the emperor, she was sent back 'in an imperial carriage
clad in fabulous embroideries'. Later made regent for a young
Wusun heir, she used the threat of Han intervention to impose
peace on this turbulent region, keep its occupants firmly in
the Chinese sphere of influence and make sure the Wusun
would never, ever have anything more to do with the Xiongnu.

North of the Great Wall, the Xiongnu's long collapse continued in twenty years of usurpation, intrigue and murder. In
59 BC, when the king of a vassal tribe in eastern Mongolia
died, the chanyu Yuan-Guidi tried to foist his young son on
them, at which the whole tribe migrated eastwards, fleeing
from the 10,000 horsemen the chanyu sent in fruitless pursuit. Driven into revolt by the violence, several tribes united
to elect a chanyu of their own, Huhanye by name, brother of

---

[1] The princess, Liu Jieyou, asked to come home in 51 BC. 'I am advancing in
years,' she said. 'I miss my homeland.' She was escorted back to Chang'an,
given a great reception and died two years later. The story, told by Sima
Guang, is quoted in Yap, *Wars*.

Yuan-Guidi. He formed an army and started a civil war. Yuan-Guidi had neither the nerve nor the manpower to fight back. He sent an urgent message to his younger brother: 'The eastern insurgents are attacking me. Can you come to my aid?' To which his brother replied, 'You have no empathy for others, you have created carnage among your own brothers and nobles. You should die where you are. Do not affront me.' At this, Yuan-Guidi realized everything was lost and committed suicide. There followed total anarchy, as tribal bosses, rebellious relatives and commanders set up local rulers – six of them in 57–56 BC – in a flurry of conspiracies, flights, attacks, defections, executions and suicides.

In Chang'an, the emperor and his advisers received reports of the chaos in astonishment. This, some urged, was a chance to finish them off. But the Imperial Counsellor advised a different course: 'The greatest virtue of a sage lord is not to take advantage of his enemies during their internal strife.' An attack now would just drive the Xiongnu further north. Better to send an envoy to express condolences and offer assistance. And stand by to welcome surrendering chieftains. That will help dealings with these and other barbarians. 'The emperor accepted the proposal.'

After two years of turmoil, the six Xiongnu claimants to the throne whittled themselves down to two: Huhanye in the centre and his elder brother Zhizhi[2] in the east. In 54 BC, it was Zhizhi who came out on top, chasing his brother from the tent-city in the Orkhon Valley that was the Xiongnu capital.

For Huhanye, there was only one source of help: China. That would mean surrender. He opened a debate with his

---

[2] Two different characters, two different tones: Zhì Zhī 郅支. What he was called in Xiongnu we cannot know.

officers. Most were appalled at the idea. Sima Guang summarizes the tumult:

> Preposterous, intolerable! We Xiongnu revere the chivalrous and brave! Surrender is utterly despicable! Our kingdom was founded on horseback and warfare! Our motto is: Wage relentless war! To perish in battle is a divine honour! Han, mighty as it is, has never prevailed! Why be disloyal to our ancestors? If we surrender, our vassals will deride us!

One of Huhanye's top officers took the floor, and called for a reality check:

> We do not have the resources to recover what we have lost. We have not seen peace for a long time. If we were to serve Han, we would be guaranteed peace, and our people would gain some respite. But we are destined to be annihilated if we choose to continue along the present path.

The tumult continued, then died. Zhizhi was on his way, with overwhelming force. What other course was open? Huhanye accepted, sending his son to Chang'an to act as a hostage, and starting several months of ambassadorial exchanges to arrange the formalities for the spring of the next year, 51 BC.

In Chang'an, news of his approach sent the court into a frenzy. Huhanye was coming to pay homage. But he was head of an independent state. How should he be treated? As guest or vassal? After much debate, the emperor decreed that Huhanye was *voluntarily* making the Xiongnu, their enemies for centuries, a subject state. This – the unforced submission of a whole empire, never mind that it was an empire divided against itself – was unprecedented, overwhelming. 'I do not possess the virtue or moral aptitude for this grand and formal procedure,' said the emperor, and would therefore 'receive the chanyu with our national ceremonial etiquettes reserved for the most distinctive and esteemed guests'.

Coming to Chang'an in the spring of 51 BC, Huhanye could hardly have believed his eyes. Built by the dynastic founder, Gaozu, 150 years previously, Chang'an was home to some 250,000, equal to a sixth of the chanyu's own people. His whole tent-capital would easily have fitted inside the emperor's main residence, the Everlasting Palace, a rectangle 8.6 kilometres around, with forty halls, standing on a platform 15 metres high. And this was only one of seven palaces. His weakened empire had a few fortresses, but nothing with walls like this – 25 kilometres around, 8 metres high. Yet he and his predecessors, with their 1.5 million people, had almost had all this and Han's toiling millions (60 million, according to one estimate) at their feet. They had been fighting to get their share for the last 200 years. Now a share was theirs for the asking.

The reception, outside the city, at which Huhanye was not required to kneel, was 'incomparable', with 'dazzling and luxuriant gifts', listed by Sima Guang: an imperial diadem, a belt and unspecified trappings, a solid gold seal fastened on to an embroidered sash, a sword with a jade-inlaid hilt, a dagger, a bow and 48 arrows (of unknown symbolic significance), 10 ceremonial halberds, a royal carriage, a saddle (no doubt ornately decorated), a bridle (ditto), 15 horses, 20 catties (about 12 kilos) of gold, 200,000 coins, 77 suits of clothes, 8,000 bales of brocade and 15 tonnes of silk.

Then, joined by aristocrats of every sort, heads of vassal

states and barbarian chieftains, Huhanye was led past tens of thousands of onlookers to the main bridge over the River Wei, where the emperor greeted him, to roars of 'Long live the emperor!' from the crowd, and led him in a formal entry into the city.

After a few days, it was time to return home, though what 'home' meant now was an open question. Huhanye asked if he and his people might settle just outside the Great Wall, north of the Yellow River, pretty much where his ancestors had been driven from by Meng Tian. And perhaps, in case of an emergency, he could find shelter inside the Wall? No problem. Off he went, with 16,000 Han troops, to his new base, where his hungry force – and presumably their families – received 34,000 *hu* of grain (which, if true, comes to 1,300 tonnes, presumably enough to last until the next harvest).

So the Xiongnu were divided in half, the southerners under Huhanye in the borderlands, in the well-funded service of the Han emperor, and the northerners under Zhizhi in control of the old heartland, nursing hopes of a revival. Obviously there was no point in Zhizhi taking on Han. Instead, revival for him meant reclaiming the west, namely Wusun territory.

It was not just the usual historians – Sima Qian, Ban Gu, Sima Guang – who recorded the split in Xiongnu leadership. There is an independent source. Among the thousands of bamboo slats that served as stationery for Han administrators in the Western Regions, one collection is a report by an official named Xi.[3] The strips were jumbled, and no one agrees on the exact order, but it is clear that Xi is apprehensive about

[3] Enno Giele, 'Evidence for the Xiongnu in Chinese Wooden Documents', in Brosseder and Miller (eds), *Xiongnu Archaeology*.

reporting bad news. 'Your utterly unworthy subject, risking capital punishment and with repeated salutation' reports that 'the captain and soldiers saw outside the defence lines to the north-east . . . fires in four places, as large as wood-piles for signalling, at a distance from the defence lines of more than 100 li [some 50 kilometres].' Xi mentions Huhanye and the Wusun king, calling them cheats, then makes a reference to Zhizhi 'not knowing about this situation'. He concludes: 'The barbarian people are greedy and inconsiderate, wicked and possessing two hearts,' and submits his report in grovelling terms suitable to his low rank: 'being foolish and stupid . . . and with forgetful speech, I bang my head to the floor'.

For Zhizhi to deal with the Wusun proved a relatively easy task, aided by the death of the emperor, a severe famine in 48–47 BC, power struggles in the new court, and cost-cutting by the frugal new emperor, 27-year-old Liu Shi, ruling as Emperor Yuan. Zhizhi also bought himself time by exchanging envoys with Han, asking for the return of his son, who had been kept as a hostage for the last decade. For the sake of a quiet life, the new emperor agreed. A general named Gu Ji volunteered to deliver the prince all the way to Zhizhi's court as a way to guarantee his gratitude. But, says Sima Guang, 'for some obscure reason' – perhaps in revenge for Han's generosity towards his brother – 'Zhizhi went berserk and ordered his men to execute Gu Ji and his retainers.'

Now Han had cause to join Zhizhi's brother Huhanye in an attack. Realizing his mistake, Zhizhi decided to lead his people further west, out of harm's way. Kangju – a small kingdom beyond Wusun in the steppes west of Lake Balkhash, on the Syrdarya River, in present-day Kazakhstan – saw a chance to assert itself by allying with Zhizhi, attacking Wusun and making Zhizhi King of the Wusun. 'Zhizhi loathed the Wusun with vile bitterness, so when he heard the proposal it was beyond his wildest aspiration.' There followed a further migration into Kangju – an unrecorded epic across 2,400 kilometres, taking three months – an exchange of daughters as wives between the chanyu and the Kangju king, and finally a successful joint attack on the Wusun.

Back in the Xiongnu heartland, Zhizhi's migration had left the centre ground vacant. Since Huhanye's people had pretty much exhausted the reserves of their new estates, he led his people north again, back to the more fertile pastures from which he had fled not long before. He was a vassal now, but safe, and with a guaranteed income from the emperor to whom he owed his power.

If you ever drive along the new motorway between Zhangye and Wuwei, turn off to the left about 60 kilometres short of Wuwei, leave the snowy peaks of the Qilian Mountains behind you, and follow the gentle slope down to the town of Yongchang. The approach road ends at a roundabout, in the middle of which is a strange sight: three lumpish concrete statues, the central one being obviously Chinese, flanked by two that are equally obviously Roman, a woman and a soldier, his hand on his armoured chest in a Roman salute.

This is the story of how these two Romans came to be here. Actually, it is three stories. The first concerns real Romans, and an astonishing suggestion that once upon a time, when the Han were building their Great Wall and reaching out westward, some Romans settled in China, not far from Yongchang. The second is the story of the story, of how a historical will-o'-the-wisp arose from nothing, and strengthened, and became an obsession – locally, nationally, internationally – and is now fixed in stone by these statues, and therefore (to many) true. The third is the continuing story of the Xiongnu collapse, which in this case involves the death of the appalling Zhizhi.

The starting point is Rome in 59 BC, when Julius Caesar, Pompey and Crassus formed a triumvirate, the first of several that governed the empire. Crassus was a property tycoon who craved military glory. In 54 BC he led an army of seven legions, some 42,000 men, against Parthia (roughly present-day Iraq and Iran). The Parthians were horse-archers, the Romans specialists in hand-to-hand combat. In May, 53 BC, they met at Carrhae (now Harran in Turkey). The Parthians kept their distance and riddled the Romans with arrows, often faking a retreat and firing over their shoulders – the famous 'Parthian shot', which English corrupted into the 'parting shot' in a war of words. The Romans gambled that the Parthians would run out of arrows. They didn't because the Parthian commander had organized relays of camels with new supplies. The Romans' only response was to form a *testudo,* a 'tortoise' of interlocking shields. Still the arrows came, lobbed in high trajectories over the shields, flashing in underneath them into Roman legs, until their feet were nailed to the ground (as Plutarch put it in his life of Crassus). Nearly 20,000 were killed and another 10,000 captured, many of whom were sent over 2,000 kilometres across Parthia to guard its eastern frontier against the Xiongnu. At this point, they drop out of western history.

And so, perhaps, into Chinese history, eighteen years later, thanks to the Xiongnu. That at least is what was claimed in a 1957 monograph by the Professor of Chinese at Oxford, the wonderfully named Homer Hasenpflug Dubs.[4] Dubs was as eccentric as his name suggests, 'well liked, but a bit odd', as a senior member of his college, University College, put it. Dubs was much struck by the possibility that a village near Yongchang had once borne the name by which (he claims) the Chinese once referred to Rome: Li Qian. Dubs gives an elaborate and ingenious explanation as to how this could have happened.

'Between 110 and 100 BC, there arrived at the Chinese capital an embassy from the King of Parthia. Among the presents to the Chinese Emperor are stated to have been fine jugglers from "Li Qian".' They were, he claimed, from Alexandria. The Chinese, who disliked polysyllables and initial vowels, dropped the *A*, transliterating the second and third syllables, *lexan*, as *lí qián*. They then used their version of Alexandria as their name for the empire of which it was a part. Thus Li Qian equalled Rome. If this was so, it didn't last long. By the sixth century, the Chinese were referring to ancient Rome and its empire as Da Qin, Great Qin, as in the dynasty and empire created by the First Emperor, and later still Luo Ma, an approximation of Roma.

Now we return to Zhizhi, in Sima Guang's account. He had set himself up on the Talas River in southern Kazakhstan, just beyond the far borders of the Western Regions, threatening to gain control of the Silk Road. He was not a popular leader, for military successes had made him 'insufferably insolent'. He argued with his royal Kangju ally, killed his wife (the king's daughter) in a fit of temper and then

---

[4] See Bibliography. It was originally a lecture given two years earlier to the China Society.

turned on the Kangju nobility, ordering hundreds to be killed, dismembered and tossed into a river. Then, in full dictatorial control, he had his subjects build a fortress. Three times, Han sent envoys to demand Gu Ji's insignia as a symbol of surrender. Zhizhi bought time by promising to submit, but never did. A Han minister warned that he should be taken out.

In 36 BC a Chinese commander of the frontier, intent on glory, led 40,000 men westward, sweeping up fifteen minor kingdoms as allies and capturing a Kangju noble who was happy to brief the commander on the layout of Zhizhi's castle, with its double palisade of huge logs, moat and rammed-earth ramparts. Hundreds of armed men crowded the battlements, yelling, 'Come and fight!' Horsemen galloped about, challenging the attackers. A band of foot soldiers drilled in close formation. In the siege that followed – engineers undermining the walls, infantry shielding crossbowmen, fires set against the wooden palisades – Zhizhi was wounded by an arrow in the face and fell down the battlement steps. Night fell, the fire spread and at dawn, to the boom of war-drums, the 'ear-splitting shrieks' of war-horns, troops piled earth against the inner ramparts, stormed up and over, and the fortress fell. Zhizhi died of his wounds, 1,518 of his force fell – a remarkably exact figure, so perhaps true – 1,000 more surrendered, and 145 were captured. With Gu Ji's imperial tallies and his silken instructions found and with Zhizhi's head sent off to Chang'an to be hoisted above the main street, victory was complete. The Han generals sent a message to the emperor suggesting he issue an imperial edict 'disseminating a message to all our vassal states reading, "Kings! Whosoever dares to flout Han, no matter how near or far-flung, we shall have you executed!" '

It was the group of foot soldiers that seized Dubs's attention. In his translation of Ban Gu's text (a source for Sima Guang's), the attackers noticed that 'more than 100 foot soldiers, lined up on either side of the gate in a fish-scale formation, were practising military drill'. This, Dubs suggested, was a Roman testudo (tortoise) of interlocking shields. In addition, he argued, the idea of a double palisade was a standard Roman design, unknown elsewhere. The 145 prisoners were – Dubs surmised – the 'more than 100 foot soldiers', spared because they were not Xiongnu. Dubs's conclusion was that these 'Romans' had escaped their Parthian masters and fled to the Xiongnu, who had taken them on as mercenaries with some interesting military insights, and now found themselves in Chinese hands.

These men would have become good frontiersmen, helping to guard the Wall, the narrow Gansu Corridor and the way west. It would have been natural for them to be settled in their own frontier town, named after themselves: Rome, or Li Qian. That's as far as the story goes.

But the threads wind on down the centuries to the present. Folklore took over. These Romans, now men in their forties with unrivalled experience, would have married local women and raised families, creating a community with looks very different from the locals. So different, perhaps, that it is possible to see their origins in some of today's 'foreign-looking' inhabitants. That was the rumour. That was what drew me to Yongchang, and onwards, to the town supposedly built by Romans 1,300 years before China established any other links with the West.

I was with Michael, seeking evidence to back the rumours. He had given me the background, so he was as intrigued as me. Those statues lent weight to his words. There they stood, the two Romans, with the heavy-duty stone plaque underneath: 'In Memory of Li Qian', challenging anyone to doubt the story.

He questioned a passer-by. Yes, everyone knew that there were people around who 'looked foreign'. We should ask at the local government office, which was just around the corner, up a side alley. There we were taken in hand by Song Guorong, a man with slicked-back hair and a silver tooth who was, by chance, an expert. He had edited a little book of papers on the subject. It had not yet been published, but he presented me with a proof copy, warning me that the subject was rather sensitive.

'If you want to see a man who looks like a foreigner,' he said, 'you have to register with the police.'

'But why?'

'Because other foreigners come here and make trouble. So many other foreigners! Italians come here and see the local foreigners and call them brothers. People are tired of them, so it becomes difficult.'

But not *too* difficult, because he immediately telephoned a friend.

'How many have come?' I asked, through Michael, as he put the phone down.

'More than hundreds. They stayed for weeks. There was an Italian film producer, talking about making a film next year. Then a scholar came from Oxford. He looked foreign, like you. Maybe he was your brother?[5] He wanted to research,

---

[5] At the time, I treated this as a joke. To Chinese, especially in areas unused to seeing many foreigners, it seemed that all of them look alike. On this non-PC basis, I could have a large number of brothers. But I was wrong. A few

but there was the SARS scare, you remember, and he couldn't travel anywhere. But you can see. Mr Luo is coming. He looks foreign. He will show you. If you want to discover the truth,' he added, 'you could pay Mr Luo, maybe fifty yuan for half a day.'

Mr Luo, who by an astonishing coincidence was waiting downstairs, was certainly anything but mainstream Chinese. He had hazel eyes, a thick head of hair, heavy black eyebrows, saturnine looks and a supercilious manner that would have served him well if he ever went for a bit part in a Mafia movie. He was a sharp dresser, too. Black polo-neck, lightweight grey jacket, black trousers, black slip-on shoes.

Luo took us in hand. We would go to his village, Zhelai, where the foreign-looking people were. There used to be many more, he said. They had mostly gone away looking for work in Lanzhou, Beijing, Shanghai. But there were still seventeen or eighteen left.

We set off along a dirt road under the motorway back towards the Qilian Mountains.

'Mr Luo, how do people feel about looking different?'

'Before 1978, they felt bad. Some had yellow hair, which they thought was bad, because people came to see them; so they dyed their hair black. But since China opened up to the outside world, they have become proud.'

As we climbed, terraced fields gave way to big, open country, with glorious views towards the snows and glaciers of the

---

years later, I was in conversation with an old friend, the travel writer and novelist Colin Thubron. I told him my story. 'It was me,' he said. He had been researching his book *Shadow of the Silk Road*. We're not far apart in age, same height, and look vaguely alike. We could indeed be brothers. Mr Song, I misjudged you. My apologies.

Qilian Mountains. A beacon tower stood guard over stubbly wheat, which meant that the Han Great Wall was, or had been, somewhere around.

'There used to be lots of towers round here,' said Luo. 'But villagers made them into fields.'

Past a stand of yellow poplars, we came to a score of mud-brick houses and courtyards and thatched barns, all of medieval simplicity. This was Zhelai, once Li Qian – Dubs's 'Rome' – where people supposedly looked foreign. It was hard to tell, because there was no one around. Bar a distant cockerel, the place was as silent as the quite large tomb which we were now approaching. It turned out not to be a large tomb, but a small section of earth wall with a fence around it. 'Li Qian Historic Ruin', said the sign, giving the impression that this was the very wall created by the Romans when they came to live here. It looked suspiciously like any other piece of the Han Great Wall, which you can see running all along the Gansu Corridor paralleling the new motorway. It must once have run right through the village. All the rest having long since vanished under ploughs, this 27-metre slab of rammed earth had been saved by being declared Roman.

The wall was the centrepiece of the village's claim to fame, a claim commemorated by one of the most incongruous pieces of architecture you can imagine. Raised on a low platform of pink granite stood four fluted pseudo-Roman columns, set in a square, supporting an architrave and a flat roof. It might have been copied from a tomb or shrine, but all it shielded was a stele recording that 'Roman troops settled here', and its date, 1994. It stood to the side of a courtyard or parade ground. Today, it seemed to be used for winnowing, for chaff blew around the waist-high walls.

Alongside the village, but across a dry ravine in a much more barren area of hard sand and tussocks, were more walls, in better shape, the remains of a substantial fortress or camp-site. It seemed a strange place to build a camp.

'In ancient times,' explained Luo, glancing round at the wasteland and raising his voice over a dusty breeze, 'this was grassland. The ravine was a big river flowing from the Qilian Shan. People called the place "Treasure Basin" and saw the shape of a sleeping Buddha in the mountains. But the population grew, and so did the numbers of sheep and cattle, and the grasslands died, and the river dried up, so the people left.'

Perhaps that explained why the place was empty?

No, it was not empty. There were still 300 people here, in twenty-eight families. We would go and see. Buffeted by the hot wind, we walked back, through clumps of brittle grass that crackled in the breeze like wildfire. Luo promised to find a girl who was the most foreign-looking of them all. Xiao Dan was her name: Little Dan. She would be in the school.

She wasn't, because the school was shut. Luo led the way to her house. Little Dan's aunt, who looked thoroughly Chinese, ushered us into a tiled compound and then into an airy marble-floored room, with a *kang,* a sleeping-platform, heated from underneath in winter, big enough for fourteen people. Little Dan was off on a picnic with the other children. She wouldn't be back until much later. We couldn't wait.

'Could I see a picture of her at least?'

The aunt hurried out, and back with a photograph. Little Dan, the most foreign-looking of all, had a fine, typical Chinese face. The only thing different about her, to my eyes, was that she had a hint of red in her dark hair. It is a little unfair to make a judgement on the basis of a one-day visit and a photograph, but the only evidence of foreignness in Zhelai seemed to be a girl whose hair was not completely jet black.

Dubs's paper might simply have become an academic oddity but for the passionate interest of an Australian writer, David Harris. As a post-graduate in Armidale, New South Wales, he heard of Dubs from a linguistics professor who had been at Oxford in Dubs's time. The story seized him with such force that he set out to find the 'lost city'. No one could have been worse prepared. He knew little of China, had no funds, and was trying to prove that westerners formed an important element in Chinese history, not a claim likely to win official support. His naivety produced some excellent material for his book, *Black Horse Odyssey*, but he managed no more than two quick visits to ex-Li Qian. He saw the bits of wall, and the ruins of the fortress, and came away determined to return, with good financial and archeological support. Bureaucracy stymied him. He never did go back.

But his conviction and his search made a great story, which broke in December 1989 when the *People's Daily* reported the Dubs–Harris hypothesis. Then local officials, among them Song Guorong, the editor of the book, took up the theme. If this could become better known, it would do wonders for local tourism, for there was really no other reason for Great Wall and Silk Road travellers to stop off at Yongchang. Up went the statues, and the fence around the old wall in Zhelai, and the Roman pavilion.

More publicity followed. Google 'Romans China' and you will see what I mean. The story almost made it to the silver screen. North of Yinchuan, on the great loop of the Yellow River, a Ming Great Wall fortress has been turned into a film lot, the China West Film Studio, which has provided settings for some eighty movies. One of them was a Chinese–British made-for-TV co-production called *Homeward Bound*, being the story of what happened to the Romans when they tried to get back to Italy (not the point of the legend, but a nice twist). Much work was done, much film shot. Then what happened? I have been unable to find out. The money ran out, or some new executive pulled the plug. In any event, nothing more has been heard of the film.

Now let's see what all this amounts to. In brief: it's a fine example of how a hypothesis becomes folklore, and then drifts towards being accepted as a historical fact.

Glen Dudbridge, Dubs's successor at Oxford, was scathing about the matter when I asked for his opinion. 'Over the years, I have received a long string of enquiries about Dubs and his Roman city in China,' he e-mailed. 'The story refuses to go away, even though Dubs's claims were methodically refuted by generation after generation of specialists during the past 50 years.'

In an unpublished paper, he summarizes the critical academic responses, both western and Chinese: 'untenable' . . . 'impossible to accept' . . . 'a historical romance' . . . 'a bizarre flight of fancy' . . . 'a work of fiction of moderate interest'. There are so many things that simply don't fit, not least that 145 men, who would anyway have been getting close to retirement, would not have been much of an addition to China's western defences. They were too few to found a city.

Look at the two fundamental claims:

- that Li Qian equals Rome. Many scholars have pointed out that there is no reason why Li Qian should equate with

Alexandria, or why Alexandria should equate with Rome, since Alexandria was Greek, and not conquered by the Romans until 30 BC, six years *after* the capture of Zhizhi's capital. Anyway, Li Qian was the name of a local administrative area a century before both the attack on Zhizhi's capital and the battle of Carrhae. The obvious conclusion was in one of the articles in the proof copy of the book Mr Song had given me: 'Therefore there is no connection between Li Qian and any Roman prisoners.'[6]

- that the soldiers formed a testudo. Dudbridge goes on to a highly technical examination of Dubs's suggestion that a 'fish-scale formation' was a Roman testudo, and finds it wanting. The translation is simply wrong, he says. Dubs misunderstood both the grammar and a technical term. What the Chinese means is: 'More than 100 foot soldiers were formed up in close order on either side of the gate, practising military [i.e. weapons] drill.'

- 'The plain fact is,' he concluded to me, 'that Dubs linked together three entirely unrelated matters – the battle of Carrhae (53 BC), the Chinese capture of a Central Asian stronghold in 36 BC, and the ancient county of Li Jian in western China (already there in 53 BC).'

No historical evidence, and no present-day evidence either. If there really are people in the area who 'look foreign', it could not be a result of Italian genes carrying their information

[6] The article is by Zhang Defang (张德芳), Director of the Gansu Provincial Archaeology Team. Other references coming to the same conclusion, for Chinese readers: Wang Shou Kuan (往受宽), *Dunhuang Journal* (1, 37), 2000; Liu Guanghua (刘光华) and Xie Yujie (谢玉杰), *2nd North-West Minority College Journal* (2, 39), Lanzhou, 1999.

down the centuries, for eighty generations. No traits particular to individuals endure that long, because any trait as general as overall appearance is the result of uncounted numbers of genes that mix randomly. Yellow hair doesn't sound very Italian. On the other hand, this was once the western frontier of China, with all sorts of contacts with non-Chinese peoples, whose genes could well have filtered down to the present, enough to produce a few families who look foreign to Chinese eyes.

But good stories like this are too appealing to be destroyed by disapproval and disproof. At the grass-roots level in China, where 'heritage' and folklore often pass as historical fact, chances are that statements by killjoy experts who prefer evidence to good stories will have absolutely no impact at all. Anyway, the story has now escaped from its roots. Four hundred kilometres to the east, in a Ming fortress that is now the China West Film Studio, is a display left over from the making of the *Homeward Bound* film. It is the house of the governor whose task it was to look after the Roman soldiers in their new home. It includes some wonderful and thoroughly authentic-looking furniture. My guess is that the statues, the plaque, the pavilion and the film set will convince many thousands every year that the story is true.

Back east, Huhanye was relieved at his brother's death, but apprehensive lest he share a similar fate. So once again, in 33 BC, he went to Chang'an to pay homage to the emperor, requesting the hand of a princess to re-establish the peace-and-kinship treaty and turn himself into the emperor's son-in-law. The emperor agreed, and selected a woman from his harem who was of a noble family and who had not yet been invited into the emperor's bed. This was the soon-to-be-famous Zhaojun, whose story and subsequent legend is told in the next chapter.

Huhanye was 'ecstatic'. 'I will be the border sentinel for Han,' he wrote. 'Not for this lifetime, but for ever. Please withdraw your troops from the border.' One minister advised the emperor against agreeing, offering ten reasons: all barbarians would take heart, they will return to war, they are not to be trusted, those who are settled here will abscond, Han profiteers will inspire them to rebel again, 'bandits, louts and riffraff' would flee to them, and so on. So, said the emperor, thanks but no thanks. To which Huhanye grovelled: 'I am dense. I never even contemplated such intricacies.'

Two years later (31 BC), Huhanye died, in looming chaos over the succession. Since the early days, the crown had gone from father to son (indeed, the stability of the system was a major reason for the endurance of the Xiongnu empire), but sons were sometimes too young, or for some reason deemed inadequate by the Xiongnu aristocracy, and it had become customary for the succession to go from brother to brother. After Huhanye's death, there were no brothers, only disputatious cousins. Civil war was inevitable. But not yet. For three decades there was peace, and riches flowed northwards, more than ever. From 6,000 bolts in 51 BC, deliveries of raw silk rose to 30,000 bolts in 1 BC, when the current chanyu, Ujiuli, came to Chang'an on an official visit. 'Whenever the Xiongnu chanyu came to pay homage,' wrote Sima Guang, 'the Han Emperor would confer upon them gifts and embroideries and bales of raw silk in ever-increasing quantities.'

Again, this – another voluntary submission by an old enemy – was a great event, marked by a banquet for 'hundreds of civic and military officers'. But it seems that the 26-year-old Emperor Ai had more than diplomacy in mind. His reign was already marked by violent rivalries between four women, all of whom called themselves empress dowagers. In addition, Ai was besotted with a man named Dong Xian, a few years his junior, whom he had presented with ever higher offices, ever greater wealth and a royal mansion. Everyone knew about the affair. Once, so they said, when the two were asleep together, clothing entwined, Emperor Ai awoke and rather than disturb his lover he cut off the sleeve of his robe to ease himself out of bed. Ever after, homosexuality was referred to as 'the passion of the cut sleeve'. Courtiers were aghast. Astrologers said that the emperor was under the malign influence of the planet Jupiter, which exuded a bad *pneuma* (air) and presaged a year of catastrophes. This needed to be countered by some grand positive gesture. Possibly the state banquet would suffice.

Into this hotbed of corruption and scandal came the chanyu, Ujiuli (reigned 8 BC–AD 13). At the banquet, he was amazed to see the honour given to the imperial favourite. 'Through the translator [please note: the chanyu did not speak Chinese] he inquired as to how a young man of his age could attain such a supreme position.' The emperor avoided details. Through the interpreter, he replied curtly, 'Whilst the Grand Marshal [one of Dong Xian's many offices] may be young, he is nevertheless a sage.' After the banquet and a night in the Lodge for State Dignitaries, which the emperor said was a great honour, the chanyu left much richer. Among the gifts was a lacquered wooden bowl – a so-called 'ear-cup' from the shape of its handle – made in the imperial workshop in Kaogong, Chang'an, and dated the fifth year of the Emperor Ai (2 BC). It was found in Noyon Uul, in Petr Kozlov's tomb

No. 6, which suggests that this tomb was Ujiuli's (though how you prove that is an open question).

In China, Ai died suddenly, and Dong Xian, stripped of all his ranks, committed suicide. In a flurry of accusations, suicides, banishments and executions, a usurper, Wang Mang, a minister-turned-emperor, seized power in a brief and bitter interregnum (AD 9–23). Described by Sima Guang as 'restive, petulant and tetchy', Wang Mang announced the birth of a new dynasty, Xin.

10

PRINCESSES FOR PEACE

In Inner Mongolia's capital, Hohhot, my hotel, which would not have been out of place in central London, or Paris, or New York, had a vast and intriguing bas relief behind the check-in desk: a woman wrapped in a large fur-lined cloak playing some sort of a lute. She was obviously important, because she was surrounded by dancing girls, soldiers and horsemen. When I asked about her, I was told the hotel was named after her, and that she was indeed important because she had brought peace to China by marrying a Xiongnu chief. Though one among many, she stood for them all. This is her story, and theirs.

Buying off the Xiongnu was expensive, not only in troops and weapons and 'gifts' but also in princesses. Twelve of them were sent north to marry various chanyus between 200 and 100 BC, one every eight years or so, and several others after that. There are few details. They get chosen, they go, they vanish.

Today, the absence of information seems dismissive, as if the women were mere pawns, offered in order to satisfy the lust of a coarse barbarian chief.

But it wasn't like that. For one thing, royal women were not objects to be moved around at the emperor's will, mothers in particular. Empress dowagers were formidable figures (Empress Lü uniquely so in her cruelty and vindictive scheming). In the words of Burton Watson, translator of Sima Qian, 'The mere suggestion that a king or an emperor had failed to treat his mother with the proper deference would be sufficient to cast a shadow of guilt over his whole regime.' He goes on to summarize the role of women at court, as recorded by Sima Qian.

> Time and again we discover them manoeuvring behind the scenes to bring pressure upon their lovers and sons; in scene after scene we see concubines dissolving into persuasive tears before their lords, or testy old women carrying on like spoiled children until they get their way ... [or] the figure of the determined matriarch contriving to dictate the lives of her offspring.

Secondly, the young women were agents with a mission – to forge links so close that the 'barbarians' would become 'civilized' and peace would be guaranteed. If things turned out well, their children would be the sons and daughters of Chinese royalty. In theory, therefore, the chanyu would become family, and filial duty would make war impossible. Sometimes it worked well, sometimes a little, sometimes not at all.

But there was no denying the burden carried by the princesses, even if they had no choice.

Handing over high-status women was an act of significance, not just for the women, who were hardly out of their teens, but for the court and for ordinary Chinese. The princesses may have had a reasonably good life in the chanyu's court, bearing in mind that it contained many bilingual officials and maybe one or two other princesses. If they were mistreated, reports would filter back to Chang'an, with consequences, like an invasion or a halt to the flow of gifts, or both. But to most of the court and the public, who knew nothing of nomad ways, it was a fate worse than death. That anyone, let alone a princess, could be sent into the land of the northern barbarians was the equivalent, in European folk tales, of sacrificing a virgin to a dragon, except this was for real.

Actually, the policy involved more than just the Xiongnu, because their empire included many other tribes, which occasionally had to be paid off with goods and a princess or two. In 108 BC, a poem was placed in the mouth of a princess named Liu Xijun – her family name defining her as a relative of Liu Bang, founder of the Han dynasty – after she was despatched to the Wusun in an attempt to prise them away from the Xiongnu. The words are not hers. It was written by someone back home, imagining what it was like to be her:

My family married me to a lost horizon,
Sent me far away to the Wusun king's strange land.
A domed lodging is my dwelling, of felt is its walls,
Flesh for food, mare's milk for drink.
Longing ever for my homeland, my heart is full of sorrow,
I wish I were a brown goose flying home.

None of the women themselves recorded their experiences, so we have no idea how they felt or what their new life was like. But the practice had such emotional clout in China that it cried out for universal expression, which it found in the story of one particular girl, who was not, as it happened, a princess. Somehow, that only added to the pathos. As often in Chinese history, the few bare facts were overtaken by multi-layered fictions. She acquired attributes, passions, and relationships that turned her first into a heroine and then a goddess, celebrated with plays, poems, memorials, a film, an opera, a tomb-park and that plush hotel in Hohhot.

Her name was Zhaojun, and her real-life story begins in 33 BC, when the Xiongnu and Han-dynasty China were at peace. This was two decades after the Xiongnu had been split between two brothers, Zhizhi and Huhanye. Zhizhi had fled and been killed. In 33 BC, the grateful Huhanye came on his second state visit, saying that he wished to 'become the Emperor's son-in-law'. He was hoping for a princess. What he got was something rather less – a nineteen-year-old lady 'of noble family background', Zhaojun.

She must have been fabulously beautiful. The *Han Shu* says that she was presented at a state banquet. 'Her beauty, dazzling in its luminosity, lit up the entire hall. The young woman casually ambled into the hall with unassuming elegance and grace, leaving those present with a feeling of profound awe and admiration.'

Huhanye was delighted. Off she went, probably by carriage, because that was how dignitaries and royal women travelled, and possibly (according to one scholar) along Meng Tian's Straight Road. She bore a son. Huhanye died two years later. Following Xiongnu tradition, she married his heir, her stepson, by whom she had two daughters, the older named Yun, the younger unnamed, but both respected enough to be useful in Chinese–Xiongnu diplomatic exchanges. Soon after, she vanished from the historical record.

Her transformation began about two centuries later, and has never stopped. She is one of the Four Beauties, women linked in legend by nothing more than their looks. Their beauty caused fish to forget how to swim, the moon to hide her face, birds to fall from the sky and flowers to wilt. Version followed version, building incident and character to serve one agenda after another, until now. Scholars list some 250 books, 780 poems and several plays about her.

Here's how the story went in its earliest form:

At seventeen, Zhaojun[1] is already a celebrated beauty, so beautiful that her father refuses all offers of marriage and presents her to the emperor. But her father has no influence at court, and she is one among many. She is put in the Palace of the Concubines, and there she lives for several years, until depression sets in and she ceases to care for herself. No wonder, then, that she is never noticed. When the Xiongnu king comes, there is to be a great spectacle of dancers, musicians and singers. Zhaojun seizes her chance, and appears at her best, wonderfully dressed, her face and figure radiating beauty. When the emperor asks the chanyu if there is anything he would like in particular, the chanyu replies, 'I have treasures enough, but the Xiongnu women cannot compare with the Chinese. Grant me one of your beauties.' At this the emperor asks for a concubine to step forward and offer herself voluntarily.

[1] As often, our heroine had many names. Originally, she was Wang Qiang. Her 'style' or 'courtesy' name was Wang Zhaojun, Zhaojun for short. At court, she became Mingfei (Shining Consort).

219

Zhaojun advances and speaks: 'Your humble servant has had the good fortune to find herself in the Palace of Concubines. Alas, alone among them, she was too ordinary to be of interest to Your Majesty. I therefore wish to offer myself to the chanyu.' The emperor is stupefied by her beauty, and filled with regrets, but cannot go back on his word. With a sigh, he lets her go. Her heart, however, stays with China. On her arrival in the wild lands of the north, she remains the image of sadness, and composes mournful songs, lamenting her fate among the swirling sands and biting winds, enduring an incomprehensible language and fermented milk that ruins her hair. She has exchanged unhappiness for pure misery. In one poem, 'Bitter Nostalgia', she sees herself as a beautiful bird, shut away in a far-off palace, tormented out of her mind, yearning to join the wild geese in their flight south.

> High is the mountain,
> Deep the river!
> Alas, my father! Alas, my mother!
> How long is the road that separates us!
> Oh, how many are the sorrows
> And the cares that afflict my heart!

She has a son, who on the death of her husband succeeds him. She asks her son whose traditions she should follow: the Xiongnu's or the Chinese. He says: Do as the Xiongnu do. So she takes poison, and dies.

Already, she has some character. She is no mere victim, but a volunteer, which makes her tragic. She is devoted to her emperor and her country, and she cannot live with her loss. But it is all rather depressing. We could do with a little more drama, which is what was added by the fifth century. Now a new character appears, one of the court painters, the evil Mao Yanshou. Since the emperor can't possibly visit all his concubines, and since he wants only the most beautiful as his consorts, it is the job of the artists to paint the portraits of all the girls so that the emperor can choose the most beautiful. Customarily, the girls bribe the painter to upgrade their charms. But Zhaojun has integrity. She refuses to pay. In revenge, Mao paints her ugly. When the chanyu asks for a Chinese girl, the emperor chooses the ugliest – Zhaojun – and only discovers his mistake as she is about to leave. He cannot, of course, go back on his word, and in his fury has all the painters executed.

The story is now much more dramatic, but she is still the epitome of suffering. Later, therefore, she not only chooses her fate: she does so bravely, for a noble cause. As she says in a letter that she is supposed to have written to the emperor: 'In a thousand years to come, and even ten thousand, it will be remembered that Your Majesty once had a woman who played the role of special envoy in a foreign court beyond the Frontier.' Now she has become the self-elected representative of a superior culture, who, like a missionary, seeks to teach the Xiongnu the ways of civilization, ensuring endless peace.

Sometime in the first millennium, she acquires another talent, and an attribute: she becomes a singer, who plays brilliantly and sadly on a pipa, a Chinese lute. The pipa, the instrument of court musicians, had special significance, as the third-century poet Fu Xuan recorded: 'The pipa appeared in the late Qin period. When the people suffered from being forced to build the Great Wall, they played the instrument to express their resentment.'

The final element in the evolving story was the addition of a love interest. The emperor hears Zhaojun playing her pipa. He falls in love with her. He confers upon her the name Mingfei (Shining Consort), which is how people usually refer to her today. The evil Mao defects to the Xiongnu, and persuades the chanyu to demand Zhaojun's hand. The emperor is weak, and must comply. The lovers part, in tears. The Xiongnu withdraw. Zhaojun, the saviour of the nation she has lost for ever, casts herself into the Yellow River.

It is in this form that the story reached maturity, in a play by the fourteenth-century playwright Ma Zhiyuan entitled *Autumn in the Han Palace*. Ma wrote with his own agenda, which could not be the established one of how Zhaojun civilized the Xiongnu, because China had recently been invaded and occupied by the Mongols, the 'barbaric' descendants of the Xiongnu. Weakness had led to unprecedented disaster. For the first time, the whole nation was under foreign rule. Beautiful women like Zhaojun get taken over by the barbarians, and China loses her very soul. This was tragedy, pure and simple.

So she entered the world of myth. After the Mongols fell, people reverted to the old theme, saying she had been sent from heaven by the Jade Emperor to make peace between the Chinese and the barbarians. To prove her divinity, people told the story of how, on her journey beyond the Great Wall, just as she comes to the Yellow River, there is a terrible storm of wind and snow. Calmly she dismounts and begins to play her pipa. There follows an astonishing transformation. The blizzard ceases, the sky clears, and on the plain flowers appear and the grass turns a wonderful spring-time green. All the places through which she travels become fertile.

When she died, it was said that everywhere the grass withered, except upon her principal tomb, which, in the seventeenth century, arose south of Hohhot. The 30-metre hummock is now the focal point of a major tourist attraction with a big new building at its entrance, its two wings sprouting from a central passageway. When I visited with my companion, Water Xu, an autumnal wind scattered leaves across the marble forecourt. There was no one around except a guard. Could we go inside? No, it wasn't finished yet. In a year or so, one of the wings would be a museum. 'You know,' he went on, 'seen from the air, this building looks like a flying goose.' Ah, yes, of course. It recalled that poem put into the mouth of one of the princesses, wishing to be at one with the wild geese flying south to the civilized world. Never mind that that particular girl had been sent off to the Wusun, not the Xiongnu, for all the princesses were Zhaojun. Everyone knows the poem, said Water, because it was turned into the theme song of a TV series about Zhaojun, 'Wild geese flying south,' he hummed. 'Over hills and mountain, how great the grasslands are, something, something, I can't quite remember.'

The park is, of course, a political statement, celebrating national unity and the fortieth anniversary of the establishment of Inner Mongolia in 1966. So Zhaojun is given royal treatment. An arch shields a statue of her in a long, flowing gown, very suitable for a Han princess, though not for the consort of a steppe-based chanyu. Statues of animals crouching in reverence line the avenue leading to the tomb-mound, all of them partly or wholly mythological, recalling oxen, deer, and a legendary creature called *xie zhi*, a cross between a goat and a sheep with the magical ability to tell right from wrong and to swallow bad officials. The animals lead to a romantic statue of Huhanye and Zhaojun on horseback – a carriage, though more truthful, would have concealed her – with a plinth captioned *he-qin*, peace-and-kinship, the policy by which Han and Xiongnu were supposedly united as members of one big happy family.

It's all fake heritage. She was probably buried somewhere on the steppes. She has eight possible burial sites, but this is the one people take most seriously, not because it's true but because it is impressive. Stairs lead steeply up the burial mound to a little pavilion containing a stele in her honour. It is a good view from up there. Looking down on hectares of parkland, an avenue of kowtowing beasts, a building symbolizing her homesickness and statues proclaiming her importance, who would dare deny that she is worthy of the words picked out in white on the stele: 'GREAT MERIT'.

11

THE SHOCK OF SURRENDER

WHAT WOULD IT HAVE BEEN LIKE FOR ZHAOJUN TRAVEL-ling to the Xiongnu capital in her four-horse carriage? We cannot know, but pictures and contemporary descriptions can release the imagination. Armoured outriders, a mixed force of Han and Xiongnu in wary cooperation, guard her on either side, and carriage-loads of silk-clad officials follow behind her, with ox-wagons full of tents for the two-month journey from Chang'an.

To put ourselves in Zhaojun's delicate shoes (though perhaps she has had the sense to put on sturdy leather boots), we should imagine her and her entourage as they make good time along Meng Tian's Straight Road for a month, take rafts buoyed up by sheepskin floats over the Yellow River, wind up and over the Yan Mountains, rest at one of the Xiongnu border fortresses where prisoners eke out a living as farmers, pick up speed over the Gobi's gravelly wastes, and then, to the growing dismay of her Chinese guardsmen, enter the enemy heartland, the flowing grasslands of central Mongolia, where herders on horseback, wielding lassos at the end of long poles, round up herds of horses, goats and sheep. What about toilet arrangements for this aristocratic beauty? Ordinary girls pee on the grass. Zhaojun has the privacy of her carriage, a tent, and handmaids with chamberpots. Occasionally, at some larger collection of tents, weather-beaten women in their all-encircling deels offer fermented mares' milk and hard curds. They are not (yet) to Zhaojun's taste, but perhaps she waves her handmaids aside to sip and nibble. After being on the road for two months, her cavalcade weaves between forested hills, along tracks similar to the ones you see today, broad patterns of parallel lines where drivers have made new tracks. Herds of sheep scatter as the outriders cut through them. Ahead, many tents fill a valley: the capital, at last. Her husband, Huhanye, has long since gone on ahead, to supervise a formal greeting. Small family tents by the hundred, with their lines of tethered horses, surround larger tents by the dozen, some of which form a corridor leading to the vast palace-tent, big enough to host 1,000 people. Lines of mounted Xiongnu warriors, fearsome in leather armour, mix with crowds of women in deels. All carry bowls of kumiss, which they flick heavenward with their third fingers, crying, 'Ura! Ura!' as she passes. Her escorts, Xiongnu and Chinese, peel away, leaving her to be welcomed to her new life. She steps carefully over the wooden threshold, for she has been warned that to touch it is a gross impropriety.[1]

---

[1] This is an ancient taboo, for reasons that no one can explain. Almost 1,300 years later, when Marco Polo attended Kublai Khan's banquets in Da Du

Inside she sees two circles of poles holding the great dome of felt, over a floor covered by felt carpets with intricate designs of semi-mythical animals, like those on the Ordos bronzes and the hangings found in Noyon Uul. Huhanye, warned of her arrival hours before, sits on a gold-plated wooden throne, flanked by advisers. Back home Han courtiers imagine her to be in misery. Far from it. She is at the heart of a rich empire, well supplied with Chinese products, and with Chinese companions chosen from the thousands of captive servants. She has wealth and authority she could never have dreamed of in Chang'an. She cannot know that the Xiongnu empire will never be what it once was. Anyway, the end will not come for another century. She has a lot to learn, and she's terrified. But it's not a bad outlook for a teenager who was until recently a tiny cog in the vast machine of the Chang'an court.

One summer a few years ago, I went to Noyon Uul with two Xiongnu experts from Ulaanbaatar's Museum of Mongolian History – Odbaatar, slim and quiet-spoken, and his boss Gelegdorj Eregzen, whose dissertation was on Noyon Uul. Travelling in a solid Russian Forgon 4 × 4, we drove north for 100 kilometres and turned on to a track, rolling like a dinghy in a swell through stands of birch and knee-high shrubs and over grass rich with yellow flowers.

Eregzen pointed to a grove of trees. Hidden by the birches and a blanket of shrubs was a circular mound, and in the side of the mound was a hole. This – Kozlov's tomb No. 1 – looked like an overgrown and abandoned well, a square pit lined

---

(Beijing), guards stood by to beat anyone who stepped on the threshold. Tourists in Mongolia are still advised to take care.

with decaying timbers. Other mounds dotted the woodlands, all practically invisible. But in a half-hour walk we came across dozens of them – Eregzen knew of 100 or so – mostly only a metre or two high, and 10 metres apart. Some were bigger. One, No. 24, was a crater that must have taken weeks to excavate. It was still 6 metres deep and a stone's throw across, with the entrance road running into it much as Kozlov's team had dug it, like an ancient sunken lane. A Chinese lacquer bowl from tomb No. 6 has an inscription dating it to 2 BC, which means it was probably a gift from the Han emperor Ai to the Xiongnu chanyu Ujiuli (Wuzhuliu in Chinese).

For decades, scholars have known that the Xiongnu élite had been extremely wealthy. They were no barbarians, at least the top people weren't, in terms of possessions and art and social structure. The Xiongnu armies and the Noyon Uul graves represented wealth on a grand scale. But no one had any idea how grand until recently.

Only since the early 1990s, with the collapse of the Soviet Union and Mongolia's Communist government, have international teams of scholars begun to reveal the true depth and range of the culture created by the Xiongnu. Mongolia is still almost virgin territory for archaeologists, so there are many international projects – fifteen in 2017, with more planned for 2018 and beyond. The Xiongnu finds are mostly from graves, a few of them from around 10,000 graves of local dignitaries, most from the so-called 'élite' or 'royal' or 'terrace' graves, with the very biggest rivalling those of Noyon Uul. There are several hundred of these, which are almost square with sloping entrance corridors up to 40 metres long pointing south. The corridors do not reach the bottom of the burial chamber, one of many mysteries. Only twenty have been excavated. All but one have been looted (or perhaps they were deliberately destroyed by successive chanyus as a way of promoting their own legacies, as new CEOs squash the projects of their predecessors). They are in ten cemeteries ranging in size from Noyon Uul's almost 2,000 hectares down to 20. Two are in the far west of Mongolia, two in southern Siberia, the rest in central Mongolia and none in China. Two are near the valley of the Orkhon River, in the centre of Mongolia, which is the best place from which to rule this region (later Turkic and Mongol empires also ruled from here). All have a penumbra of subsidiary graves, hundreds of them, about half being circular, the others rectangular. Most are on gentle slopes that were probably used as winter pastures. The majority of the really big ones – the élite tombs – are raised about 1 metre inside a low stone wall. The graves, dug in soft earth, have sloping walls, in steps, so that they did not collapse as they were dug. The depths range from 5 to 20 metres.

All the élite tombs vary, but there are similarities in size and structure, and also in content: animal bones (skulls, legs and tailbones of horses, cows, sheep and goats); horse paraphernalia of iron; Chinese carriages; the end bits or 'ears' of bows; bronze cauldrons; ceramic pots (almost 300 of these, made in local kilns); bronze mirrors, Chinese, many deliberately broken (more on these later); textiles; many types of ornament and personal possession, typically beads, belt-buckles like the ones found in Ordos, in bronze of course, but also in bone, stone and wood; and sticks of bone that may be chopsticks, often found near Chinese lacquered bowls and cups (occasionally with Chinese characters defining their function, suggesting that the Xiongnu adopted eating habits from China). One cup has a Chinese dedication to 'sons and grandsons', as if it were a marketing slogan. These cups show that the Xiongnu aristocracy were fussy: when the Eastern Han came to power in AD 25, lacquered ware in China gave way to downmarket ceramics, but the Xiongnu élite didn't go for the new style and did not put much of it in their graves. Ankle bones of sheep[2] are common. These little rough cubes, with their six different faces, were used as dice for games and telling the future (still are actually). Often, the smaller objects were wrapped in cloth. The burial chambers were of logs, sometimes a double chamber, containing the coffin, all covered with layers of pine cones and brush, which were set on fire before the pit was refilled. Coffins were often decorated with lozenges outlined in gold, reminiscent of the folding walls of Mongolian *gers* (tents) today. Perhaps the shapes represented spirit-gers.

What all this means is obscure. Do some items have special significance? Does their position in the tomb? Does size matter? Were the grave-sites sacred? Why the difference between circular and rectangular tombs? Did the entrance ramps serve a practical or ritual purpose, or both? So many questions, so few answers.

Take one small mystery among many, but worth a look because it is so odd. In 1996–9, an eight-man team[3] excavated a burial in a cemetery of sixty-six graves bordering the Egiin Gol, a river in the forested hills of northern Mongolia near the Russian border. The graves date from the fourth century BC to the second century AD. One grave was a rough circle of stones. In the centre 1.7 metres down was a cow or

---

[2] Astragali, to give them their technical name.
[3] Including Diimajav Erdenebaatar and Tsagaan Törbat, both of whom reappear shortly.

bullock skull. A little further, under three layers of flat stones, scattered by looters, lay a coffin with two skeletons, male and female. With the man's bones were bits of a bow, a spear-head, arrow-shafts and arrowheads, and bits of textile. But the bones themselves were a mess, scattered by the looters (one assumes), with some missing. He was between thirty and forty-five when he died. Beside him lay the woman, on her back, aged about thirty at death. Her skeleton was intact, her head supported by a leather pillow. She was buried with not much – a couple of hairpins, a mirror placed on her stomach. Above the two of them was an 'offering box', containing some cattle bones and – this is the puzzle – the woman's hyoid bone. The hyoid bone, at the top of the throat, is a peculiar thing. It is not strictly a bone, but a semi-circular piece of cartilage that is attached only by muscle, with no other link to the skeleton. It is a foundation for tongue-movements. To get it out and put it in its place of honour, the woman's tongue had been removed before burial. Why? Your guess is as good as mine. The eight authors of the paper reporting the find[4] make none, but point out that there is no clue as to whether the operation was done post- or pre-mortem. Post-, I would guess, because pre- would have been excruciating. In any event, she was buried with care and consideration, as was her hyoid bone.

To get an idea of the Xiongnu in life and death, I went to see the doyen of Mongolian archaeologists, Diimajav Erdene-baatar, professor in Ulaanbaatar's National University. A burly man with a thatch of grey hair and a drooping moustache, he

---

[4] P. Murail et al., 'The Man, the Woman and the Hyoid Bone' in *Antiquity* (see Bibliography).

has a passion for his subject, and experience to match, having shared in the excavation of the vast cemetery known as Gol Mod 1 and masterminded work on its twin, Gol Mod 2 (Gol Mod means 'river-wood', recalling their surroundings of mountainous fir forests and streams). His finds really need a large-scale, state-sponsored museum, which does not exist, so Erdenebaatar has made his own in the university. It is a jewel-box of treasures.

His main focus is Gol Mod 2, which he talks about with pride, because he discovered it in 2001. He had started with Gol Mod 1 working with a team of French archaeologists. He had told them where it was and collaborated on its excavation. One day, wanting to get to another site he was working on, he decided to take a short cut, and asked a local to come along to guide him. 'You know,' his guide said, 'we have another place, very like Gol Mod.' So they went to check it out, and he was astonished to see, in among the scattering of fir trees, a vast pile of rocks, with numerous smaller piles alongside.

'Obviously it was a cemetery,' he said. And the main grave was not only bigger than the one at Gol Mod 1, it was richer – though looted, the robbers had left many more artefacts in place. 'It was like a gift from Heaven,' he added – from the Mongol god, Khökh Tenger, the Blue Sky. This was Gol Mod 2, comprising not just one large grave – the largest known so far – but 400 subsidiary graves as well. He then worked for three years on the main tomb, a massive operation, in which up to 200 people, digging down 21 metres, found the array of objects now in his museum.

There is, for instance, the iron rim of a chariot wheel, now laid out on the floor of his museum as if waiting to be refitted. About 1.25 metres across, it was part of one of sixteen or seventeen carriages, all broken and all but one burned as part of the burial rituals (the number of chariots was an estimate based on the number of wheel-hubs). That's a cavalcade of chariots, almost enough to rival those of the Qin and Han courts, certainly enough to transport a royal Xiongnu family and top officials south across Ordos. Chariots, covered in black lacquer and drawn by two or four horses, were an important part of the 'gifts' sent by the Han emperors, and equally important as the official means of transport of Han envoys and Han princesses. Though once widely used in warfare, their military importance had faded. Mounted archers could run rings round chariots. The Xiongnu made their own, but they were wagons for domestic use. As the remains of many chariots in other graves suggest, these were status symbols not just for the chanyu but for all Xiongnu aristocrats, the equivalents of limousines for a modern head of state. Most of them had parasols or roofs to keep off the rain and sun. Rock drawings and paintings of chariots show their horses prancing along, tossing their heads as if they had not a care in the world.

How did they get there, these Chinese chariots with their iron-rimmed wheels? They would not have travelled well through mountains, but they were suited to the steppe, and fortunately there was a steppe close by that led due north–south – Ordos – where the difficult parts had been made easy by Meng Tian's road. Perhaps even under Xiongnu rule (206–120 BC) it was kept in good condition to speed the delivery of gifts and princesses.

To return to Erdenebaatar's museum: the most valuable objects (found in tomb No. 20) are fourteen gold-coated plaques used to decorate horse-straps – gorgeous little cartouches and

13-centimetre discs with bas reliefs of two mythological creatures, a sort of a unicorn with a deer's body, a horse's head and a single huge, curling horn; and a *bers* (as it is known in Mongolia today), with the face of a snarling snow leopard, a single horn, a dragon's neck, wings and camel's feet. The Xiongnu liked gold, of which Mongolia has an abundance, probably collecting it in minute traces from rivers, so these are almost certainly a Xiongnu product, not Chinese. Other objects reveal international connections with China and beyond. Small gold ornaments with turquoise inlays recall similar ones found in Afghanistan (ancient Bactria), and were quite possibly made there.[5]

The most intriguing of his discoveries, found in a large circular grave beside the main tomb, is a small blue glass bowl, only 7.5 centimetres high. It has white lines painted round the rim, and the delicate bulge of the body is strengthened with raised ribs. Glass is not a material used by the Chinese at this time. So where did it come from and when? The surprising answer is: Rome in about AD 50. That's certain because there are six other similar pieces in western museums.[6] But how and why was it in the grave of an eminent Xiongnu?

'I thought it had been traded all the way across Asia,' said Erdenebaatar, 'but when I was in Berlin a professor there said no, it was too rare and delicate for trade. It must have been a gift.' His words set the imagination to work. Could it be

---

[5] Ursula Brosseder, 2007, quoted in Miller, *Power Politics*. The Chinese knew about Bactria (Da Xia) from the traveller Zhang Qian, so the Xiongnu would surely have known of it as well. There is a detailed chemical analysis of Gol Mod gold in Desroches et al., *Mongolie: Le Premier Empire des Steppes* (see Bibliography).

[6] Cologne Museum and Corning Museum, New York.

evidence for those 'Romans' saved from the ruins of Zhizhi's fortress in 36 BC? Could a Roman have travelled all the way across Asia, like a precursor of Marco Polo? It seems impossible. Remember that Herodotus, in his description of the Scythians, said that it took seven sets of interpreters to cross Asia. More likely, local leaders had handed on this prize possession as a gift, until it landed in the hands of some leading Xiongnu, perhaps the chanyu himself.

A few days later, I set off for the two Gol Mod cemeteries. There were three others with me – Batmõnkh, a guide with a passion for history, Tsend, one of Erdenebaatar's PhD students, and the driver, Mönkhöö, master of our 4 × 4 Forgon van. We headed west from Ulaanbaatar on tarmac, then north over the open steppe. They call this an ocean of grass, with good reason – distant horizons, a vast blue sky, no fences and a track-network hundreds of metres wide, as if a giant had run a comb across the grass. After 400 kilometres and a night in a friendly tent, we splashed through a stream, crunched through a snow-filled gully, wove between firs and arrived at Gol Mod 2.

Dominating a plateau surrounded by hills, what had once been a deep pit had been completely filled in. Stones outlined a shape like a giant paddle, the shaft marking what had once been a descending ramp and a square over the grave itself. Archaeologists commonly refer to tombs with entrance passageways as 'terrace' tombs. Larger ones are said to be those of the 'élite', while smaller ones are termed 'aristocratic', and the smallest, whether circular or rectangular, are 'satellite tombs'. The élite tomb we were looking at is the biggest yet discovered.

'It wasn't like this when I first saw it,' said Tsend. 'Those stones over there' – he pointed to piles of them a few metres away under fir trees – 'were all on top of the grave,' which raised it to make a platform. It had taken a team of about 200 soldiers, released from duty, to clear the rocks and prepare the tomb for excavation. Twenty-one metres down, they found a coffin, broken by looters and then crushed under a protective carapace of rocks. The only human remains were a skull and a femur.

The main grave was part of a huge necropolis. There were 190 smaller terrace tombs nearby, along with 85 circular burials and 250 others. To one side of the main grave were twenty-seven circular tombs, forming a regular, gentle curve, for officials or relatives killed to attend their leader in death. Excavations showed that the coffins were laid out to follow the line of the arc, suggesting that this was a single ritual, all the killings and burials done together. Today, seeing the size of the main grave and the carefully placed subsidiary graves, you get an idea of the power of the chanyu to command in this world and the next, matching that of the Chinese emperor he fought and emulated.

Concealment would have been impossible. This burial site covers a square kilometre, made over many decades, by a people confident that they could protect their tombs from looting or destruction by enemies. The way to do this, it seems, was to build big and deep. What looter with a basic pick made of deer-antlers could dig down 15 or more metres? Quite a few as it happens, but the Xiongnu could not have known that. So this was chosen as a fine place for aristocratic funerals – plenty of pasture, protected from winds by mountains, a nearby stream for drinking water and cooking, and lots of trees for fires, tomb-props and coffins. And beautiful, whether in high summer with the sandy earth unfrozen and soft for digging, or on a crisp autumn day, as this was, with the smell of the firs and a cold breeze sighing through the pine needles. Mongolians called this mysterious place Balgasin Tal, the City Steppe. I imagined myself as a time traveller, leaving the present for the world 2,000 years ago, watching sixty generations of Mongol herders flicker past, and then as the centuries slip by, seeing ghostly parades from earlier cultures – Jurchens, Kitans, Uighurs, Turks and half a dozen others – all pausing to wonder at this evidence of long-vanished predecessors.

I paced the outline of the main grave, not to record it – all the measurements are in the reports – but to feel its scale. Six paces across at the entrance, a 40-metre passageway, sometimes called 'the pathway to the other world', becoming wider as it approached the 40-metre-per-side grave, which (as the excavation showed) dropped 21 metres in a series of steps. Imagine a stepped pyramid with a sloping ramp leading almost to the top, and then in your mind turn it upside down. The stepped structure and the sloping walls were to prevent the soft soil collapsing. A back-of-the-envelope calculation suggests that the diggers – probably Chinese prisoners of war and criminals, not ordinary Xiongnu – had to shift 14,000 cubic metres of earth, about 21,000 tonnes. How did they do it? With wooden shovels, loading slings carried on a yoke by two men? Today, a manual worker can dig 5 tonnes a day. The numbers of diggers and sling-carriers would have been constricted as they worked their way down, but in round figures it suggests 400 men working for 10 days, or 200 working for about three weeks.

Nothing to match the First Emperor's tomb (16,000 men

working for 10 months),[7] but still quite an operation, with no way to keep it secret. Digging was just the start. The tomb would have been fitted with timbers, dressed with tapestries and finally filled with the objects now in Erdenebaatar's museum, before the coffin was carried down the entranceway and lowered into its final resting place. The grave, once filled in, was made even more obvious by covering it with hundreds of stones and giving it a low masonry wall, roughly cut into blocks. These people or their captives knew how to dress stones, a skill normally connected with city-dwellers. A layer of cinders near the surface showed that fire had played some part in the funeral rites.

Sunset and a biting wind drove us away. With the low sun turning car-tracks into shadowy claw-marks, we arrived at the nearest town, a scattering of plywood shacks either side of a stretch of steppe corrugated by car-tracks. A two-storey flat-pack building proclaimed: 'Food Place. Hotel. Karaoke. People's Shop'. Someone came from the nearby village to cook mutton and rice. We were the only occupants. Next morning, we were off at dawn. Two hours later, splashing through the half-frozen Khünüi River, climbing a steep and forested ridge, descending through trees flaming an autumnal orange, we came to Gol Mod 1.

This was a place with a long history of archaeology. A Mongolian scientist, Dorjsuren (1923–97), started work here in 1956, listing over 200 graves, half a dozen terrace tombs and several other satellite graves, opening twenty-six of the smaller circular ones. An attempt to excavate the massive

[7] My own calculation in *The Terracotta Army* (Bantam, London, revised edition 2018).

main tomb ended when the sides of his 8-metre hole col-lapsed. Then in 2000 came the French, headed by Jean-Paul Desroches and the Mongolians under Erdenebaatar, who continued Dorjsuren's work, identifying 316 tombs (since then the count has risen to over 393), of which 214 were aris-tocratic or élite ones, with entrance pathways. The entrances are aligned roughly north–south, so that as you descended into the grave you headed north, in the direction of the seven stars that make the Great Bear, though whether this is signifi-cant is anyone's guess. Perhaps we should switch the point of view. Perhaps the dead were supposed to exit the tomb uphill and enter the afterlife by heading south, which (if traditional Mongolian practice is anything to go by) is the direction their tents faced.

The team cut the intruding firs, cleared wind-blown sand, and excavated two élite tombs and another seven satellite burials. The most significant was the largest, labelled T1, which was carbon-dated between AD 20 and 50. With the occasional help of a mechanical digger, 800 volunteers care-fully scooped out 4,000 tonnes of soil, revealing two layers, bronze and iron relics in the upper one, gold and semi-precious objects below. A rock floor was apparently designed to frustrate looters, but a deer-horn, used as a pickaxe, showed that looters had entered anyway, presumably by dig-ging a long-gone tunnel. Seventeen metres down, the team found a double coffin of larch-wood planks, one inside the other – empty, looted, except for a few small bits of jewellery.

Why loot it? Was there a market in buried jewellery? Unlikely, given that nomads did not use cash. And why go to all the trouble of digging up old stuff when new stuff was available more easily by trade or pillage or from local workshops?

Some scholars suggest that the looting was driven by the ideology of successor groups eager to possess or destroy the symbols of prestige displayed by the predecessors. We have no answers.

Anyway, in this case, the looters must have given up, because from the area round the coffin, the team gathered hundreds of items – fragments of vases, gold plaques, a bit of a bronze mirror, bones, silver ornaments, iron wheel-rims, chariot decorations, horse accoutrements, arrowheads, and several pieces of material – silk, wool and felt. A Chinese jade pendant drilled by a local artisan to make two holes for gold decorations. A multi-coloured bead made by fusing pieces of different coloured glass – a complex operation, perhaps done in Europe, involving the use of manganese, copper, iron and barium.

The fragment of a bronze mirror deserves a note. Some thirty bits have been found in other tombs, most of them belonging to women. They were highly polished on one side and decorated on the other. Only *fragments*, not whole mirrors. They had been broken deliberately, for burial. Why? Many objects were broken, a shamanistic practice intended perhaps to 'release the essential spirit of the object, thereby rendering it useful in the after-life'.[8] Mirrors, though, seem to be in a class of their own. The fragments suggest a combination of Chinese and nomadic rituals. Scholars speculate that mirrors represented the cosmos (many mirrors from Chinese graves have sky symbols, like clouds and dragons, on their reverse sides) and were thought to capture images, as the eye does, or to emit the light 'absorbed' above ground. In China,

[8] Eregzen (ed.), *Treasures*.

they were commonly placed on the dead, facing upwards, to lighten the darkness and drive away evil spirits. I once saw a house near Xian with a mirror over the door, so that evil spirits would see their own reflection and be scared away. Mirrors were objects of 'reverence and prestige within nomadic cultures and, moreover, retained sacred symbolism', being passed down the generations or smashed into pieces that were divided between different burials.[9] Even today, when burying a deceased woman in Mongolia, her beloved items are often shown to the mirror before it is placed in the coffin, so that she can have them with her in the afterlife.

(The belief in the magic of mirrors is not limited to Mongolia and China. As everybody who has watched a vampire movie knows, vampires do not get reflected in mirrors. In *Sleeping Beauty*, the evil stepmother's mirror reveals truths. In Aachen, in the early fifteenth century, gullible pilgrims used little concave mirrors to 'collect' the healing power of Christ's robes when they were shown to the public. Johannes Gutenberg, inventor of printing with moveable type, planned to make his fortune by turning out these mirrors by the thousand, before a plague cancelled the pilgrimage and forced him to turn his attention to something more significant.)

A lacquered tray offers rare support for written sources, like a torch spotlighting a find in a cave. The tray had a Chinese inscription recording its origins: made by, or under the supervision of, someone called Wu, working under seven other layers of

---

[9] Tsagaan Törbat, 'A Study on Bronze Mirrors in Xiongnu Graves', in Brosseder and Miller (eds), *Xiongnu Archaeology*.

supervision[10] – *seven!* This was the product of a vast and complex bureaucracy in the Imperial Workshop, Chang'an, in 16 BC. As the authors of the article deciphering the inscription say, 'This is important as it is only the fifth absolutely dated object excavated from Xiongnu élite tombs.' It is also further proof that the Xiongnu aristocracy was in thrall to the Chinese after their submission in the mid-50s BC (more about that shortly). If this correlates with the burial, it dates from the reign of a chanyu named Seuxie (or Souxie, transliterations vary), who ruled 20–12 BC. Perhaps it is even the tomb of Seuxie himself.

After removing everything they found, they re-covered the grave and replaced the low surrounding wall, stone by well-dressed stone, each one carefully numbered.

The second élite tomb – T20, just over 18 metres deep – contained the partial remains of sixteen horses, notably their heads, all arranged to look north. Their teeth reveal that they were killed during the summer, supporting the idea that tombs were dug then. Their legs were placed to suggest that they were walking, as if to accompany the dead into the afterlife, perhaps also to provide them with food, because the limbs were laid on a bed of burning charcoal. One small item was missing. 'It is important to note,' writes Hélène Martin in a report on the finds,[11] 'that no trace of the hyoid bone was found,' whereas in the case of a human (see p. 231), it had

---

[10] Yeruul-Erdene Chimiddorj and Ikue Otani, 'The Chinese Inscription . . .', in *The Silk Road* (see Bibliography). The inscription reveals the size of this operation and the complexity of the bureaucracy controlling it. For production, there was a production inspector, an assistant clerk, a workshop overseer, a head secretary and an executive officer. For overall inspection, a deputy director of the right, and a director, in this case a provisional director.

[11] Hélène Martin, 'The Animal in the Xiongnu Funeral Universe', in Brosseder and Miller (eds), *Xiongnu Archaeology*.

been carefully preserved – a symbol of something that will probably forever remain a mystery.[12]

For an overview, we drove to the top of a little hill, which turned out to be a sand dune fixed in place by a covering of grass. From there it was obvious that the two cemeteries were remarkably similar, of equivalent size, in places of equal beauty, set in forests and protected by forested mountains. Sixty kilometres apart as the crow flies, they were linked by culture, family and ritual. Perhaps leaders from Ordos came here with other delegates from across the empire to take part in the burials and memorial rites.

Surely, with cemeteries of this size, there would have been a capital city nearby?

'Yes,' agreed Tsend, 'because, of the ten thousand known Xiongnu graves, about one-third were in this area, near the Tamir River.' Within 100 kilometres, river valleys and natural highways connect to the Orkhon River, the main artery for later empires. This was the Xiongnu heartland. But, Tsend added, even at its height when there was little chance of an invasion, the capital must have been no more than a tent-city. If there are remains of stone – well cut like those surrounding the tomb in front of us and final proof that this region was in fact the administrative heart of the Xiongnu empire – they await discovery.

There was a mystery here. The two Gol Mod cemeteries, Noyon Uul and the other élite tombs were radically different from the graves in Ordos, where there were none of the big, deep terrace tombs with sloping entrances and Chinese

---

[12] Human remains were also found in four graves, in such a bad state that they revealed little except their sex (male), age (20–25) and size (average). One was bow-legged, from years of riding.

chariots; radically different too from the thousands of other Xiongnu tombs in Mongolia.

Back in Ulaanbaatar, Tsagaan Törbat of the Mongolian Academy of Sciences gave me an explanation.

'All Mongolian élite graves date from the end of the second half of the first century soon after the Xiongnu submitted to Han, to the first century AD,' he said. We were in his office, which was cluttered with the books and papers to do with his current research into the Xianbei, successors to the Xiongnu. 'So we're talking about a short period, only a few decades. In Mongolia, we have only eight places with these élite graves. They are in the shape of Chinese royal graves' – though the Chinese tradition was to make mounds over the graves, as did the Scythians, something that the Xiongnu did not do. 'We have to ask why we suddenly get these big Chinese-style graves full of Chinese – or Chinese-style – objects: chariots, buttons, jade discs, mirrors, ceramics.'

He paused, then answered his own question.

'I think something happened to Xiongnu ideology. It was to do with the balance of power. In 51 BC, the Xiongnu under Huhanye accepted peace, acknowledging China as the superior culture. It must have been a severe shock, tolerable only because they received so much from China. I think that's why they adopted Chinese-style tombs and burial rites.'

It sounds right. Written evidence supports the suggestion of a radical change. The chanyus started to call themselves *ruodi* (or *jodi*), which may be a Chinese version of the Xiongnu for 'filial' or 'loyal'. Members of the aristocracy, who like most Xiongnu had names that were hard to transliterate into Chinese, started to give themselves simple Chinese names: Zhi, Dong, Zhu, Bi. As the American scholar Bryan Miller writes, 'They chose to appease the Chinese with whatever language became necessary, in exchange for a peaceful southern frontier and a steady increase in gifts.'[13]

It's remarkable that a warrior people should so suddenly adopt elements of their conquerors' culture, but two modern examples back him up. At the end of the Second World War, both West Germany and Japan embraced western democratic norms with astonishing speed. The United States, the overwhelming western Great Power, was a modern equivalent of old China, backing its political agenda with massive infusions of aid (though driven by the need to confront the Soviet Union, not the sort of Cold War rivalry that existed in Asia in the first century AD). Five years after the war's end, both West Germany and Japan were internationalist, demilitarized, stable, democratic and on their way to remarkable economic growth. At the outbreak of war in 1939, who would have dared predict such changes? When the Xiongnu were at their height, who could have foreseen their collapse into subservience and dependency?

One piece of evidence, or rather an absence, supports Törbat's hypothesis. Despite the Xiongnu's history of warfare, these are not the graves of men eager to proclaim themselves as warriors. As Ursula Brosseder says in her paper on terrace tombs,[14] 'As far as we can tell, weaponry does not play a significant role among the grave-goods, since bows and arrows or swords are mostly missing.'[15] Of course, these may have

[13] Miller, *Power Politics*.

[14] Ursula Brosseder, 'Xiongnu Terrace Tombs and their Interpretation as Elite Burials', in Jan Bemmann et al. (eds), *Current Archaeological Research in Mongolia* (see Bibliography).

[15] Mostly. There are some remains of weapons, e.g. in Khudgiin Tolgoi. See Hyeung-Won Yun, 'The Xiongnu Tombs in Khudgiin Tolgoi', in Bemman et al. (eds), *Current Archaeological Research*.

been taken by looters. But wooden bows and arrows decay, and looters would have had their own, and even decayed bows would have left traces of their shapes. Chances are they were never there, suggesting that the later chanyus had decided to set aside symbols of their violent past.

Not that they abandoned all their own ways. They kept their own ceramics factories, while importing Chinese lacquerware. Their tombs have a shell of rocks that shielded and defined them, unlike the Chinese earthen funeral mounds. As Bryan Miller puts it, 'The presence of Chinese goods reflects not a comprehensive adoption of Chinese traditions, but rather a utilization of the exotic within local traditions.'

It seems that the Xiongnu élite were driven to overcome feelings of inadequacy and inferiority by collecting wealth and displaying it in 'ostentatious graves', in the words of the German pre-historian Georg Kossack (1923–2004), widely considered the 'father' of today's top German archaeologists. He relates this to other élites who adopted aspects of foreign cultures (like Roman aristocrats who adopted Greek art). His theory, quoted by Ursula Brosseder, suggests that the Xiongnu's new subservience seemed 'to stimulate the inner need to demonstrate that one is a member of an Elite by borrowing foreign material goods and customs'. Hence the Xiongnu obsession with Chinese carriages, lacquered bowls, horse accessories and clothing.

For the chanyus and their élitist retinues, the system worked. Sure, they were subservient, but they were rich. Gifts continued to flow. As the graves themselves reveal, the chanyu's authority remained intact – for a while.

12

A CRISIS, A REVIVAL AND THE END OF THE XIONGNU

YES, A PROFITABLE PEACE. BUT THEN CAME A BRIEF RETURN to the old days of profitable war, leading to a very unprofitable end. War returned thanks to the disastrous rule of Wang Mang, the man who usurped the Han throne and set up the very short Xin dynasty, which divided two long periods of Han rule.

Wang Mang's dynasty was disastrous from the start. His idea of restoring universal confidence was to bring in a currency reform – six different materials (gold, silver, tortoiseshell, seashell, and two types of other metal) in twenty-eight different denominations. The people were so bewildered they refused to use the new system, which was promptly rescinded, leading to a boom in counterfeiting and illicit trading, which in turn led to arbitrary arrests and banishments.

Another of his more foolish acts was to tell the Wuhuan of Manchuria, who had been paying tribute to the Xiongnu for

200 years, that they did not need to pay any longer, presumably in an attempt to gain their support. The chanyu was furious. He invaded Wuhuan, seized 1,000 women and children as hostages, and demanded payment in full – 'Bring your horses, cattle, leather, fur and clothes in exchange for your women and children' – took delivery, and then held on to the hostages.

In a strange incident told by Sima Guang, Wang Mang then tried to impose his will on the Xiongnu by deception. A delegation of twelve generals, 'dressed in their most elaborate and luxuriant trappings', each in a carriage, each with his own military escort, had been told to tour the kingdom to display scrolls and other 'exhibits' to back Wang Mang's claim to authority. In AD 10, they arrived at the Xiongnu court laden with gifts, and bearing a new imperial seal, an incised stone beautifully wrapped in silk. The old seal was a formal acknowledgement that the Han emperor and the chanyu (Wuzhuliu in Chinese, Ujiuli in Mongolian) were equals, naming him as 'Emperor of the Xiongnu'. The new seal was inscribed with the words 'Xin – Xiongnu chanyu seal', naming the new dynasty, with no statement of equality. The envoys obviously hoped to hand it over and leave, without any fuss. Not so easy, as it turned out. There was to be an exchange of seals, and an official banquet. First came the banquet, with the increasingly anxious envoys eager to complete official business and get to bed. A Xiongnu officer warned the chanyu that he had better examine the new seal, but he brushed aside the idea. 'It really doesn't matter,' he said. 'How could they change the wording of a seal?' So he made the exchange, handing over the old seal, receiving the nicely wrapped new one and setting it aside for the next day. The banquet resumed. Many hours into the night and many toasts later, the nervous (and probably groggy) generals retired to their tent. One of them pointed out that when the chanyu finally saw the new seal, he would be furious and demand the old one back. Better make that impossible. How? By smashing it at once. So they did, giving the task to a junior officer. And next day, sure enough, the chanyu unwrapped the new seal, had it translated by his interpreter, objected bitterly that 'you have reduced the chanyu to a commoner!' and demanded the old seal back. The five envoys showed the bits of the broken seal, and had the nerve to claim total ignorance of how it happened. Nothing to do with us, they said, 'it had destroyed itself spontaneously'. What was the chanyu to do? To accuse them would at least cause a diplomatic incident, at worst a pitched battle with the envoys' military escort. In any event, no more gifts. All he could do was swallow his anger, and accept the new seal. Back in Chang'an, Wang Mang was well pleased. He ennobled the generals, the commanders of their military escort, and the junior officer who smashed the seal.

Trickery like this was no way to ensure friendly relations. When the chanyu heard of what had happened he was beside himself with rage. The Han emperors had been good to Huh-anye, he said, but this one 'is an imposter and has no right to be on the throne'.

Word spread. Minor tribes in the Western Regions defected to the Xiongnu, who regained control of their traditional lands. In response, Wang Mang broke off diplomatic relations with the Xiongnu and 'decided to flaunt the opulent wealth of his coffers and to demonstrate the awe-inspiring might of the Xin kingdom' by arbitrarily changing the chanyu's title to a Chinese term meaning 'Surrendered Slaves', and by trying to make this true by preparing for a massive, five-pronged invasion with an army of 300,000 that included 'every convict, prisoner, youth and warrior in the kingdom'. The aim was nothing less than the total destruction of the Xiongnu, forcing them out over their northern border and then dividing their territory into fifteen mini-states – all this to be funded by an economy still reeling from the effects of his currency reform.

A year later (11 AD), the troops still had not been fully gathered or deployed. In the border camps, as one general wrote in a memo to the emperor listing a catalogue of problems, 'the morale of the soldiers has deteriorated and their weapons have become blunt'. Moreover they had turned the border regions – made rich with pastures and cattle by decades of peace – into a wilderness while waiting for supplies that never came. 'The land is sandy and salty, there is no water and no grassland for miles . . . the autumn and winter months are bitterly cold and in the spring and summer months there are colossal sandstorms.' The horses and oxen were dying, the men so weakened by carrying cooking utensils, logs and charcoal that they were prey to pestilence and unable to fight, even if they could advance. Discipline broke down. Troops were becoming 'uncontrollably rowdy . . . and insufferably malicious'. Newly appointed officers 'exacted bribes from the populace'. An attempt to co-opt other border tribes to fight the Xiongnu turned vassals into enemies and drove them to defect to the Xiongnu. Since an attack by the gathering force would have almost certainly been catastrophic, no invasion was ordered and the demoralized troops stayed in their camps.

So: a precarious peace held between the empires, guaranteed

in part because Huhanye's grandson, Deng, was held in Chang'an, with an honorary title of 'Little Chanyu'. But at a lower level, violence ruled. Xiongnu raids continued. A general told Wang Mang that the 'Little Chanyu' had instigated them. In a fury, Wang Mang summoned all the representatives of his vassal states, 'and in front of the dignitaries, he had [Deng] decapitated'. Somehow, this was kept secret.

In AD 13, the chanyu died, succeeded by his younger brother, Ulei-Jodi, father of the boy-hostage Deng in Chang'an. Wang Mang used this as a chance to seek better relations by sending another gift-laden delegation to the Xiongnu, but again with a hidden agenda. The envoys were instructed to say that Deng was still alive, and then demand the release of twenty-seven Chinese officers who had defected to the Xiongnu. So it happened. The returning officers – caught, fettered and delivered – were treated as traitors, and roasted alive on some kind of 'torture device'. With peace of a sort declared, Wang Mang was finally able to disband most of the long-suffering border force that had been in camp for the last two years, awaiting orders for the never-to-be invasion. Wang Mang's deception backfired, of course, when the new chanyu discovered that his son had in fact been executed.

But still gifts trumped the death of his son. Ulei-Jodi offered to keep the peace, in exchange for the remains of his son. A delegation – headed by the daughter of Zhaojun – went to the border to receive not only Deng's remains but also those of several other Xiongnu nobles executed in unrecorded circumstances.

In China, the dynasty plunged on towards its chaotic end. Wang Mang was obsessed with the idea that ancient rites would save the day, if only they could be understood correctly.

Ministers ignored their duties to struggle with impenetrable texts. The emperor, trusting nobody, insisted that all decisions came from him or his compliant corps of eunuchs. The court was plagued by executions, plots and suicides. Civil servants went unpaid, and relied on bribes. Prices rose, and so did taxes. Ordinary people took to crime. 'Itinerant bands of marauders plundered, pillaged and robbed.' Commoners prostrated themselves outside the palace, begging for relief from injustice. Revolts multiplied. But to bring the emperor bad news was to court execution; the way to promotion was to say that all was well.

In 18 AD, Ulei-Jodi died, being succeeded by his younger brother Hudurshi. Wang Mang remained as treacherous as ever. When the new chanyu offered to come to Chang'an to pay homage and sent a delegation to the border to discuss terms, the two leaders – another of Zhaojun's daughters and her husband Xubu Dang – were ambushed, kidnapped and taken to Chang'an as prisoners, the idea being that assassins would be sent to kill the chanyu and replace him with the kidnapped Xubu Dang. When the chanyu heard the news, 'he was greatly infuriated by the sordid and appalling behaviour of Wang Mang', and stepped up the raids.

In response, Wang Mang turned to ever more desperate measures. He offered rewards for anyone who could suggest new ways to invade and conquer the Xiongnu. Ideas flowed in, each more crazy than the last. Anti-hunger medication was one; another was a flying machine that would act as a spy-in-the-sky over Xiongnu territory. Sima Guang says the device was shown to Wang Mang. If even partially true, and discounting the Greek legend of Daedalus and Icarus, this could have been the first attempt at manned flight. This is an adaptation of Ban Gu's version of the incident, as translated in Joseph Needham's *Science and Civilisation in China* (Vol. 4, 2):

> One man said that he could fly a thousand *li* in a day, and spy out the movements of the Xiongnu. Wang Mang tested him without delay. He took the pinions of a great bird for his two wings. His head and whole body were covered over with feathers, and all was interconnected by means of rings and knots. He flew a distance of several hundred paces, and then fell to the ground. Wang Mang saw that the methods could not be used, but wishing to gain prestige from these inventors he ordered that they should be given military appointments and presented with chariots and horses.

Could there be any truth in this? Not a chance. There is no way he could have left the ground. No bird-man or wing-flapping machine has ever flown, and no flying bird, reptile or mammal of more than 72 kilos[1] has ever existed (that we know of yet). With wings of the right size, shape, weight and structure, could the inventor have glided, leaping from a tower or cliff, or being towed by galloping horses? No, because no one would understand the principles of powered or gliding flight for another 1,800 years.[2] If the Birdman of Chang'an was real, he would have been good for a laugh, but not for a flight.

---

[1] Seventy-two kilos is the top estimated weight of *Argentavis magnificens*, the biggest bird so far discovered. It became extinct between about 7 and 11 million years ago. Some large pterosaurs may have weighed more, but estimates vary too widely to be accepted.

[2] The first man-carrying glider was built by Sir George Cayley in 1804.

Wang Mang was not put off by failure:

On one occasion the emperor visited the Tower of the Golden Phoenix to receive Buddhist ordination. He caused many prisoners condemned to death to be brought forward, had them harnessed with great bamboo mats as wings, and ordered them to fly down to the ground from the top of the tower. This was called a 'liberation of living creatures'. All the prisoners died, but the emperor contemplated the spectacle with enjoyment and much laughter.

Then, in AD 22–23, Wang Mang, to show that he was still in control, dyed his grey hair and beard black, selected 120 new concubines for his harem, freed all the criminals in his kingdom, and offered the rebels a last chance to surrender, or face total destruction at the hands of his million-strong army, reinforced with 'large numbers of tigers, leopards, rhinoceroses, elephants and other wild beasts'. He was living a fantasy. In the countryside, rebel groups, determined to reinstate the Han dynasty, united to form an army. In the summer of 23, a great siege (Kunyang, in central China)[3] ended with the total defeat of the government forces. Everywhere, ordinary people joined in the revolt. On the first day of September, rebels broke into Chang'an. 'Rebels, looters and insurgents, moving like a tidal wave' set fire to the palace doors, yelling for Wang Mang, who hid in a back room, delirious with panic, trying to decide with his astrologer what seat would be the most auspicious. Early next day, with his last loyal troops and family members being slaughtered by the mob, he fled to

[3] Now in Ye County, Pingdingshan Prefecture, Henan.

an island in the middle of a lake, where, finally, he was found, stabbed and beheaded. His head was set on a spike and displayed in the provisional capital of the restored Han dynasty, until 'angry mobs viciously wrenched away the head, kicking it hither and thither'. So ended the shortest dynasty in Chinese history, leading to two years of chaos until the Eastern (or Later) Han (25–220) brought stability once more.

All of which left the Xiongnu in excellent spirits. Their renewed self-confidence lasted through the overthrow of Wang Mang, the chaos that attended the return of the old dynasty as the Eastern Han, and the violence that followed. Once, two top Han officials demanded some woodland near Zhangye on the Xiongnu side of the border. 'What is this?' the outraged chanyu replied. This land had been passed from father to son for five generations! They used these woods 'for making domed huts and carts . . . it is the land of our forefathers and we dare not discard it.'[4] For a while, it looked as if the Xiongnu were about to restore Modun's empire.

But rivalry undermined them. An heir apparent named Bi (actually, Khailoshi-Jodi, renamed on the insistence of the Chinese, who had passed a law that people should have only a single name, a Chinese one) was pushed from the succession in AD 48 and took off with his followers to Ordos, where he was recognized as chanyu. He should have returned to claim the throne, but he remained, in security and comfort. His action split the Xiongnu into a northern, Mongolian branch and a southern, Chinese-based one, which became one of several 'barbarian' hordes living inside the Great Wall.

[4] Miller, *Power Politics.*

The northern branch – wealthy with Han gifts, their aristocrats burying each other in lavish Han-style graves – lived on, in obscurity, because no one in China thought them worth recording. For forty years, chanyus came and went, occasionally raiding, once again becoming an affront to the Han, more so now that the southern Xiongnu were family members inside the Great Wall. In AD 87, a chanyu stepped briefly from the shadows. His name was Youliu, and the only other thing known about him is that the up-and-coming tribe from Manchuria, the Xianbei, reached his capital, caught him, beheaded him and skinned him.

That was the beginning of the real end. Tens of thousands of Xiongnu fled south. In Chang'an, a ten-year-old, He, had just become emperor. It happened that an ambitious and arrogant general, Dou Xian, brother of the empress dowager and the boy-emperor's uncle, was in prison after being implicated in an assassination. To regain his freedom and influence, he offered to crush the Xiongnu and end a 300-year menace for good and all. His sister agreed. In AD 89, he headed north with a huge army of Han, Southern Xiongnu, Xianbei and several other barbarian contingents.

What happened next is worth telling in detail, because the campaign was well recorded and because hard evidence for it recently emerged. Almost always, historical sources are marred by distortion and exaggeration. But here the source is backed by an inscription discovered in 2017. So the story is actually two stories: the events and the discovery.

To record his coming victory, Dou Xian had with him Ban Gu, imperial librarian and the most eminent historian of his time. At fifty-seven, Ban Gu had been working on his monumental *Han Shu* (*Book of Han*), his history of the previous dynasty, for thirty years. History was a delicate business. Earlier in his life, he had been imprisoned just for starting his work, but he had deeply impressed the emperor and been encouraged to continue. He would eventually die in prison, accused by a jealous rival, but right now he was at the height of his prestige, acting as historian-at-large.

He could not have been thrilled at the prospect. His advice was exactly the reverse of what was happening. The way to deal with the Xiongnu was to maintain 'hostile vigilance': keep clear, but if you have to deal with them, be tough. Here is his uncompromising opinion: Those who live beyond the Wall . . .

> . . . are greedy and desirous of gain; they wear their hair down their backs and fasten their garments on the left; they have human faces but the hearts of wild beasts . . . They are separated from us by mountains and valleys and cut off by the desert. By these means did Heaven and Earth divide inner from outer. Therefore the Sage Kings treated them like birds and beasts, neither concluding treaties with them, nor going forth and attacking them. To conclude agreements with them is to waste gifts and suffer deception. To attack them is to exhaust our armies and provoke raids. Their land cannot be cultivated so as to produce food; their people cannot be made subjects and tamed. For these reasons they are kept outside and not taken as relatives, they are kept distant and not accepted as kin.

Yet here he was, crossing what ought not to be crossed, attacking a people who had often been treated as kin, and recording an invasion that should not have been. He kept quiet, and did what his emperor wanted.

Things worked out well. Advancing in three columns across the Gobi in the summer of 89, Dou Xian first met the Xiongnu east of the Three Beauties range, where the Altai Mountains dip into gravel, sand and gnarled saxaul bushes.[5] There are few details, but the allies sent the Xiongnu, under a chanyu named Bei (note the Chinese-style name) in headlong retreat north-west. Dou Xian pursued them for 180 kilometres, out of the Gobi, across grasslands into the Khangai Mountains. The Xiongnu regrouped on gently billowing plains near a 140-metre hill named Yanran. Again, a great victory; again, no details, except that it was great.

To mark the victory, Dou Xian ordered his tame historian, Ban Gu, to write a memorial and have it inscribed in stone on a cliff face near the top of the nearby hill. When Ban Gu got home, he recorded what he had written: an account of the battle ending in a formal, traditional verse of five lines and seven characters per line.

This is the account that he wrote:[6]

In the first year of Yung Yuan's reign [Emperor He as he became], in the autumn [actually July], the National Maternal Uncle, Dou Xian, was appointed the Commander-in-Chief to show the power of Han over the Xiongnu. Among his subordinate generals – as powerful as eagles and tigers – were troops from the Southern Xiongnu, Tenger Khan [the chanyu of the

---

[5] Near the Three Beauties is the canyon of red sandstone known as Bayan Zag, 'Rich in Saxauls'. Here, in 1923, the American explorer Roy Chapman Andrews and his team discovered the dinosaur fossils that are now in the American Museum of Natural History in New York. He called the place the Flaming Cliffs.
[6] With thanks to Alatan, Professor of English, Inner Mongolia University of Technology, for his translation.

Southern Xiongnu][7] and Shi, Rong and Di khans. The 30,000 horsemen and 3,000 chariots divided into four parts. When the troops were on the march, the dust covered the sky and the earth, flags flying, their armour outshining Heaven. They came to the Gobi, and killed many of the enemy, so that their bodies lay scattered here and there. Then passing mountains and rivers, they came to Yanran Mountain. They followed the footprints of the Xiongnu and set fire to their tents wherever they found them, expressing their anger against them. They comforted the souls of their ancestors, and fortified their rule so it could be passed down to their descendants, expressing the power of the whole land. This one victory assured peace for ever. Thus Our victory is inscribed on the rock of this mountain top, as an expression of Our royal power and virtue.

The verse, reproduced in the fourth-century *Hou Han Shu* (*Book of the Later Han*), roughly translates as:

The fine Sovereign's armies campaigned into the desolate
   remote [regions],
Destroyed the fierce and cruel, brought order to beyond
   the seas,
Far-reached those distant [places], joined the territories
   and borders,
Made *feng* [offerings] at Spirit Mount, erected a glorious
   tablet,
Recorded the splendour of the Emperor, renowned for
   ten thousand generations.[8]

[7] This was his title, Heavenly Khan. His name was Xiulan Shisu-quuti (in pinyin), Syuulan Shiju-Khoudi (in Mongolian); he ruled 88–93.
[8] Translation by Miller in *Power Politics*.

An inscription was not enough. This victory needed a spiritual dimension. That meant ritual sacrifices, the *feng* rituals mentioned in the poem. Sima Qian devotes a long chapter to the subject. These hugely significant rites, usually linked with others known as *shan*, were performed from the earliest times, since at least 2200 BC. Unfortunately, rulers had to qualify to perform them, as Sima Qian writes: 'When each dynasty attains the height of its glory, then the *feng* and *shan* are celebrated, but when it reaches a period of decline, they are no longer performed.' So there had been long gaps of hundreds of years, or even 'as many as a thousand', between enactments of these rites, with the result that 'the details of the ancient ceremony have been completely lost'. Never mind. There was a sacrifice of some kind to mark the height of Han glory, which was enough for it to be called *feng*.

The Yanran Inscription became famous as a memorial to the final, stamping-on-the-head-of-the-snake end of the Xiongnu menace. There was one problem: no one knew where the Yanran Mountain was, so no one could check that Ban Gu's record was a true copy of the inscription. Perhaps the cliff recorded a different version of events. There were several attempts to find it, with no success. In 1990, two herders avoiding a rainstorm sheltered beneath the cliff, noticed the inscription and reported their find. But Mongolia was embroiled in the collapse of Communism. No one could do anything. But at least Mongolian scholars knew the position. Now they needed Chinese involvement to help with the language.

In 2014, they contacted Professor Jakhadal Chimeddorj, an archaeologist and Vice-President of the Inner Mongolia University in Hohhot. In July 2017, a joint Chinese and Mongolian expedition went to the spot and took rubbings. The following month, Chimeddorj and other team members from Chinggis Khan University in Ulaanbaatar announced that they could read 220 of the 260 legible characters (another 32 having been eroded away), and yes, the one recorded in historical sources was the same as the inscription devised by Ban Gu, almost to the day 1,928 years previously.

Actually, it wasn't quite the end for the Northern Xiongnu. The so-called 'last of the chanyus' was killed in 93. 'So-called' because sources do not agree on his name, and Mongolian sources list a further dozen pretenders to the title, on into the third century. But sixty years before that, by the mid-second century, the Xianbei ruled Mongolia, and if any northern Xiongnu remained free, they were nothing but robber bands. The rest had vanished into the hidden heart of Central Asia, never to be heard of again – until two hundred years later, on the far side of the continent, there appeared a tribe with a similar lifestyle and a strangely similar name. That's another story, told in the next chapter.

But the Southern Xiongnu remained. After the Han dynasty ended in 220 and China collapsed into a muddle of mini-states (between the third and the fifth centuries), they briefly (311–349) took much of north China. Almost a century later, to revive and extend this mayfly empire, a Xiongnu leader founded a new kingdom.

His name was Helian Bobo, chanyu of a state he called Da Xia (Great Xia, after an ancient dynasty, and also a name taken on 600 years later by the Tangut empire of West Xia). His claim to fame is that he built the only known Xiongnu city, in 413–19, a few years after the formation of Da Xia in 407. Standing on the south-east border of Ordos, it is called

Tong Wan Cheng (Ruling Ten Thousand Cities). Today, the area is part of Shaanxi, but only because in the 1940s the provincial boss was in debt to the top man in Shaanxi, so he simply claimed a slab of Ordos, transferred it to Shaanxi and redrew the border. History, however, tells us that this is really an Ordos story.

Actually, it is two stories. The first belongs to the city, the second to the guide who met me in the car park, a large one, for this place is beginning to attract a lot of visitors. The car park overlooked an impressive sight – an off-white tower and a wall hundreds of metres long. Looking for information, I glanced at a stall selling tourist items. Nearby stood a fine-looking old man with a weather-beaten face and short-cropped grey hair. He introduced himself as Ma Junwang, local resident all his life, and author of a pamphlet on the history of the city. There it was, for sale on the stall. He was the perfect guide.

The ruins – the 40-metre watch-tower, the 30-metre wall, the bulwarks known as 'horse-faces' – had the colour of whipped cream. That, Mr Ma explained, was because Bobo's capital, built by 40,000 labourers, was not made of bricks but of layer upon layer of quartz sand and white clay, turned into a sort of cement with rice flour. This was the local equivalent of the rammed earth used to build the Han Great Wall, the ruins of which you can still see today weaving across southern Ordos.

It had survived the last 1,600 years pretty well. 'Yes,' said Mr Ma as we were about to go inside, 'that's because the Red Guards didn't blow it all up during the Cultural Revolution in the late 1960s.'

'*What?*'

'It was part of the campaign against old things. The Red

Guards blew up some of the wall over there, and found some cannonballs, so they became afraid and left the rest alone.'

This was fascinating. Why would they become afraid? And if Ma had been in this area all his life, did he see them do it?

He seemed a little embarrassed to go on. Intrigued, I pressed him to describe his experience, and his story became more and more extraordinary. 'We were living in a cave at the time, and . . .'

'Living in a *cave*?'

'Yes, lots of families did that. In caves we had dug at the bottom of the wall. This place was our home. The grass in the city was good pasture. We had two caves. We kept pigs in the other one.'

In 1967, their lives were interrupted by the local effects of the Cultural Revolution. Red Guards arrived. As a poor farmer, aged only twenty, he was not going to fight these badly educated teenagers revelling in their power to destroy.

'They made me join them, so I saw it all. They discovered these cannonballs, and the leader thought they had better tell the authorities. Archaeologists came and said it was probably the arsenal, and told them to leave it alone. So they did.'

As we walked up the slope to the entrance, Ma finished his story. He went on living in the ruined city, and developed such an interest in it that he became the local expert, and eventually the guide.

By now we were inside the city, on a raised platform which may have been used by Bobo to review his troops. A few buried cannonballs broke the surface. From there you could see the whole city, a square of walls and corner-towers that measured 6 kilometres around. That's where his family's cave had been, Ma said, pointing to a far wall, beyond the trees and shrubs that covered the undulating ruins. Once, 100,000 people had lived here, around a long-gone lake, and continued to do so for many generations after Bobo's short-lived realm was conquered in 431 by Northern Wei, a 'barbarian' state controlled by the Xianbei, one of the half-dozen kingdoms of a divided China. Da Xia lasted only twenty-four years, but the Xiongnu inhabitants remained there for another four hundred years, after which the city was abandoned and forgotten and the last of the Xiongnu merged with local populations and finally faded from view.

Ma led the way, winding between slender trees to the West Gate, unearthed in 2008. The excavation made an 11-metre pit, around which I picked my way precariously in search of a good angle for a picture. Other than the towers and the walls, it was about the only sign of the city's former glory.

Its rediscovery dates from 1845, when a Ming general came and called the place the White City, which is what locals sometimes call it today, Tsagaan Balgasun in Mongolian. No one knows what the city was called originally, because Da Xia did not record its history. It was the first scholars, arriving in the 1950s, who named the place Tong Wan Cheng, picking it up from a phrase in a Chinese source about Bobo's ambitions to rule 10,000 cities.

As Ma guided us back to the car park, a crowd of tourists came past, clicking cameras and picking up bits of roof tiles, a hint of growing interest in a site that will soon, surely, get the attention it deserves as the last and grandest memorial to the Xiongnu.

13

FROM XIONGNU TO HUN, POSSIBLY

Meanwhile, some (perhaps most) of the northern Xiongnu had vanished into the depths of Central Asia. Or possibly not. For, two hundred years later, there emerged from the great sweep of grassland on the other side of Central Asia a tribe with a similar lifestyle – tent-dwellers with wagons, supreme mounted archers – and a similar name: the Huns, who, a century later still, would be a major force in the collapse of the Roman empire. It is a process worth looking at in detail, because it was a mirror image of what had been going on in China, a repeat of the old confrontation between mobile, acquisitive barbarians and stable, rich urbanites. The difference between the two confrontations is that China hit back and survived; Rome couldn't and collapsed.

Did the Xiongnu become the Huns? Chinese historians make no distinction between the two, and both are 'Hunnu' in Mongolian, so in China and Mongolia there is no doubt. Others are less certain.

For centuries, no one in Europe had any idea of where the Huns came from. As Rome declined and fell, people said their homeland was somewhere beyond the edge of the known world, east of the Maeotic marshes – the shallow and silty Sea of Azov – on the other side of the Kerch Straits that link this inland sea to its parent, the Black Sea. But otherwise, all was a blank, filled by folklore. They were sent by God as a punishment. Or they had fought with Achilles in the Trojan War. They were any of the Asian tribes named by ancient authors, 'Scythian' being the most popular option. Any or all of these.

Come the Enlightenment, a French Sinologist, Joseph de Guignes, filled the hole. De Guignes – as he is in most catalogues; or Deguines, as he spelled himself – usually appears in academic footnotes, if anywhere. He deserves more, because his theory about Hun origins started the controversy.

Born in 1721, de Guignes was still in his twenties when he was appointed 'interpreter' for oriental languages at the Royal Library in Paris, Chinese being his particular forte. He at once embarked upon the monumental work that made his name. News of this brilliant young polymath spread across the Channel. In 1751, at the age of thirty, he was elected to the Royal Society in London – one of the youngest members ever, and a foreigner. He owed this honour to a draft of his major work, displaying, as the citation remarks, 'everything that one might expect from a book so considerable, which he has ready for the press'. Well, not quite. It took him another five years to get his work on the press, and a further two to get it off; his *Histoire générale des Huns, des Turcs et des*

Mogols was published in five volumes between 1756 and 1758. His big idea was to prove that all eastern peoples – Chinese, Turks, Mongols, Huns – were actually descendants of Noah, who had wandered eastwards after the Flood. This became an obsession, and the subject of his next book, which sparked a sharp riposte from sceptics, followed by an anti-riposte from the impervious de Guignes. He remained impervious up to his death almost fifty years later.

His history was never translated into English. But one aspect of his theory took root, and flourished. Attila's Huns, he said, were descendants of the 'Hiong-nou'. He does not argue his case, simply stating as a fact that the 'Hiong-nou' were the Huns, period. 'First Book,' he starts, 'History of the Ancient Huns'. A warlike nomadic tribe had vanished from Central Asia in the mid-second century. Two hundred years later, the Huns emerged at the other end of Central Asia, similar in lifestyle and name. That was enough for de Guignes, and for his successors, the weightiest of whom was Edward Gibbon in his *Decline and Fall of the Roman Empire*. In Gibbon, de Guignes found magisterial backing. The Huns who threatened Rome were descendants of the Xiongnu made . . .

> . . . formidable by the matchless dexterity with which they managed their bows and their horses; by their hardy patience in supporting the inclemency of the weather; and by the incredible speed of their march, which was seldom checked by torrents or precipices, by the deepest rivers, or by the most lofty mountains.

Gibbon used words as artillery, blasting doubt before it had a chance to grow. For the next two centuries, it was taken as a fact that the Huns were the Xiongnu, reborn in poverty. The 1911 edition of the *Encyclopædia Britannica* relies on the misspelled 'de Guiques'. René Grousset, the great French expert in Central Asia, writing in the 1930s in *L'Empire des Steppes* (and in the English edition of 1970, see Bibliography), refers to the 'Hsiung-nu of the west' – that is, the remnants of those under Zhizhi who were defeated in 36 BC – 'who under the name of Huns were to be the adversaries of the Roman world'. In his Historical *Atlas of China* of 1935, the German orientalist Albert Herrmann has a spread on the 'Hsiung-Nu or Huns'.

About the same time, it occurred to some sceptical scholars that there was absolutely no evidence to bridge the gap between the two. Indeed, the difference between the sophisticated nobility buried in Gol Mod and Attila's impoverished hordes is striking. The theory fell into limbo. As Edward Thompson, one-time Professor of Classics at Nottingham University, baldly wrote in his 1948 book on the Huns,[1] 'This view has now been exploded and abandoned.'

In fact it was never exploded, just never established, and it has recently regained lost ground. The two tribes were briefly so close in time and place that it is hard to believe they were separate. The remnants of the Xiongnu, fleeing from central Mongolia int the 90s along trade routes that led through the Ili Valley in southern Kazakhstan, would have reached the Syrdarya River by about 120. In round figures, that's 2,800 kilometres in thirty years, or a mere 90 kilometres a year. In 160, the Greek polymath Ptolemy mentions the 'Khoinoi', commonly equated with the Chuni, the initial *ch* sounded as

---

[1] E. A. Thompson, *A History of Attila and the Huns* (see Bibliography).

in the Scottish *loch*, which makes them sound pretty much like 'Huns'. These people he placed between two other tribes, the most distant of which, the Roxelani, probably lived on the Don, thus putting the Huns just north of the Sea of Azov – the 'Maeotic marshes' mentioned later by Roman authors. The gap has narrowed to 2,000 kilometres and forty years – a gap easily crossed at the slow pace of 50 kilometres a year.

The Huns moved a lot further and faster than that. They were wanderers, in need of a base and pastures. But with every kilometre westward, they would find pasturage increasingly reduced by other nomads and by settled communities. With little to offer other than wool, felt and domestic animals, their only remaining option would have been theft. They turned from pastoral nomads into a robber band, for whom violence would be as much a way of life as it became for wandering Vikings.

Conquest demanded unity and direction, and for that we come at last to the final element in their rise to fame and fortune: leadership. Some time in the fourth century the Huns acquired their first named leader, the first to bring himself and his people to the attention of the outside world. He was called something like Balamber or Balamur, and hardly anything at all is known about him except his name. It was he who inspired his people and focused their fighting potential to attack tribe after tribe, establishing a tradition of leadership that would, in the end, produce Attila. In AD 350 the Huns crossed the Volga and approached the outer fringes of the Roman world, dislodging a host of other tribes as they went.

In the mid-fourth century, this grassland was dominated by the Sarmatians, a loose confederation of Iranian people who had taken over from the Scythians more than 500 years before. The Sarmatians specialized in fighting with lances, their warriors protected by conical caps and mailed coats, but no match for the Hun tornado.

One group of Sarmatians were the Alans, a wide-ranging sub-federation known as As to the Persians. (It is from their name, by the way, that 'Aryan' is derived, *l* shifting to *r* in some Iranian languages; thus the tribe so admired by Hitler turns out not to be Germanic at all.) Now we are getting into a region and a tribe that became known to the Romans. Ammianus Marcellinus, the fourth-century Roman historian, says they were cattle-herding nomads who lived in wagons roofed with bark and worshipped a sword stuck in the ground, a belief that Attila himself would adopt. They were terrific riders on their tough little horses. The Alans, more European than Asian, with full beards and blue eyes, were lovers of war, experts with the sword and the lasso, issuing terrifying yells in battle, reviling old men because they had not died fighting. They were said to flay their slain enemies and turn their skins into horse-trappings. Theirs was an extensive culture – their tombs have been found by the hundred in southern Russia – and a flexible one, happy to assimilate captives and to be assimilated. The Huns blew them apart, clan by clan. The Alans then formed fragments of the explosion of tribes that tore the Roman empire to pieces. They also had a talent for retaining their own identity. In the slurry of wandering peoples, the Alans were like grit, widely mixed but always abrasive. Within a couple of generations, different clans would in some cases become useful recruits for the Huns, in others allies of Rome. Their remnants in the Caucasus would transmute into the Ossetians of southern Russia and Georgia: the first two syllables of this name recall their Persian appellation, As, with a Mongol-style plural -*ut* (so the current name of the little Russian enclave known as North Ossetia–Alania doubly emphasizes its roots). At the other end of the empire, they would join both the Goths on their march into Spain – some derive the name Catalonia from a combination of Goth and Alan – and the Vandals, who swept them up on their flight to North Africa in about 420.

Across the Dnieper lived the Ostrogoths – 'Eastern' Goths – members of a huge Germanic tribe that had wandered into eastern Europe and southern Russia two centuries before, and had now divided into two branches, the others being the Visi- ('Western') Goths. The Ostrogoths were settled farming folk, but their venerable chief, Ermanaric,[2] would have been something of a role model for an aspiring Hun leader. He was the central figure of an estate that straggled from the Black Sea to the Baltic, from its core, which Ermanaric ruled directly, out to an ever looser network of vassals, allies, tribute-payers and trade partners. Balamber, with his Hun and Alan cavalry, smashed Ermanaric's army just north of the Black Sea in about 376. The loose federation of tribes collapsed like a burst balloon; the old Ostrogoth committed suicide; and Balamber took a Gothic princess in marriage to seal the takeover.

At the Dniester, the Visigoths of today's Romania were next in line. These had become a proud and sophisticated people, now settled in towns, with a respect for law and order

---

[2] Ermanaric's name probably derives from Hermann-Rex, King Hermann, the Gothic having adopted the Latin word and turned it into *reiks*, which, when retransliterated, became *ric*. It was a common ending for the names of Gothic aristocrats.

administered by their ruler. Rome, having given up thoughts of direct rule, treated the Visigoths as trade partners, valuing the supply of slaves, grain, cloth, wine and coins. After the Roman Emperor Valens acknowledged Visigothic independence in 369, it seemed both would benefit: their agreement established a mutual trade link, mutual respect, a buffer state for Rome against the barbarian hordes of Inner Asia.

Rome could be resisted, but not the advancing Huns. A line of defences along the Dniester was easily bypassed when the Huns ignored the Gothic army, crossed the river by night and made a surprise assault on the Goths from the rear. After a hasty retreat across present-day Moldova, Gothic morale collapsed, driving them across the Danube into Thrace. Behind them, advancing from the Ukrainian lowlands, came Attila's immediate forebears, on a 75-kilometre march over the Carpathians, winding uphill along the road that now leads from Kolomyya through the Carpathian National Nature Park, spreading wagon-trains and herds over the Hungarian grasslands, which became their base.

Hungary is a long way from where the Xiongnu vanished, and links are hard to find. There are arguments both for and against.

In 1986 a joint Russian–Mongolian expedition excavated a grave-site in the far west of Mongolia, in the Altai Mountains. Their report refers to the find as a 'Hun' site, reflecting the Mongolian eagerness to equate Xiongnu and Hun, but it is clearly Xiongnu. The five graves were remarkable because they had not been thoroughly vandalized. All contained wooden coffins, and four of the five held the remains of bows: bits of bone or horn, used as 'ears' at the end of the limbs and to reinforce the central section. Oddly, the graves contained no actual bows or the remains of any, only ears. The four graves had in turn three ears, three ears, two ears and four ears, and each grave also contained a varying number of the horn strips used to reinforce a bow's wooden body. Many bits of different bows, but no complete bows. There can be only one conclusion: the bits were never part of a bow, or bows. Speaking of one of the graves, one of the greatest of experts on the Huns, Otto Maenchen-Helfen, concluded: 'The people buried the dead warrior with a sham bow.'[3] A ghost bow, more like. Once suggested, the idea is obvious. Bows took years to make. And these were not the graves of wealthy chieftains. It was natural that grieving families would not waste such precious, life-and-death objects by burying them. For our purposes, though, the finds had particular significance. The ears were of different lengths, from which the authors concluded that the bows were asymmetrical, the upper limb being longer than the lower limb. Both Xiongnu bows and Hun bows were asymmetrical – for reasons that remain obscure – which suggests a link between Hun and Xiongnu.

There's more indirect evidence in cauldrons. You cannot discuss Huns and avoid cauldrons. There are some 150 examples of these heavy, metre-high, round-bodied, cylindrical objects, found all across Eurasia, from Ordos and northern Mongolia and Siberia to Hungary (with one bit from France, where Attila campaigned in his later years). About twenty of them are considered Hunnish. It sounds like evidence to link east and west, Xiongnu and Hun. One problem is that they

[3] Otto J. Maenchen-Helfen, *The World of the Huns* (see Bibliography).

are very varied in design – no two are exactly alike; some have legs, some a small stand, some no support at all, and they have many different types of handle and decoration Another problem is that many groups made them. They seem to have been used for boiling up vast clan meals and/or for funeral ceremonies. They are solid, practical objects, with none of the sophistication of Chinese bronzes. There are some individual features – Hun cauldrons are thinner, with rectangular handles, some with mushroom-shaped additions; Sarmatian ones are wider-bellied with semi-circular handles. Some scholars see a progression from Xiongnu to Hun based on handle-decorations, but it is impossible to date cauldrons unless they are found in a dateable tomb. As Otto Maenchen-Helfen puts it, 'The crude, often barbaric copper cauldrons link the Huns with the area of the Xiongnu confederacy,' which is almost, but not quite good enough to equate the two.

Similar arguments are made about other objects – bronze mirrors, which are mostly Chinese, but were also made by nomads; gold plaques; glass beads used in embroidery, along with coral, mother-of-pearl, lapis lazuli – all were used by all Eurasian cultures, including Xiongnu and Hun, though none can be used to prove a link between the two.

If Hun and Xiongnu are not quite joined by archaeology, what about folklore? If there was a link, isn't it odd that the Huns did not seem to have a folk memory of it? The Xiongnu's Turkish successors in Mongolia were happy to claim them as ancestors until they, too, were driven westwards in the eighth century; but Attila, much closer to the Xiongnu in time, apparently never did. He had his bards, but no eyewitness recorded them singing of all-conquering forebears. Again, the argument can be made to run both ways.

Sometimes folkloric information is astonishingly enduring – the Trojan War remained alive in oral accounts for centuries before Homer wrote it down. Sometimes it fades fast, especially during a long migration. The Mongols, too, forgot their origins: their great foundation epic, *The Secret History of the Mongols*, says only that they sprang from a wolf and a doe, and had crossed an ocean or lake to arrive in Mongolia perhaps around 500 years before the *Secret History* was written, probably in 1229. The Huns seem to have forgotten much faster – in 250 years – recalling nothing of their forebears; nothing, at least, that anyone recorded.

Perhaps there was something more active than mere forgetfulness at work, if Xiongnu turned to Hun. Once reduced from imperial grandeur to impoverished bands, perhaps the Huns became ashamed of their decline, and simply refused to mention their former greatness to their children. I have never heard of such a process being recorded; but then, it wouldn't be, would it? One generation of taboo – 'Don't mention China!' – would be enough. That is the way some languages are lost, obliterated by the higher status of a dominant culture.[4]

There's very little help from language. Though Attila employed interpreters and secretaries, no one wrote Hunnish, only Latin or Greek, the languages of the dominant culture, with its inbuilt prejudice against barbarian tongues. The Mongolians look on the Xiongnu as ancestors, and recent DNA analysis of Xiongnu bones reveals a genetic link between the two. There must have been an overlap between incoming Mongols

---

[4] It almost happened to Basque in post-war France, where the government insisted that Basque made children stupid and banned its use in schools. In the 1950s and 1960s, many Basques grew up not speaking the language of their parents and grandparents. There has been a revival since.

and some remaining Xiongnu. But very few words that are absolutely, undoubtedly Hunnish or Xiongnu have survived. Some names, yes – but they are Sinified or Latinized.

To tally the possible, the probable and the certain: the Huns were probably of Turkic stock, probably spoke a Turkic language (which shared distant roots with Mongolian), were possibly a remnant of migrating Xiongnu, and were certainly nothing whatever to do with the Slavic and Germanic tribes into whom they so rudely barged. It will take DNA analysis, I think, to tell whether Attila's genes owed anything to Modun's 500 years earlier.

Let's assume that the Huns were descendants of the Xiongnu, much changed by their epic journey across Eurasia. Even if they weren't, they were a part of the multiple migrations caused in part by the Xiongnu's rise, fall and flight. The Huns were something new in history: a juggernaut that could live by pillage. Like sharks, they had become expert predators, honed to fitness by constant movement, adapted to roam the inland sea of grass, blotting up lesser tribes, until they emerged from the unknown and forced themselves on to the consciousness of the sophisticated, urbanized Europeans. Their impact was catastrophic, at first indirectly and then extremely directly. Lacking anything from Hun sources, this part of the story can only be told from the Roman point of view.

In 376, disturbing news reached the Emperor Valens in Constantinople. Valens, co-ruler with his brother of the Roman empire, was familiar enough with troubles on his frontiers, but there had never been anything like this. Far to the north, beyond the Balkans, on the marshy northern banks of the Danube, refugees were gathering by the thousand, destitute and starving, fleeing their farms and villages in terror. In the words of the historian Ammianus, 'a hitherto unknown race of men had appeared from some remote corner of the earth, uprooting and destroying everything in its path like a whirlwind descending from high mountains'.[5] These aliens were mounted archers, horsemen such as no one in the Empire had ever seen before, riding as if forged into their saddles, so that man and mount seemed one, like the centaurs of old.

In Roman eyes, these were the vilest creatures imaginable. Their opinions, all wrong, were even more prejudiced than Chinese ones of their barbarians. The Huns came from the north, and everyone knew that the colder the climate was, the more barbaric the people were. To paraphrase Ammianus, who never saw a Hun himself, they were squat, with thick necks, so prodigiously ugly and bent that they might be two-legged animals, or the figures crudely carved from stumps which are seen on the parapets of bridges. There was nothing like them for cruelty and ugliness, the one accentuating the other, because they cut their baby boys' cheeks so that, when they became men, their beards grew in patches, if they grew at all. They knew nothing of metal, had no religion and lived like savages, without fire, eating their food raw, living off roots and meat tenderized by placing it under their horses' saddles. No buildings, of course, not so much as a reed hut; indeed, they feared the very idea of venturing under a roof. Once they had put their necks into some dingy shirt, they never took it off or changed it until it rotted. Granted, they were wonderful horsemen; but even this was an expression of barbarism, for they practically lived on horseback,

[5] Ammianus Marcellinus, *The Later Roman Empire* (see Bibliography).

eating, drinking, sleeping, even defecating in the saddle. Their shoes were so shapeless, their legs so bowed that they could hardly walk. Jordanes, the Gothic historian, was no less insulting. These stunted, foul and puny tribesmen, offspring of witches and unclean spirits, 'had, if I may say so, a sort of shapeless lump, not a head, with pin-holes rather than eyes'.[6] It was amazing they could see at all, given that 'the light that enters the dome of the skull can hardly reach the receding eyeballs . . . Though they live in the form of men, they have the cruelty of wild beasts.' These are judgements that have echoed down the ages. Practically everyone is happy to quote everyone else, including Gibbon, in condemning the Huns as smelly, bandy-legged, nasty, brutish and short.

It would take some years for the 'unknown race' to appear en masse, under their most effective and devastating leader, Attila, but already their eruption across the steppes of today's southern Russia and Ukraine had shunted tribe against tribe, the last of which now clamoured on the Danube's banks.

Valens's immediate concern was not the thud of alien hooves but the horde of refugees. They were Visigoths. Valens, approaching fifty and with twelve years of ruling behind him, knew a good deal about the proud and independent Visigoths, and had reason to be wary of them. Having settled in what is now Romania, they had supposedly become allies of the empire, supplying soldiers for the armies of Rome and Constantinople. But they would not stay put and, ten years before, Valens himself had gone to war to pen them into their homeland. Things hadn't gone to plan. As guerrillas they

[6] Charles Mierow (trans. and ed.). *The Gothic History of Jordanes* (see Bibliography).

were unbeatable. Three years into the war, Valens – bow-legged, paunchy, with a lazy eye – had to talk peace on a boat in the middle of the Danube, as if emperor and barbarian leader were equals. They agreed that the Danube was the natural border, and that neither side would cross it. But now here were the Visigoths, about to invade not as warriors but as a whole nation of asylum-seekers: families, children, sick and aged, by the wagonload. Advisers urged Valens to see his former foes not as refugees but as recruits for the emperor's overstretched army. Officials journeyed north, not to oppose, but to help, with transport, food and allocations of land in the frontier provinces.

So as the spring of 376 turned to summer, the destitute Visigoths came over the low-lying northern banks, taking to the river in boats and dug-out canoes, hauling rafts bearing their wagons and horses. So many all at once would have overwhelmed the Thracian countryside. They had to be kept where they were. The southern banks of the Danube turned into a vast holding camp for the bedraggled refugees. To the Visigoths, it seemed that they had fled one frying pan only to land in another. They muttered about taking direct action to seize the lands they thought they had been promised. The regional commander, Lupicinus, ordered up more troops from Gaul to quell disorder.

But time was running out. The Visigoths' eastern cousins, crowds of Ostrogoths also fleeing the unnamed menace to the east, arrived at the Danube, saw it weakly held, and crossed, without waiting for permission. Pushed and re-inforced by the new influx, the Visgothic king Fritigern led his own people 100 kilometres south, to the local provincial capital, Marcianople (the ruins of which lie half-exposed near

Devnya, 25 kilometres inland from the Bulgarian Black Sea resort of Varna). The Romans invited the Visigothic leaders to a lavish dinner, ostensibly to discuss an aid package, while outside the walls the mass of their people, kept at bay by several thousand Roman soldiers, seethed with rumour and resentment. Suspecting their chief had been lured to his downfall, the Visigoths attacked a contingent of Romans and seized their weapons. When news of this reached the dinner table, Lupicinus had some of Fritigern's attendants killed in revenge, and probably had plans to kill them all. But that would have been suicidal. The rioters were now an army. Fritigern had the presence of mind to point out that the only way to restore peace was for him to return to his people, sound, healthy and free. Lupicinus saw his point, and released his guest – who at once, as Ammianus says, 'took horse and hurried away to kindle the flame of war'. Across Lower Moesia – northern Bulgaria today – outraged Visigoths robbed, burned and looted, seizing yet more weapons. A pitched battle ended with more Romans dead, more arms seized, and Lupicinus cowering in the sacked streets of Marcianople.

Then, in an act of sheer idiocy, Valens, afraid that Goth would side with Goth, ordered the long-established and peaceful Visigothic colony in Adrianople to leave, at once. He intended to secure the place, and achieved the exact opposite. The colonists lost their tempers, killed a number of their oppressors and, leaving the city, threw themselves into the arms of their fellow Goths, who, in the autumn of 377, broke through the Roman blockade to loot their way south into present-day Turkey.

The prospect of reinforcement was not good. Though the empire had perhaps 500,000 men under arms, half of these

were frontier garrisons watching for trouble in the Barbaricum, leaving only half as mobile field armies. Besides, many
of the troops were non-Roman mercenaries, and any order to
move inspired desertions. Troops could come only from the
Gaulish frontier, under the command of Valens's young
nephew Gratian, who had been co-ruler and Emperor of the
West for the last two years. Still only eighteen, he had a growing reputation as a leader, but it was all he could do to keep
the peace along the Rhine and the Danube. The plan to shift
troops from Gaul to the Balkans leaked across the frontier,
inspiring German raids that demanded Gratian's attention all
that winter. It was not until early 378 that he set out to aid
his uncle.

The empire was already a tattered entity. Though still nom-
inally united by history and family, it had begun to split: Rome
and Constantinople, two capitals, two worlds, two languages
and two creeds (each fighting its own sub-creeds of pagan-
ism and heresy). To the east lay the great imperial rival, Persia;
in Africa, Moorish rebels; and right across northern Europe
and the frontiers of Inner Asia the Barbaricum, inhabited by
those who spoke neither Greek nor Latin. With continual barbarian incursions across the Rhine and the Danube, Rome – the
term sometimes included Constantinople and sometimes didn't,
depending on the context – tried to defend itself with a range
of strategies from outright force to negotiation, bribery, inter-
marriage, trade and, finally, controlled immigration. This
last was in the end the only possible way to stave off assault,
and yet it also led inexorably to further decay.

Barbarians were good fighters; it made sense to employ
them, with confusing consequences for both sides. Enemies
became allies, who often ended up fighting their own kin.

Peace came always at the price of continued collapse: the army was strengthened by an influx of barbarians, but taxes rose to pay for them; faith in government declined, and corruption spread. By the late fourth century the empire's borders resembled a weakening immune system, through which barbarians crept, in direct assault or temporary partnership, while the army – the ultimate arbiter of political authority and the guardian of the frontiers – was like the blood platelets of this ageing body, always rushing to clot some new wound, and never in sufficient numbers.

This, then, was the glorious, vast and diseased structure that Valens was once again preparing to defend as he marched north from Constantinople in the early summer of 378, planning to join up with his co-emperor and rival, his ambitious nephew Gratian.

Now Valens's battered ego took the reins. He, who had demanded Gratian's help, had become jealous of his nephew's success, and eager for a victory of his own. Marching north to Adrianople in July, he was told by his scouts that a Goth army was approaching, but that it consisted of only 10,000 men, a force rather less than his own of some 15,000. Outside Adrianople, he made his base near the junction of the Maritsa and Tundzha Rivers, around which over the next few days arose a palisade and a ditch. Just then an officer arrived from somewhere up the Danube with a letter from Gratian urging his uncle not to do anything hasty until the reinforcements arrived. Valens called a war council. Some whispered that Gratian just wanted to share in a triumph that should belong to Valens alone. That suited Valens. Preparations continued.

Fritigern, laagered in his wagons some 13 kilometres away

up the Tundzha, was himself wary of giving battle. Around him were not just his warriors, but their entire households as well: perhaps 30,000 people, with an unwieldy corps of wagons, all arranged in family circles, impossible to re-form in less than a day. To fight effectively – away from the encumbering wagons – he would need help; and so he had sent for the heavily armoured Ostrogothic cavalry. Meanwhile he played for time, sending out scouts to set fire to the sun-scorched wheat fields between his encampment and the Romans' – and a messenger, who arrived in the imperial camp with a letter: yes, 'barbarian' leaders were quite capable of using secretaries fluent in Latin to communicate with the Roman world, as the Xiongnu chanyus used secretaries to write in Chinese. The letter was an official plea to revert to the status quo: peace, in return for land and protection from the whirlwind approaching from the east. Valens would have none of it. He wanted victory: Fritigern captured or dead, the Goths cowed. He refused to reply.

Next morning, 9 August, the Romans were ready. All non-essential gear – spare tents, treasure chests, imperial robes – was sent back into Adrianople for safety, and the horsemen and infantry set off to cover the 13 kilometres to the Visigothic laagers. It was a short march, but a gruelling one, over burned fields, under a scorching sun, with no streams in sight.

After a couple of hours the Roman horsemen and infantry approached the Visigothic camp and its huddles of wagons, from which rose wild war-cries and chants in praise of Gothic ancestors. The sweaty approach had caused the Romans to straggle, with one wing of the cavalry out in front and infantry behind blocking the way of the second. Slowly they pulled themselves into line, clattering their weapons and beating their shields to drown out the barbarians' clamour.

To Fritigern, still awaiting help, these were unnerving sights and sounds. Again, he played for time, sending a request for peace. This time Valens was about to agree when a band of Roman outriders, hungry for glory, perhaps, made a quick lunge at the Visigothic flank. At that moment the Ostrogothic cavalry came galloping in along the valley. The Roman cavalry moved forward to confront this new menace. That was what Fritigern had been waiting for. His infantry burst from the wagons, firing arrows, throwing spears, until the two lines clashed and locked in a heaving scrum of shields, broken spears and swords, so tightly packed that soldiers could hardly lift their arms to strike – or, having done so, lower them again. Dust rose, covering the battleground in a choking, blinding fog. Outside the mêlée, there was no need for the Visigothic archers and spearmen to aim: any missile thrown or fired at random dropped through the dust unseen, and had to find a mark.

Then came the heavy cavalry, with no opposing Roman cavalry to stop them, trampling the dying, their battleaxes splitting the helmets and breastplates of infantrymen weakened by heat, weighed down with armour and slipping on the blood-soaked ground.

Within the hour, the living began to stumble away from the Roman lines over the corpses of the slain. 'Some fell without knowing who struck them,' writes Ammianus. 'Some were crushed by sheer weight of numbers; some were killed by their own comrades.'

As the sun set, the noise of battle died away into the silent, moonless night. Two-thirds of the Romans – perhaps 10,000 men – lay dead, jumbled with corpses of horses. Now the dark fields filled with other sounds, as the cries, sobs and groans of the wounded followed the survivors across the burned-out crops and along the road back to Adrianople.

No one knows what happened to Valens. He had been lost or abandoned by his bodyguard and found his way to the army's most disciplined and experienced legions, holding out in a last stand. A general rode off to call in some reserves, only to find they had fled. After that, nothing. Some said the emperor died when struck by an arrow soon after night fell. Or perhaps he found refuge in a farmhouse nearby, which was surrounded and burned to the ground, along with all those inside – except one man who escaped from a window to tell what had happened. Thus the story came to Ammianus. True or not, the emperor's body was never found.

The violence continued, and the empire had no answer to it. At dawn, the Visigoths advanced beyond the battlefield, to Adrianople, hot on the heels of the survivors seeking refuge. But there was no safety to be had, for the defenders, scrabbling to prepare for a siege, refused to open the gates to their fleeing fellows. By midday the Visigoths had encircled the walls, trapping the terrified survivors against them. Some 300 surrendered, only to be slaughtered on the spot.

Luckily for the city, a thunderstorm washed out the assault, forcing the Visigoths back to their wagons and allowing the defenders to shore up the gates with rocks and make ready their trebuchets and siege bows. When the Visigoths attacked the next day, they lost hundreds crushed by rocks, impaled by arrows the size of spears and buried under stones tipped from above.

Giving up the assault, they turned to easier targets, looting their way across 200 kilometres to the very gates of Constantinople. There the rampage died, killed by the sight of the vast walls, and then by a horrifying incident. As the city mounted its defence, a Saracen contingent suddenly erupted from the gates. One of these fearsome warriors, carrying a sword and wearing nothing but a loincloth, hurled himself into the fray, sliced open a Gothic soldier's throat, seized the corpse and sucked the streaming blood. It was enough to drain what remained of the Goths' courage and force a retreat northwards.

The war dragged on for four more years, ending in a treaty that gave the Goths almost exactly what had been agreed in the first place: land just south of the Danube and semi-independence, with their soldiers fighting for Rome under their own leaders. It would not last, for the Goths were a nation on the move, the greatest of the many barbarian migrations that would undermine the empire. A Visigoth who fought at Adrianople could have lived through another revolt, a slow advance deeper into the empire, the brief seizure of Rome itself in 410, a march over the Pyrenees and a final return over the same mountains to find peace at last in south-west France.

And all this chaos – the refugee crisis, the rebellion, the disaster of Adrianople, the attack on Constantinople, the impossible peace, the slow erosion by barbarians – had been unleashed by the 'unknown race' to the east. Still no one in the empire or even the nearer reaches of the Barbaricum knew anything of them.

Perhaps they should have done. For, as Ammianus mentions in passing, among the cavalry that had come to Fritigern's rescue was a contingent of these lightly armed horse-archers, no more than a few hundred, probably operating as outriders for the main Goth force. It was their arrival the previous year that had forced the Romans to withdraw, allowing the Goths to break through into Thrace. No doubt they had been doing very nicely as freebooters and spies, harassing enemy flanks. If they had been in the battle outside Adrianople, no one would have taken much notice of these few coarse creatures with their minimal armour; but they were seen afterwards, during the looting. Then they vanished, for few cities had fallen and the pickings would have been meagre.

They left, however, with another sort of treasure: information. They had seen what the West had to offer. They had witnessed Rome's worst day since the defeat by Hannibal at Cannae 594 years before. They might even have guessed that Rome would in future rely more on heavy cavalry, which, as they knew, was no match for their own type of warfare. They had seen Rome's wider problems: the difficulty of securing a leaky frontier, the impossibility of gathering and moving large armies to fight fast-moving guerrillas, the arrogance of the 'civilized' when confronting the 'barbarian'. While the whole Balkan sector of the empire collapsed into rioting, these swift mounted archers galloped back northwards and eastwards with their few stolen items, and their vital intelligence: the empire was rich, and vulnerable.

These lightly armed, fast-moving horsemen were the first Huns to reach central Europe. Shortly, under the most ruthless of their leaders, they too would cross the river, with consequences for the decaying empire far in excess of anything wrought by the Goths.

In the 380s, some groups of Huns were inside the empire, first as mercenaries-as-peacemakers, then as robber barons leading hit-and-run raids, then as allies bribed with grants of land. Back in Hungary, the Huns took to raiding across Turkey and into Syria, where monasteries provided rich pickings. 'Dead are the merchants, widowed the women,' mourned a Christian priest, Cyrillonas, in 395. In 408 they first turned on Western Europe. In about 430, they raided the Rhineland, attacking a small tribe known both as Burgundians and Nibelungs (after a chief, Niflung), thus providing future German-speakers with the roots of an enduring folk tale, epic poem and Wagner's operatic saga. A new leader, Ruga, came up with a system that bore remarkable similarities to the Xiongnu agenda: raids, and promises to stop raids in exchange for gifts, in Ruga's case gold. Ruga died in 435.

His successor was Attila, who took raiding and blackmail to a whole new level. He was a scary little man, moody and brutal, but also capable of being 'sympathetic in council' – in the words of Greek official Priscus, who actually visited Attila in his capital, with its wooden walls, wooden buildings, and Roman-style stone bath-house. Attila hired secretaries. Raids became invasion across the Balkans to the great walls of Constantinople. Ambassadors made demands. There was lavish hospitality, and equally lavish payments (2,000 pounds of gold annually). These funded Attila's army, which built siege engines. Empire followed, down the Balkans, across to the Caspian, up to the Baltic, an area half the size of the USA.

And then in 450, ambition got the better of him. He planned to head west, into Gaul, and then to Rome itself. His excuse was that the Emperor's sister, Honoria, seeking revenge for being deprived of a lover, came up with a daft scheme involving the Hun ruler. In Gibbon's florid account, she 'offered to deliver her person into the arms of a barbarian of whose language she was ignorant, whose figure was scarcely human and whose religion and manners she abhorred'.[7] She sent her ring as proof of her good faith.

Attila raised a massive army and crossed France to Orléans. A Christian source claims that on the way he introduced himself to a priest in Latin with the words 'Ego sum Attila, flagellum Dei', 'I am Attila, the scourge of God', sent to punish a wayward Christendom. In fact, his scourging days were numbered. Turned back by a Roman army, he backtracked to the flat, rolling Catalaunian Plains near Troyes, where, in one of the most famous battles in European history, he was defeated, and returned to Hungary. After another campaign into Italy, stymied by plague and famine, he retreated again and took solace in the arms of a new young wife named Ildico. After a drunken wedding night, he suffered some sort of a seizure – possibly a burst ulcer – and drowned in his own blood. He was found dead the next morning, with poor Ildico (in Priscus's words) 'weeping with downcast face beside him'.

With their helmsman gone, the Huns, torn apart by rival successors, sank with very little trace. By 470 they were gone, vanishing back into the eastern steppes. Rome itself was also vanishing. In 476 the last Roman emperor, Romulus, was replaced by a barbarian, Odoacer. By a strange coincidence, the fathers of both men had been officials at Attila's court. His ghost haunted the end of the empire he had sought to conquer.

Other traces lingered, like dust left over from the great Xiongnu explosion. Attila remained 'God's scourge' in Christian legend, which also credited God for destroying him. As

---

[7] In *Decline and Fall of the Roman Empire*, Book 5 (see Bibliography).

Etzel, he entered German folklore. His name lives on in the Norfolk village of Attleborough. In France, schoolchildren learn to quote him, spuriously: '*Là où mon cheval passera, l'herbe ne repoussera pas.*' ('Wherever my horse passes, the grass will not regrow.') A thousand years after his death, Vikings put 'Atli' in their lays, and sang of him in Iceland, Greenland and their short-lived colony in Newfoundland. There have been bad plays, Verdi's opera, films, a couple of forgettable TV series. He remains a standard cliché attached to any leader accused of mindless devastation.

Epilogue

A LASTING LEGACY

THE XIONGNU VANISHED, DIFFUSED ACROSS ASIA, EVIDENCE for their existence buried and gathered in Chinese histories. Travelling across their imperial lands now, you would not know they had ruled an empire almost twice the size of Rome's, from Lake Baikal to the Great Wall, from Manchuria to the heart of Eurasia. But take a closer look, and they emerge from the past like a forest revealed by rising mist. What would China be without the Great Wall, built to keep out the Xiongnu and now a symbol of the nation? Without the Xiongnu, there would no panorama of the Wall to greet you at passport control in Beijing International, and China would be short of a few million tourists. Open an atlas or check an online map of China: the far north-west – Xinjiang, or the Western Regions as it once was – is part of China only because of Emperor Wu's determination to seize it from the Xiongnu. And what would the nation be without the certainty that their culture is the essence of refinement, a bastion against the forces of barbarism?

Then look at Mongolia itself. True, it was once part of China, sort of; or rather part of the Mongol empire which had made China part of Mongolia. In China, that still rankles: China under barbarian rule! For a century (1279–1368), the world turned upside down! Then it righted itself, and Mongolia really did become part of China for 500 years. Finally, in the early twentieth century, Mongolia regained its independence. For Chinese, this is against the natural order of things. Mongolians say the opposite. They boast of two ancestral empires that made China tremble. The later one was the creation of Genghis Khan, of course, the father of the nation. But he looked back 1,000 years, to a tradition of empire started by the Xiongnu.

To the Chinese, the appearance of Halley's Comet in 240 BC was an omen of change, and possibly catastrophe. The rise of the Xiongnu brought both, with the death of uncounted ten thousands and the reshaping of Asian history – reasons enough for these people and their empire to get the attention they deserve.

BIBLIOGRAPHY

The following are the works I consulted for this book. There are many others. Barfield's *The Perilous Frontier*, Di Cosmo's *Ancient China and its Enemies* and *Xiongnu Archaeology* (see Brosseder, below) all have excellent bibliographies. *Xiongnu Archaeology* is a wonderful guide to current archaeological research. Di Cosmo's 'Selected Bibliography on Xiongnu Archaeology and Related Subjects', which surveys the field up to 2008, is available online.

Alexeyev, Andrei Yu., et al.: *Scythians, Warriors of Ancient Siberia*, Trustees of the British Museum/Thames & Hudson, London, 2017.

Ammianus Marcellinus: *The Later Roman Empire*, trans. and ed. Walter Hamilton, Penguin, Harmondsworth, 1986 (and later editions).

André, Guilhem et al.: 'L'un des plus anciens papiers du monde exhumé récemment en Mongolie', *Arts Asiatiques*, Vol. 65, 2010.

Ban Gu: *The History of the Former Han Dynasty*, Waverly Press, Baltimore, 1938–1955.

Barfield, Thomas J.: *The Perilous Frontier: Nomadic Empires and China, 221 BC to AD 1757*, Blackwell, Cambridge (Mass.) and Oxford, 1989.

Barfield, Thomas J.: 'The Hsiung-nu Imperial Confederacy: Organization and Foreign Policy', *The Journal of Asian Studies*, Vol. 41, No. 1, November 1981.

Baumer, Christoph: *The History of Central Asia, Vol. II: The Age of the Silk Roads*, I. B. Tauris, London and New York, 2014.

Bemmann, Jan, et al. (eds): *Current Archaeological Research in Mongolia, Bonn Contributions to Asian Archaeology*, Vol. 4, Rheinische Friedrich-Wilhelms-Universität Bonn, 2009.

Benjamin, Craig G. R.: *The Yuezhi: Origin, Migration and the Conquest of Northern Bactria*, Brepols, Turnhout, Belgium, 2007.

Brosseder, Ursula, and Bryan K. Miller (eds): *Xiongnu Archaeology: Multidisciplinary Perspectives of the First Steppe Empire in Inner Asia, Bonn Contributions to Asian Archaeology*, Vol. 5, Rheinische Friedrich-Wilhelms-Universität Bonn, 2011.

Buchwald, Tony: *Sima Qian's Self-Conception in Claims of Legitimacy*, GRIN Verlag, Norderstedt, 2012.

Chimiddorj, Yeruul-Erdene, and Ikue Otani: 'The Chinese Inscription on the Lacquerware Unearthed from Tomb 20, Gol Mod Site 1, Mongolia', *The Silk Road*, Vol. 13, 2015.

Chin, Tamara T.: 'Defamiliarizing the Foreigner: Sima Qian's Ethnography and Han–Xiongnu Marriage', *Harvard Journal of Asiatic Studies*, Vol. 70, No. 2, December 2010.

Cosmo, Nicola Di: *Ancient China and its Enemies: The Rise of Nomadic Power in East Asian History*, Cambridge University Press, New York, 2002.

Cosmo, Nicola Di: 'Ancient Inner Asian Nomads: Their Economic Basis and Its Significance in Chinese History', *The Journal of Asian Studies*, Vol. 53, No. 4, November 1994.

Cosmo, Nicola Di: 'Han Frontiers: Toward an Integrated View', *Journal of the American Oriental Society*, Vol. 129, No. 2, April–June 2009.

Crespigny, Rafe de: *Northern Frontier: The Policies and Strategy of the Later Han Empire*, Australian National University Faculty of Asian Studies Monographs, New Series, No. 4, Canberra, 1984. An edited version: *The Division and Destruction of the Xiongnu Confederacy in the First and Second Centuries AD*, available as an Internet edn, 2004.

Davis-Kimball, Jeannine, and C. Scott Littleton, 'Warrior Women of the Eurasia Steppes', *Archaeology*, Vol. 50, No. 1, 1997.

Desroches, Jean-Paul, et al., *Mongolie: Le Premier Empire des Steppes*, Actes Sud, Mission archéologique française, Paris, 2003.

Dubs, Homer H.: 'History and Historians Under the Han' (review of Burton Watson's *Ssu-ma Ch'ien: Grand Historian of China*), *The Journal of Asian Studies*, Vol. 20, No. 2, February 1961.

Durrant, Stephen W.: 'Self as the Intersection of Traditions: The Autobiographical Writings of Ssu-ma Ch'ien', *Journal of the American Oriental Society*, Vol. 106, No. 1, January–March 1986.

Erdenebaatar, Diimajav: *Хүн Улсын Соёлын Өв/The Cultural Heritage of Xiongnu Empire*, Munkhiin Useg Publishing House, Ulaanbaatar, 2016.

Eregzen, Gelegdorj (ed.): *Хүннүгийн Өв/Treasures of the Xiongnu* (exhibition catalogue), National Museum of Mongolia, 2011.

Gibbon, Edward, *The History of the Decline and Fall of the Roman Empire*, many edns.

Giscard, Pierre-Henri, and Tsagaan Turbat (eds): *France-Mongolie: Découvertes Archéologiques – Vingt Ans de Partenariat* (exhibition catalogue), Institute of History and Archaeology, Ulaanbaatar, 2015.

Grousset, René: *The Empire of the Steppes*, Rutgers University Press, New Brunswick and London, 1970.

Hanks, Bryan: 'Archaeology of the Eurasian Steppes and Mongolia', *Annual Review of Anthropology*, Vol. 39, 2010.

Honeychurch, William: 'Alternative Complexities: The Archaeology of Pastoral Nomadic States', *Journal of Archaeological Research*, Vol. 22, No. 4, December 2014.

Honeychurch, William: *Inner Asia and the Spatial Politics of Empire: Archaeology, Mobility, and Culture Contact*, Springer, New York, 2015.

Honeychurch, William: 'The Nomad as State Builder: Historical Theory and Material Evidence from Mongolia', *Journal of World Prehistory*, Vol. 26, No. 4, December 2013.

Kessler, Adam T.: *Empires Beyond the Great Wall*, Natural History Museum of Los Angeles County, 1994. A shorter version: 'Beyond the Great Wall of China: Archaeological Treasures from Inner Mongolia', *Minerva*, Vol. 5, No. 3, May/June 1994.

Khazanov, Anatoly: *Nomads and the Outside World*, Cambridge University Press, Cambridge, 1984.

Klopsteg, Paul E.: *Turkish Archery and the Composite Bow*, Simon Archery Foundation, Manchester, 1987.

Lattimore, Owen: *Inner Asian Frontiers of China*, American Geographical Society, New York, 1951.

Lattimore, Owen: *Studies in Frontier History*, Oxford University Press, 1962.

Leslie, D. D., and K. H. Gardiner, 'Chinese Knowledge of Western Asia during the Han', *T'oung Pao*, Second Series, Vol. 68, Livr. 4/5, 1982.

Loades, Mike: *The Composite Bow*, Osprey, Oxford, 2016.

Loades, Mike: *The Crossbow*, Osprey, Oxford, 2018.

Loewe, Michael: *Crisis and Conflict in Han China*, George Allen & Unwin, London, 1974.

Loewe, Michael: *Records of Han Administration*, 2 vols, Cambridge University Press, Cambridge, 1967.

Maenchen-Helfen, Otto J.: *The World of the Huns*, University of California Press, Berkeley, Los Angeles and London, 1973.

Man, John: *Attila*, Bantam, London, 2005.

Man, John, *The Great Wall*, Bantam, London, 2008.

Markley, Jonathan: *Peace and Peril: Sima Qian's Portrayal of Han–Xiongnu Relations*, Brepols, Turnhout, Belgium, 2011.

Mierow, Charles (trans. and ed.): *The Gothic History of Jordanes*, Princeton University Press/Oxford University Press, Princeton and Oxford, 1915.

Miller, Bryan K.: *Power Politics in the Xiongnu Empire*, University of Pennsylvania Dissertation, published online 2009.

Miller, Bryan K.: 'Xiongnu "Kings" and the Political Order of the Steppe Empire', *Journal of the Economic and Social History of the Orient*, Vol. 57, No. 1, 2014.

Miniaev, Sergei S.: 'Production of Bronzeware among the Xiongnu', *The Silk Road*, Vol. 14, 2016.

Murail, P., et al.: 'The Man, the Woman and the Hyoid Bone: From Archaeology to the Burial Practices of the Xiongnu

People (Egyin Gol Valley, Mongolia)', *Antiquity*, Vol. 74, No. 265, September 2000.

Murphy, Eileen M.: 'A Bioarchaeological Study of Xiongnu Expansion in Iron Age Tuva, South Siberia', *The Archaeology of Power and Politics in Eurasia*, ed. Charles Hartley et al., Cambridge University Press, Cambridge, 2012.

Murphy, Eileen M.: *Iron Age Archaeology and Trauma from Aymyrlyg, South Siberia*, Bar Publishing, Oxford, 2003.

Paludin, Ann: *Chinese Sculpture: A Great Tradition*, Serindia, Enfield, Chicago, 2007.

Psarras, Sophia-Karin: 'Exploring the North: Non-Chinese Cultures of the Late Warring States and Han', *Monumenta Serica*, Vol. 42, 1994.

Psarras, Sophia-Karin: 'Han and Xiongnu: A Reexamination of Cultural and Political Relations', in two parts: (1) *Monumenta Serica*, Vol. 51, 2003, and (2) *Monumenta Serica*, Vol. 52, 2004.

Rachewiltz, Igor de (trans. and ed.), *The Secret History of the Mongols: A Mongolian Epic Chronicle of the Thirteenth Century, translated with a historical and philological commentary*, 2 vols, Brill, Leiden, Boston and Cologne, 2004; supplementary vol., 2013.

Rogers, J. Daniel: 'Inner Asian States and Empires: Theories and Synthesis', *Journal of Archaeological Research*, Vol. 20, No. 3, September 2012.

Rudenko, Sergei I.: *Frozen Tombs of Siberia: The Pazyryk Burials of Iron Age Horsemen*, trans. M. W. Thompson, J. M. Dent & Sons, London, 1970.

Selby, Stephen: *Archery Traditions of Asia*, Hong Kong Museum of Coastal Defence, Hong Kong, 2003.

Selby, Stephen: *Chinese Archery*, Hong Kong University Press, Hong Kong, 2000.

Sima Qian: *Records of the Grand Historian: Qin Dynasty*, trans. Burton Watson, The Chinese University of Hong Kong and Columbia University Press, Hong Kong and New York, 1993.

Sinor, Denis: 'The Inner Asian Warriors', *Journal of the American Oriental Society*, Vol. 101, No. 2, April–June 1981.

So, Jenny F., and Emma C. Bunker, *Traders and Raiders on China's Northern Frontier*, Smithsonian Institution, Washington, 1999.

Thompson, E. A.: *The Huns* (revised by Peter Heather from original edn, *A History of Attila and the Huns*, Oxford University Press, 1948), Blackwell, Oxford, 1999.

Törbat, Tsagaan: *Khunnugiin jiriin irgediin bulsh*, Mongolian State Educational University, Ulaanbaatar, 2004.

Trever, Camilla: *Excavations in Northern Mongolia (1924–1925)*, Leningrad, 1932.

Turchin, Peter: 'A Theory for Formation of Large Empires', *Journal of Global History*, Vol. 4, Issue 2, 2009.

Watson, Burton, *Han Fei Tzu: Basic Writings*, Columbia University Press, New York and London, 2001.

Watson, Burton: *Ssu-ma Ch'ien, Grand Historian of China*, Columbia University Press, New York and London, 1958.

Yap, Joseph: *Wars with the Xiongnu: A Translation from Zizhi Tongjian*, AuthorHouse, Bloomington, Indiana, 2009.

Yetts, W. Perceval: 'Discoveries of the Kozlov Expedition', *The Burlington Magazine for Connoisseurs*, Vol. 48, No. 277, April 1906.

ACKNOWLEDGEMENTS

Special thanks to Ge Jian and all at the Grasslands Foundation in Beijing and Hohhot, notably Water Xu, Tselmeg and Han. And, as so often in the past, I thank Alatan, Professor of English, Inner Mongolia University of Technology, Hohhot, without whose trilingual help I would feel lost. Others who helped in the creation of this book are: Goyo Reston, Tsendee and Batmunkh, who provided vital help in Mongolia; Professor Diimajav Erdenebaatar in Ulaanbaatar, chief archaeologist of Gol Mod 2; Professor Wang Zhihao and Zhang Ziyang ('Mr Shark') in the Bronze Museum, Ordos City; Ursula Brosseder, Rheinische Friedrich-Wilhelms-Universität, Bonn; Tsagaan Törbat, Mongolian Academy of Sciences, Institute of Archaeology, Ulaanbaatar; Odbaatar and Gelegdorj Eregzen, National History Museum, Ulaanbaatar; Ding Ding of the Oriental Holding Group, Ordos City; and finally the late and very deeply lamented Igor de Rachewiltz, School of Asian

ACKNOWLEDGEMENTS

and Pacific Studies, Australian National University, Canberra. Finally, thanks to Henry Vines and his team at Transworld; to Richenda Todd for her meticulous editing; and to Michele Topham and all at Felicity Bryan Agency.

PICTURE ACKNOWLEDGEMENTS

All photos in the illustration section are courtesy of the author unless otherwise stated. Every effort has been made to obtain the necessary permissions with reference to copyright material. We apologize for any omissions in this respect and will be pleased to make the appropriate acknowledgments in future editions.

Page 1: Coronet photograph courtesy of the Inner Mongolia Museum, Hohhot.

Page 3: Weapon imagery: © G. Ganbold and S. Enkhbold, in Gelegdorj Eregzen (ed.), *Treasures of the Xiongnu* (see Bibliography).

Page 5: Gol Mod grave excavations: © Diimajav Erdenebaatar; cutaway of Noyon Uul 'terrace tomb': © Natalia Polosmak.

Page 6: Textile imagery: © *Treasures of the Xiongnu* (see above); bronze cauldron photograph: © Diimajav Erdenebaatar.

Page 7: All images: © Diimajav Erdenebaatar.

INDEX

ABOUT THE AUTHOR

John Man is a historian with a special interest in Asia and the nature of leadership. His books, published in over twenty languages, include bestselling biographies of Genghis Khan, Kublai Khan and Attila the Hun, as well as histories of the Great Wall of China, the Mongol Empire and the Amazons.